Litigation Against Schools:
Implications for School Management

Litigation Against Schools:
Implications for School Management

Edited by

Dympna Glendenning

and

William Binchy

Published in 2006 by
FirstLaw Limited,
Merchants Court,
Merchants Quay,
Dublin 8

Typeset by
Gough Typesetting Services
Dublin

Printed by
Johnswood Press Ltd.

ISBN 1-904480-33-0

All rights reserved.
No part of this publication may be
reproduced or transmitted in any form or by any means,
including photocopying and recording,
without the written permission of the publisher.
Such written permission must also be obtained before any
part of this publication is stored in a retrieval system of any nature.

© Editor and contributors, 2006

PREFACE

The modest aim of this book is to help school principals and others involved in school management in the task of coming to terms with the new legal culture. Until recently, there was a relative dearth of legislation governing the management of schools. Today there is a raft of legislation, accompanied by important judicial decisions, handed down by the Irish Supreme Court and High Court, but also by courts in Strasbourg and Luxembourg. School managers must have familiarity with a range of legal areas, such as constitutional and administrative law, international human rights law, tort, contract and criminal law. Very few practising lawyers would claim complete mastery over such an intimidatingly vast legal landscape, yet school managers are expected to have an unerring competence.

We are delighted that a number of legal experts are willing to share their insights. The team is indeed a strong one. Dr Neville Cox is a leading expert on sports law. Professor Gerry Whyte has written authoritative texts on constitutional and public interest law, as well as labour law. Dr Ciaran Craven, Barrister at Law, has authored influential works on medical and tort law. Estelle Feldman has written widely on freedom of information law in Ireland and internationally. We are honoured also to have a contribution on aspects of English law from Professor Neville Harris of the University of Manchester.

One of the challenges facing school management is to integrate the philosophy underlying the several disparate areas of law. Negligence law and health and safety law require schools to take care of their pupils. International human rights law and equality legislation oblige schools not to discriminate on a range of grounds. Recent legislative initiatives are designed to protect the interests and welfare of vulnerable groups of pupils. These different goals must be achieved in harmony with each other -by no means an easy task in some cases. The best advice to schools is to have an open and supportive philosophy, but most of all to have confidence that the law is ultimately their friend, not their adversary. What we believe emerges from the book is that courts, far from being at war with school principals and teachers, are striving to deepen the common good by supporting educationalists in their noble vocation.

Dympna Glendenning and William Binchy

January 2006

CONTENTS

Preface v
Table of Cases xiii
Table of Legislation xxii

The School's Duty of Care to its Pupils:
Recent Developments in the Law (William Binchy) 1
   THE SCHOOL'S DUTY OF CARE TO ITS PUPILS 1
      The "careful parent" test 3
      The duty of care in supervision 3
         Injuries sustained off the premises 25
         Supervision outside hours 26
         School transport 32
         Supervision on school tours 33
   THE OCCUPIERS' LIABILITY ACT 1995 35
      Some guiding cases 36
      Occupiers/supervision/activity characterisation 38
      Modifying the scope of liability 40
      The duty of school management to trespassers 42
      Criminal entrants 43
Concluding observations regarding the 1995 Act 47
   THE SAFETY, HEALTH AND WELFARE AT WORK ACT 2005 47
   OTHER ACTS OF NEGLIGENCE 52
   EMERGING ISSUES 54
      Pupils with disabilities 54
      Pupils, autonomy and privacy 57

Secondary School Sports and the Law (Dr. Neville Cox) 63
   THE GENERAL STANDARDS REQUIRED OF SPORTS TEACHERS 64
      Case One 65
      Case Two 65
      Case Three 65
   DUTIES WHEN TEACHING OR COACHING SPORT 66

Ensuring that a pupil has adequate instruction in
    "injury avoidance" principles 67
Ensuring that a pupil is fit to engage in sporting
    activity 68
Appropriate matching of players 70
Weather permitting? 71
Duties in respect of equipment 75
Supervision 76
Premises 84
Generally – the role of insurance 89
CONCLUSION 90

The Delivery of Minimum Education and the Common Good

(Dympna Glendenning) 92
INTRODUCTION 92
MINIMUM EDUCATION AND EARLY SCHOOL LEAVING 93
MINIMUM EDUCATION: A CONSTITUTIONAL RIGHT 95
MINIMUM EDUCATION: THE CONSTITUTIONAL STANDARD 97
LIMITS TO STATE'S OBLIGATIONS 101
MINIMUM EDUCATION: LEGISLATIVE PROVISION 102
    The Education Act 1998 102
THE EDUCATION (WELFARE) ACT 2000 103
    The National Educational Welfare Board (NEWB) 104
    Educational Welfare Officers 106
    Prosecutions for failure to attend school 107
    Duties on Schools and Principals 109
    Obligations to young persons in employment 110
THE SEPARATION OF POWERS DOCTRINE 111

Implications for Schools of Irish Equality Legislation

(Gerry Whyte) 118
INTRODUCTION 118
EQUAL STATUS ACTS 2000–2004 120
    Grounds of discrimination 120
    Context in which Acts are to apply 121
    Meaning of discrimination for the purposes of the Acts 121
    Meaning of harassment for the purposes of the Acts 123
    Consideration of section 7 of the Act 124
    Enforcement procedures and remedies 126

EMPLOYMENT EQUALITY ACTS 1998–2004 130
   Grounds of discrimination 130
   Contexts in which Act applies 131
   Meaning of discrimination for the purposes of
      the Acts 132
   Meaning of harassment for the purposes of the Acts 138
   Enforcement procedures and remedies 139

Bullying and School Discipline (Dr. Ciaran Craven) 145
   INTRODUCTION 145
   PUPIL EXCLUSION FROM CLASS 145
   VIOLENT AND AGGRESSIVE PUPILS IN THE SCHOOL 146
   CRIMINAL LIABILITY 146
      General 146
      Assault 147
      Assault causing harm 147
      Assault causing serious harm 148
      Other offences 148
      Defences 148
      "Use of force" 148
      Self-defence and the defence of property 149
      Use of force in arrest 150
      Reprise 151
   CIVIL LIABILITY 151
      General 151
      Basis of liability 152
      Two related issues 152
   LIABILITY IN NEGLIGENCE 153
      The duty 153
      The standard of care 155
      Small children and supervision 155
      Balancing supervision and humaneness 156
      Exclusion may be necessary 158
      Discipline may also be necessary 159
      Reprise 165
   DISCIPLINARY PROCEDURES 166
      General 166
      Acting immediately – fairness of procedures 167
      Acting fairly – scope of judicial review 169
      Wrongdoing off school premises 170

Injunctive relief 173
Reprise 175
THE STATUTORY MECHANISMS 175
General 175
Education Act 1998 176
Education (Welfare) Act 2000 177
Appeals by National Education Welfare Board of
decision of boards of management 178

**School Discipline: Balancing Individual Student Rights and
the Common Good** (Dympna Glendenning) 180
INTRODUCTION 180
PRELIMINARY POINT 181
SCHOOL POLICIES ON DISCIPLINE 182
EXPULSION FROM A RECOGNISED SCHOOL 182
FAIR PROCEDURES AND NATURAL JUSTICE CONSIDERATIONS 186
SECTION 29 APPEALS 188
DETENTION OF CHILDREN 190
HEALTH AND SAFETY 190
RECENT HOUSE OF LORDS CASES 191
The Case of "L" and In-School Detention 191
The Case of "P" and the Legality of Strike Action 192
STUDENTS WITH SCHOOL ATTENDANCE PROBLEMS 194
THE LEGALITY OF EXCLUSION 195
THE CONCEPT OF REASONABLE FORCE 198

**Making Parents Pay: The Legal Enforcement of School
Attendance in England** (Neville Harris) 202
INTRODUCTION 202
THE RIGHT TO EDUCATION AND SCHOOL ATTENDANCE 204
IS PROSECUTION THE ANSWER? 213
ALTERNATIVES TO PROSECUTION 215
CONCLUSION 219

The Office of Ombudsman for Children in Ireland
(Dympna Glendenning) 222
INTRODUCTION 222
ORIGINS OF THE OFFICE OF OMBUDSMAN FOR CHILDREN 224

    Human Rights in the UNCRC 224
    **Recent Reforms in Ireland : Children's Rights and
    Welfare** 225
  Role and Functions: Ombudsman for Children 226
    Promotional Function of Ombudsman 227
    Investigatory function of ombudsman 228
    **Complaints taken against Schools and Voluntary
    Hospitals** 229
    **Functions of a School: Section 9 of the
    Education Act 1998** 230
  Exclusions and Limitations 232
    Exclusions under the 2002 Act 232
    Further Limitations on the Ombudsman's Powers 233
  Independence of Office of Ombudsman: Ministerial Veto 235
  First Annual Report of Ombudsman 237

**Freedom of Information Act and Schools: Balancing Education
and Secrecy** (Estelle Feldman) 239
  Introduction 239
  The Freedom of Information Acts 1997 and 2003 241
    The Amendment Act 241
    Administering the Act 242
    Fees: A requester's nightmare 243
    What is personal information? 243
    **To which Schools does the Freedom of Information
    Act apply?** 243
    Accurate record-keeping and sensible procedures 244
    Sound management practice 245
  Principal Rights under the Act 246
    Process of releasing information 247
    Rights of third parties 247
  Department of Education and Science and the
    Freedom of Information Act 247
    Openness and transparency 248
    Education Act 1998 248
  School League Tables or the Clash of the Acts 248
    Denying parents information 249
    Legislative opportunism 249
    League tables emerge 250

Primary School league tables 250
Contents of Tuairiscí Scoile 251
High Court appeal 252
Section 21(1) FOI exemption if access might prejudice
   future reports 252
Section 26(1) FOI exemption if information given in
   confidence 253
Supreme Court appeal 254
Discretionary nature of section 256
SEPARATED PARENTS' RIGHTS OF ACCESS TO RECORDS 256
Access to minor's records shall be granted 257
Strained family relationship irrelevant 258
Parental primacy 259
Supreme Court appeal 259
PARTNERS IN EDUCATION 260
Relationship of Department of Education and Science
   with Boards of Management and with teachers 260
All records held by the Department of Education and
   Science are subject to the Act 261
Parents 261
SELECTION OF INFORMATION COMMISSIONER'S DECISIONS
   INVOLVING SCHOOLS 262
Request by a newspaper for release of records relating
   to Whole School Evaluation (WSE) 262
Poor working atmosphere in school 263
Teacher's request for personal files 264
Complaint against a teacher 266
SECTION 21 DECISIONS 268
Requirement to identify potential harm that
   might arise 268
Access refused to internal audits of Department
   of Education and Science 269
UNDERSTANDING REALITIES 271
Data versus information 271
Secret versus confidential 271
CONCLUSIONS 272

Subject Index 273

TABLE OF CASES

A (A Minor) v. Leeds City Council, unreported, March 2, 1999
(Leeds County Court) 79, 80
A Parent v. A Primary School, DEC–S2003–135 .... 127 *et seq.*
A v. Head Teacher and Governors of Lord Grey School
[2004] E.L.R. 169, CA 207
Abbey Films v. Attorney General [1981] I.R. 158 112
Affutu-Nartoy v. Clarke, *The Times*, February 9, 1984 .... 70, 71
Ali v. The Head Teacher and Governors of Lord Grey School
[2004] E.W.C.A. Civ. 382 .... 195 *et seq.*
Anufrijeva v. Southwark LBC [2004] 1 All E.R. 833 198
Article 26 and the Employment Equality Bill 1996 [1997]
2 I.R. 321 119
Article 26 and the Equal Status Bill 1996 [1997] 2 I.R. 387 119
Article 26 and the School Attendance Bill 1942, in re
[1942] I.R. 334 97

Banks v. Bury Borough Council [1990] C.L.Y. 384 87
Barfoot v. East Sussex CC, unreported, 1939 83
Barnfather v. London Borough of Islington Education Authority and
the Secretary of State for Education and Skills [2003]
E.L.R. 263, Q.B.D. 208
Barry v. Board of Management (Aisling Project), DEC–E2001/031 135
Bath and North-East Somerset District Council v. Warman
[1999] E.L.R. 81 .... 208, 210
Bauer v. Minidoka, 116 Idaho 586, 778 P. 2d 336 (1989) .... 45 *et seq.*
Beaumont v. Surrey Co. Co., 112 Sol. J. 704 at 704
(per Geoffrey Lane J., 1968) 3
Best Travel t/a Cypriano Holidays, unreported, Supreme Court,
November 18, 1997 34
Bethel School District No 403 v. Fraser, 478 US 675 (1986) .... 58 *et seq.*, 60
Bleach v. Our Lady Immaculate Senior School and the Department of
Education and Science, DEC–E2003/028 136
Boland v. an Taoiseach [1974] I.R. 338 112
Bolger v. Governor of Mountjoy Prison, Ireland & Attorney General,
unreported, High Court, O'Donovan J.,
November 12, 1997 .... 154, 157 *et seq.*
Boyd & Boyd v. Ireland and the Attorney General, unreported,
High Court, Budd J., May 13, 1993 157

Bradford-Smart v. West Sussex County Council[2002] 1 F.C.R. 425;
 The Times Law Reports, January 29, (Court of Appeal, Judge
 and Hale L.JJ. & Sir Denis Henry) 2002, Judge L.J. .... 25, 156, 164 *et seq.*
Brady v Cavan County Council [1999] 4 I.R. 99 113
Brady v Sunderland FC, unreported (Court of Criminal Appeal),
 November 17, 1998 64
Brown v. Board of Education (1954) 347 US 483 92
Byrne v. Dun Laoghaire County Council, 20 Irish Law Times (New Series)
 16 (Circuit Court Dublin, Judge Smyth, November 13, 2001) 47
Byrne v. Ireland [1972] I.R. 241 112
Cahill v. St. John the Baptist School, Dublin Circuit Court,
 March 6, 2001, The Irish Times, March 7, 2001 5
Cahill v. West Ham Corporation, 81 Sol. J. 630 (1932) 83
Carabba v. School District 81
Carmarthenshire County Council v. Lewis[1953] A.C. 549 26
Carroll v. Monaghan VEC, DEC–E2004/003 137
Case 000238, The Irish Times and the Department of Education and
 Science, March 5, 2003 251
Case 000365,– Ms ACH and Others and the Department of Education
 and Science, October 16, 2001 .... 243, 264
Case 030693, Deputy Enda Kenny and the Department of Education
 and Science, May 24, 2004. .... 269 *et seq.*
Case 031109, Ms Madeleine Mulrennan and the Department of
 Education and Science, August 10, 2004 268
Case 98020, Mr AAF and the Office of the Civil Service and Local
 Appointments Commissioners, October 12, 1998 240
Case 98082, Mr ABD and the Office of the Local Appointments
 Commissioners, February 11, 1999 240
Case 98099, Mr John Burns and the Department of Education and Science,
 September 13, 2000 263
Case 98169, Ms ABY and the Department of Education and Science,
 July 6, 2000 .... 260, 261, 266 *et seq.*, 268
Case 98187, Ms ABH and the Office of the Local Appointments
 Commissioners, March 30, 1999 240
Case 99173, Mr X and the Department of Education and Science,
 July 17, 2001 .... 260, 266
Chilvers v. L. C. C. 32 T.L.R. 363 (K.B. Div., Bailhache J. (with jury, 1916) 11
Chittock v. Woodbridge, *The Times*, July 15, 2002 .... 76, 82
Clare v. Minister for Education and Science, unreported, High Court,
 July 30, 2004 .... 122, 125
Clark v. Bathnal Green Corporation, 55 T.L.R. 519 (1939). 77
Clark v. Monmouthshire Co. Co., 52 L.G.R. 246 (C.A., 1954) 11
Clarke v. O'Gorman, Supreme Court, February 13, 1996 .... 9 *et seq.*
Coffee v. St Pius National School, Circuit Court, Dublin,
 October 18, 1999 9

Table of Cases

Comer v. Governors of St Patrick's RC Primary School, Court of Appeal,
 November 13, 1997 .... 65, 66
Conway v. Irish National Teachers Organisation
 [1991] 1 I.R. 305 .... 54, 194
Cronin v. Minister for Education [2004] 3 I.R. 205 .... 115 116
Crotty v. An Taoiseach [1987] I.R. 713 112
Crowley v. Co. Cork VEC, DEC–E/2000/10 135
Crowley v. Ireland [1980] I.R. 102 .... 54, 96, 194
Crump v. Gilmore (1970) 68 L.G.R. 56 208

DEC–S2003–042/043 128
DEC–S2004–028 128
DEC–S2004–086 128
DEC–S2004–162 128
Delaney v. Board of Management, Drumshanbo N.S.,
 DEC–E2004/067 .... 137 *et seq.*
Delaney v. O'Dowd [1997] IR L Log W 157 (CC) 69
Dibble v. Carmarthern Town, unreported, Queen's Bench, 2001 85
Director of Public Prosecutions v. Best (the Best case)
 [2000] 2 I.R. 17 .... 96 *et seq.*, 102
Dolan v. Keohane and Cunningham, unreported, Supreme Court,
 February 8, 1994, affirming High Court, February 14, 1992 .... 29 *et seq.*
Doyle v. Little, Circuit Court, August 2, 2002 78
Duffy v. St. Joseph's National School, Coolock, Circuit Court Dublin,
 January 30, 2003, Irish Independent, January 31, 2003 5
Dunbar v. Good Counsel College, New Ross, DEC–E2003/051 127
Dunne v. National Maternity Hospital [1989] I.R. 91 25
Durham v. Public School Bd. Of Township School Area of North Oxford,
 22 H v. Pennell, 46 S.A.S.R. 158 (Sup. Court 1987) 11

East Donegal Co-Operative Livestock Mart Ltd v. Attorney General
 [1970] I.R. 317 112
Eriksson v. Sweden, Series A no 156 (1989) 12 E.H.R.R. 183 §93 204

Family H v. U.K., Application No. 10233/83 (1984) D.R. 105 205
Farrant v. Thames District Council, unreported Queens' Bench Division,
 June 11, 1996 87
Flesk v. King, Doyle's Personal Injury Judgments, Trinity and Michaelm
 as Terms 1996, p.87 (High Court Laffoy J., October 29, 1996) 7
Flynn v. O'Reilly [1999] 1 I.L.R.M. 458 .... 36, 85, 89
Foran v. Caherleheen National School, Circuit Court, Tralee,
 March 3, 2004 2
Fosberry v. Roscommon VEC, DEC–E2004/036 136
Fowles v. Bedfordshire County Council [1995] P.I.Q.R. 380 67

Gannon v. Rotherham MBC, Halsbury's Monthly Review (1991)
    91/1717 66
Garvey v. Ireland and Others [1981] I.R. 750 186
Geyer v. Downs (1977) 138 C.L.R. 91 154
Gibbs v. Barking Health Authority[1936] All E.R. 115 .... 80, 81
Glennon v. Board of Management, St Clare's Comprehensive School
    and the Minister for Education and Science, DEC–E2003030 137
Gorringe v. Calderdale MBC [2004] 1 W.L.R. 1057 88
Gow v. Glasgow Education Authority [1922] S.C. 260 11
Graves v. London Borough of Islington [2004] E.L.R. 1 215
Greene v. Mundow, Circuit Court, Judge McMahon,
    January 20, 2000 .... 12, 28 et seq.
Greening v. Stockton-on-tees BC, unreported, Queen's Bench, 1998 86

Haines v. Warren NSW Court of Appeal (CA 85 of 1986,
    CL 348 of 1984) Glass, Samuels and Priestly JJ.A.,
    December 23, 1986 .... 154, 158, 161 et seq.
Hall v. Kennedy, unreported, High Court, Morris J.,
    December 20, 1993 .... 158 et seq.
Hall v. Meehan, unreported, High Court, Gilligan J.,
    December 17, 2004 .... 36 et seq.
Hamilton v. Independent School District No. 114, 355 NW 2d 182 (1984)
    Minn. App., September 25, 1984 (C9–84–1012), Popovich C.J.,
    Sedgwick, and Lansing JJ., *per* Popovich C.J. .... 159 et seq.
Harrison v. Shields, unreported, High Court, November 15, 1996 75
Haughey, in re [1970] I.R. 217 186
Hayes v. Ireland [1987] I.L.R.M. 651
Hazelwood School District v. Kuhlmeier, 484 US 260 (1988) 59, 60
Healy v. Dodd [1951] Ir. Jur. Rep. 22 (High Court, O'Byrne J.) 6
Heaves v. Westmeath County Council, 20 Irish Law Times (New Series)
    236 (Circuit Court, Mullingar 2001) 36
Hill v. Durham County Council, Court of Appeal, unreported,
    January 31, 2000 67
Hinchley v. Rankin [1961] 1 All E.R. 692 209
Hosback v. Sacred Heart Boys' National School, Circuit Court,
    May 24, 2000, The Irish Times, May 25, 2000 2
Hosty v. McDonagh, unreported, Supreme Court,
    May 29,1973 25
Hunter v. Perth and Kinross Council (2001) S.C.L.R. 856 .... 26 et seq.
Hurley v. INTO [1991] 2 I.R. 328 194

Jarman v. Mid-Glamorgan Education Authority, *The Times*,
    February 11, 1985
Jenkins v. Howells [1949] 2 K.D. 218 .... 210 et seq.
Julius v. Lord Bishop of Oxford (1880) L.R. 5 Appeal Cases 214/3 95

Table of Cases xvii

Kane v. Kennedy, unreported, High Court, March 25, 1999 .... 64, 88
Kavanagh v. Governor of Arbour Hill Prison, Ireland & Attorney General,
  unreported ,High Court, Morris J., April 22, 1993
  (1988/9683P). .... 156 *et seq.*
Kearn-Price v. Kent County Council [2002] E.W.C.A. Civ. 1539;
  [2002] All E.R. (D.) 440, October 30, 2002 .... 27 *et seq.*, 90
Kelly v. Gilhooley, Doyle's Personal Injury Judgments, Trinity and
  Michaelmas Terms 1994, p.86 (High Court, November 1, 1994) 3, 12
Kenny v. Board of Management, Comprehensive School, Tallaght,
  DEC–E2005/001 135
Killilea v. Information Commissioner [2003] I.E.H.C. 63 242
Kjeldesen, Busk Masden and Pedersen v. Denmark (1979-89)
  1 E.H.R.R. 711 205
Kwiotek v. NUI Galway, DEC-S2004–176 122

L, (a Minor) [2003] U.K.H.L. 9 .... 191 *et seq.*
Langham v. Wellingborough School, 101 L.J.K.B. 513 (C.A., 1932) 11
Leatherland v. Edwards, Queen's Bench, November 28, 1998 71
Lennon v. McCarthy, unreported, Supreme Court, 13 July 1966 .... 4, 8, 36, 85
Liennard v. Slough Borough Council [2002] E.W.H.C. 398 (Q.B.) 54
Long v. Gardner, 144 D.L.R. (3d) 73 (Ontario High Court Smith J., 1983),
  23 D.L.R. (2d) 711 (Ontario C.A., 1960) 11
Lunenburg (County) Dist. School Board v. Peircy (1998) 41 C.C.L.T.
  (2d.) 60 (N.S.C.A.) 81
Lynskey v. Coolmine Community School, DEC–E2002/035 .... 135 *et seq.*

MacCabe v. Westlock (1998) 226 A.R. 1 (QB) 81
Magrowski v Guy's & St. Thomas's NHS Trust 52
Maher v. Board of Management of Presentation Junior School
  [2004] I.R. 337 195
Maher v. The Board of Management of Presentation Junior School,
  unreported, High Court, Peart J., October 22, 2004 .... 18 *et seq.*
Mapp v. Gilhooley, unreported, High Court, Barr J., November 7, 1989 .... 7, 9
Maunsell v. Minister for Education [1940] I.R. 213 186
McGinn v. Board of Management, St. Anthony's Boys N.S., Kilcoole,
  DEC–E2004/032 138
Meade v. Haringey London Borough Council [1979] 2 All E.R. 1016 .... 206.
Minister for Education and Science v. the Information Commissioner
  (Schools League Tables case) [2001] I.E.H.C. 116 .... 248 *et seq.*, 262
Morrell v. Owen, *The Times*, December 14, 1993 65
MS Grewal v. Deep ChandSood [2001] 1289 L.R.I. 4 34
Muldoon v. Ireland & Attorney General [1988]
  I.L.R.M. 367 (HC) .... 153 *et seq.*, 155, 160
Mulligan v. Doherty, unreported, Supreme Court,
  May 17, 1966 79

Mulvey (a minor) v. McDonagh[2004] 1 I.R. 497 .... 155 *et seq.*
Mulvey v. McDonagh, unreported, High Court, Johnson J.,
  March 26, 2004 .... 22 *et seq.*
Murphy v. Dublin Corporation [1972] I.R. 215 112
Murphy v. County Wexford VEC, unreported, Supreme Court,
  July 29, 2004 .... 12 *et seq.*, 19
Murtagh & anor v. Board of Governors of St Emer's National School
  [1991] 1 I.R. 482; [1991] I.L.R.M. 549 .... 167, 169 *et seq.*
Myers v. Peel County Board of Education, 123 D.L.R. (1981) 80

Nagle v. South Western Health Board and the Minister for Education,
  unreported, High Court, Herbert J., October 30, 2001 115
NicFhlannchada v. Coláiste Mhuire, DEC–E2004/058 135
Nix v. Board of Management, Oola N.S., EE2/1999 .... 134 *et seq.*
NMcK v. Information Commissioner [2004] I.E.H.C. 4 .... 240, 256 *et seq.*
North Western Health Board v. H.W. [2001] 3 I.R. 622 259

O, Re (A Minor) (Care Proceedings: Education) [1992] 4 All E.R. 905 216
O'Gorman v. Crotty[1946] Ir. Jur. Rep. 34 (High Court, O'Byrne J.) 6
O'Neill v. Board of Management, St. Gabriels' N.S, DEC–E2005/007 138
O'Neill v. Tipperary S.R. V.E.C.[1996] Irish Law Log Weekly 369
  (Circuit Court, Judge O'Donnell) .... 4 *et seq*
O'Reilly v. Limerick Corporation [1989] I.L.R.M. 181 .... 113 *et seq.*
O'Shea v. Royal Borough of Kingston Upon Thames Council,
  unreported, Court of Appeal, 1995 87

P (a Minor), re [2003] U.K.H.L. 8 [2001] E.W.C.A. Civ. 652 .... 192 *et seq.*
People v. O'Shea [1982] I.R. 384 96
Phelps v. Hillingdon London Borough Council [2000] 3 W.L.R. 776;
  [2001] 2 A.C. 619, *The Times*, July 28, 2000 .... 54, 165
Phelps v. London Borough of Hillingdon, HSE, July 27, 2000 195

R (Jones) v. Ceredigon County Council [2004] E.L.R. 506 212
R (SB) v. Head Teacher and Governors of Denbigh High School
  [2005] E.L.R. 198, CA .... 207.
R .v Inner London Education Authority ex parte Ali and Murshid
  [1990] 2 Admin.L.R. 822 206
R v. Bedfordshire County Council ex parte DE, July 1, 1996, Q.B.D.
  (unreported) 212
R v. Carmarthenshire County Council ex p White [2001]
  E.L.R. 172, Q.B.D 212
R v. Devon County Council ex parte Paul George [1988]
  3 All E.R. 1002 212
R v Dyfed CC ex p S [1994] F.L.R. 320; Re S
  [1995] E.L.R. 98 212

Table of Cases

R v. Essex County Council ex p EB [1997] E.L.R. 327 212
R v. Head Teacher of Fairfield Primary School and others ex parte W,
 Q.B.D. CO/541/97, July 18, 1997, Scott Baker J. .... 166 *et seq.*
R v. Kent County Council ex p C [1998] E.L.R. 108, Q.B.D 212
R v. Newham London Borough Council, Ex parte X [1995] E.L.R. 303,
 The Times, November 15, 1994 165
R v. Rochdale MBC ex p Schemet [1994] E.L.R. 89; Re C
 [1994] E.L.R. 273 212
R (S.B.) v. Denbeigh High School[2005] 1 F.C.R. 530,
 March 2005 .... 128 *et seq.*
Ralph v. LCC, 63 T.L.R. 546 82
Rawsthorne v. Ottley [1937] 3 All E.R. 902 (K.B.D.) 4
Regina v. East Sussex C.C. ex p. Tandy [1998] A.C. 714 116
Rhind v. Astbury Waterpark [2004] E.W.C.A. (Civ.) 756 (June 16, 2004) 88
Riney v. Co. Donegal VEC, DEC–E2001/030 135
Rogers v. Essex County Council [1986] 3 All E.R. 321 212
Ryan v. Madden[1944] I.R. 154 (High Court, O'Byrne J.) 4

Scott v. Lothian Regional Council, unreported, Outer House, Scotland,
 September 29, 1998 156
Scott v. The Lothian Regional Council Court of Session, Outer House,
 Scotland (September 29, 1998) 23, 24, 25
Sheedy v. Information Commissioner, unreported, High Court,
 Gilligan J., May 20 2004 .... 250 *et seq.*, 252
Sheehan v. INTO [1997] 2 I.R. 327 194
Simonds v. Isle of Wight Council [2003] E.W.H..C. 2303 77
Sinnott v. Minister for Education and Ors [2001] 2 I.R. 505 .... 52, 113
Sinnott v. Minister for Education, unreported, Supreme Court,
 per Geoghegan J., July 12, 2001 .... 52 *et seq.*
Smith v. Jolly, Court of Appeal, May 1984 65
Smith v. Martin [1911] 2 K.B. 775 52
Smoldon v. Whitworth, Court of Appeal, December 18, 1996 71
Spiers v. Warrington Corporation [1954] 1 Q.B. 61 209
State (Gleeson) v. Minister for Defence [1976] I.R. 280 186
State (Quinn) v. Ryan [1965] I.R. 70 112
State (Smullen & Smullen) v. Duffy & Ors [1980]
 I.L.R.M. 46 (HC) .... 165, 167 *et seq.*, 173, 174, 187
State of Victoria v. Bryer (1970) 44 A.L.J.R. 174 154
State(Quinn) v. Ryan[1965] I.R. 70 112
Student A & Student B v. Dublin Secondary School
 [1999] I.E.H.C. 47 (November 25, 1999) .... 170 *et seq.*, 174, 187
Sweeney v Duggan [1997] 1 I.L.R.M. 21 64

T.D. v. Minister for Education [2001]
 4 I.R. 259 .... 101 *et seq.*, 112, 113 *et seq.*, 190

Taylor v. Bath & NE Somerset District Council, unreported,
   Court of Appeal, 1999 86
The Commonwealth v. Introvigne, 150 C.L.R. 258
   (High Court of Australia 1982), affirming, 48 F.L.R. 161
   (Fed. Court A.C.T. Dist. Reg. Gen. Div., 1980) .... 12, 13, 38 *et seq.*, 154
The Queen (R) v. Leeds Magistrates Court and Others[2005]
   E.W.H.C. 1479 (Admin.) 210
The Queen on the application of B v. Head Teacher of Alperton Community
   School and Others; The Queen v. Head Teacher of Wembley High School
   and Others ex p. T; The Queen v. Governing Body of Cardinal
   Newman High School and Others ex p. C [2001] E.L.R. 359 207
The Queen on the application of J v. Vale of Glamorgan County Council
   [2001] E.L.R. 758, C.A 212
The School's Duty of Care to its Pupils 53
Thornton v. Board of School Trustees of School District No. 57
   (1976) 73 D.L.R. 3d. 35 81
Tinker v. Des Moines Independent Community School District,
   393 US 503 (1969) .... 57 *et seq.*, 61
Tomlinson v. Congleton BC [2003] All E.R. 1122 88
Two Named Female Teachers v. A Boy's Secondary School,
   DEC–E2001/05 139

Van Donselaar v. Central Coast Grammar School Ltd[2003]
   N.S.W. C.A. 241 .... 55 *et seq.*
Van Oppen v. Clerk to the Bedford Charity Trustees [1989]
   1 All E.R. 273 (Q.B.); [1989] 3 All E.R. 389 (Court of Appeal) 64, 67
VK v. Norfolk County Council and the Special Educational Needs and
   Disability Tribunal [2005] E.L.R. 342, Q.B.D 205
Vowles v. WRFU, Court of Appeal, March, 2003 68
Vowles v. WRFU, Queen's Bench, December 13, 2002 67

Wallace v. Batavia School District, 68 F. 3 d 1010: see
   104 Ed. Law Rep. 132 199
Wallace v. Flynn, unreported, High Court, Kelly J., May 1, 2002 159
Walsh v. Board of Management, Ballinrobe Community School,
   DEC–E2004/041 137
Walsh v. Ryan, unreported, High Court, Lavan J.,
   February 12, 1993 154
Ward v. Donegal Vocational Education Committee, unreported,
   High Court, Keane J., May 1993 70
Waters v. Commissioner of Police of the Metropolis [1997] I.C.R. 1073;
   [1997] I.R.L.R. 589 (CA) (Evans, Waite, Swinton-Thomas LJ.J.) 155
Watson v. Haines, unreported, Supreme Court of NSW, April 10, 1987 68
Weir Rodgers v. The SF Trust Ltd. [2005] 1 I.L.R.M. 471
Williams v. Eady (1893) 10 T.L.R. 41 (CA) 3, 52

Williams v. Rotherham, *The Times*, August 6, 1998 69
Woodroffe-Hedley v. Cuthberston, unreported (Queens Bench),
    June 20, 1997 64
Wright v. Board of Management of Gorey Community School
    [2000] I.E.H.C. 37 (March 28, 2000) .... 173 *et seq.*., 187
Wright v. Cheshire County Council[1952] 2 All E.R. 789 80

X (Minors) v. Bedfordshire Co. Co. [1995] A.C. 766 54
X Minors v. Bedfordshire C.C. and other cases [1995] 2 A.C. 633 195

TABLE OF LEGISLATION

IRELAND

Bunreacht na Éireann 1937 .... 57, 95, 224, 237
    Preamble 115
    Art.6.1 116
    Art.15 111
    Art.15.2.1 111
    Art.28 111
    Art.26 97
    Art.34 186
    Art.40.1 54
    Art.40.3 .... 54, 186
    Art.40.1 118
    Art.40.6.2 118
    Art.41 .... 229, 259, 260
    Art.42 .... 95, 96, 102, 113, 259, 260
    Art.42.3.2 .... 93, 95 *et seq.*, 103
    Art.42.4 .... 53, 95, 103
    Art.42.5 .... 54, 95, 101, 103, 115
    Art.44.2 118
Adventure Standards Authority Act 2001 73
Anti-Discrimination (Pay) Act 1974 118
Child Care Act 1991 .... 110, 140
Child Trafficking and Pornography Act 1998 225
Children Act 2001 43
    s.52 150
Criminal Law Act 1997 150
Education (Ireland) Act 1892 93
Education Act 1998 .... 97, 102 *et seq.*, 105, 107, 137,
                                                            176 *et seq.*, 181, 188. 246, 248
    s.7(2)(a) 183, 184
    s.7(4)(b) 184
    s.9 .... 229, 230 *et seq.*
    s.9(a) 183, 184
    s.9(g) 248, 257
    s.10 .... 102, 181
    s.11 102
    s.12 102

Education Act 1998—*contd.*
- s.13 .... 253, 254
- s.15(2) 231
- s.15(2)(d) 109
- s.15(2)(g) 183, 184
- s.22(1) 232
- s.28 .... 176, 181, 230
- s.29 .... 176, 180, 188 *et seq.*
- s.29(1)(d) 188
- s.29(2) 188, 189
- s.29(3) 189
- s.29(5) 189
- s.29(7)(b) 189
- s.30 102
- s.49 233
- s.50 233
- s.51(1)(f) 233
- s.51(2) 233
- s.53 .... 249 *et seq.*, 254
- pt VII 105

Education for Persons with Special Educational Needs Act 2004 .... 102, 108, 123, 181, 184 *et seq.*
- s.1 184
- s.2 .... 184, 185
- s.3 .... 186, 195
- s.4 186
- s. 8(1) 185
- s.10 108
- s.10(1) 185
- s.10(3) 185
- s.10(6) 194
- s.14 185
- s.14(1)(a) 184
- s.14(1)(c) 184
- s.14(2)-(14)(4) 184
- s.18 195
- s.19 184
- ss.19–37 184
- s.36 184
- s.38(1)(b) 186
- s.38(7) 186
- s.39 110
- s.40 110
- ss.40–44 184
- ss.45–49 185

Education for Persons with Special Educational Needs Act 2004—*contd.*
ss.45–49 5
ss.50–53 184
Education (Welfare) Act 2000 .... 93, 96 *et seq.*, 102, 103 *et seq.*,
177 *et seq.*, 181, 185
s.2 103
s.4(4) 122
s.10 104
s.10(2) 104
s.10(3) 104
s.10(4)–(8) 106
s.12 106
s.13 104
s.17 107
s.17(2) .... 107 *et seq.*
s.19 109
s.20 109
s.21 109
s.21(a) 109
s.21(4) 109,110
s.21(5) 110
s.23 .... 177, 182, 184, 237
s.23(3) 182
s.23(4) 182
s.23(5) 182
s.24 .... 109, 178, 188, 197
s.24(1) 197
s.24(4) 183
s.24(2) 183
s.24(1) 183
s.24(5) 183
s.25 105
s.25(6) 108
s.25(8) 110
s.26 .... 110, 178
s.27 .... 110, 179
s.28 110
s.29 110
s.29(2) 110, 111
s.29(3) 111
s.29(5) 111
s.29(9) 111
s.30 110
s.32 .... 104, 105
s.33 104

Table of Legislation xxv

Education (Welfare) Act 2000—*contd.*
    s.41 104
    s.37 103
    s.40 103
Employment Equality Act 1977 118
Employment Equality Act 1998–2004 .... 130 *et seq.*, 139
Employment Equality Act 1998 .... 119, 135, 137
    s.6 132
    s.6(1) 132
    s.11 131
    s.12 131
    s.13 131
    s.14A 138
    s.14A(1)(a) 139
    s.16 132
    s.19(4) 132
    s.22(1) 132
    s.29(4) 132
    s.31(1) 132
    s.36(3) 133
    s.37(1) 133, 134
    s.37 134
    s.74(2) 136
    s.78(6) 140
    s.78(7) 140
    s.85 140
    s. 85(4) 140
    s. 85A 131
    s. 86 140
Employment Equality Act 2004
    s.4 131
    s.9 1312
    s.12 132
    s.13 132
    s.19 132
    s.20 132
    s.38 .... 131, 140
Equality Act 2004 119
    s.8 138
    s.48 121
    s.50 128
    s.51 123
    s.54 126
    s.64 127
Equal Status Acts 2000–2004 .... 120 *et seq.*, 181, 183, 185

Equal Status Act 2000 .... 102, 119 *et seq.*, 127
    s.2 .... 120, 123
    s.3 .... 120, 123
    s.3(3) 120
    s.4 .... 121 et se, 183, 184
    s.4(2) 121
    s.4(3) 121
    s.4(4) 122, 184
    s.4(5) 122
    s.5 .... 121, 124, 142 *et seq.*
    s.6 121
    s.7 .... 120, 124 *et seq.*, 140 *et seq.*
    s.7(1) 124
    s.7(2) 124
    s.7(3) .... 124 *et seq.*
    s.7(4) .... 124 *et seq.*
    s.11 124
    s.11(2) 123
    s.11(5) 123
    s.14(b) 125
    s.21 126
    s.21(1) 126
    s.23 126
    s.23(3) 126
    s.24 126
    s.24(2) 126
    s.25 126
    s.25(5) 127
    s.25(6) 127
    s.27 127
    s.31 127
Freedom of Information Act 1997 .... 239 *et seq.*
    s.3 244
    s.6 246
    s.6(9) 244
    s.7 247
    s.7(7) 262
    s.8 245
    s.8(4)(b) 250
    s.9 245
    s.14 247
    s.15 248
    s.15(6)(d)(ii) 241
    s.16 248
    s.17 .... 243, 246

Table of Legislation

Freedom of Information Act 1997—*contd.*
    s.18 .... 242, 243, 246
    s.21 .... 253, 254, 268 *et seq.*
    s.21(1) 252
    s.21(1)(a) 268
    s.21(1)(b) 253, 268
    s.21(1)(c) 253
    s.21(2) 253, 268
    s.26 .... 247, 254, 255
    s.26(1) .... 253 *et seq.*
    s.27 247
    s.28 .... 247, 251, 262
    s.28(1) 251
    s.29 247
    s.34 .... 247, 255
    s.39(10)(a) 252
    s.42 247
    sch.1 244
Freedom of Information (Amendment) Act 2003 .... 241 *et seq.*, 247
    s.10(b) 241
    s.14(1) 242
    s.14(1)(f) 242
Health (Eastern Regional Authority) Act 1999 223
Health Act 1999 229
Health Act 2004 226
Illegal Immigrants (Trafficking) Act 2000 226
Local Authorities (Higher Education Grants) Acts 1968–1992 142
Non-Fatal Offences Against the Person Act 1997 .... 146 *et seq.*, 199 *et seq.*
    s.2 .... 147 *et seq.*
    s.3 147
    s.4 148
    s.17 150
    s.18 149
    s.20 149
    s.20(2) .... 149 *et seq.*
    s.22 148
    s.24 .... 1468, 225
Occupiers' Liability Act 1995 .... 3, 35 *et seq.*, 66, 88, 154
    s.1(1) 36, 44
    s.4(1) 40, 45
    s.4(2) 42
    s.4(3) 43
    s.4(3)(a) 43
    s.4(3)(b) 43
    s.4(4) 45

Occupiers' Liability Act 1995—*contd.*
    s.5 .... 39, 41
    s.5(1) 40
    s.5(2) 40
    s.5(2)(b)(i) 39, 40
    s.5(2)(b)(ii) 41
    s.5(2)(c) 41
    s.5(3) 41
    s.5(5) 41
    s.8(a) 44

Ombudsman Act 1980
    s.7 .... 228, 233
    s.8 233
    s.9 233

Ombudsman for Children Act 2002 .... 181, 223, 226 *et seq.*
    s.6(1) 226, 236
    s.6(2) 227
    s.7 .... 227 *et seq.*, 236
    s.8 .... 223, 229
    s.9 .... 223, 230
    s.9(1)(ii) 232
    s.9(2) 230
    s.11(1)(a) 232
    s.11(1)(f) 233
    s.11(1)(b) 238
    s.11(2)(a) 235
    s.11(4) 235
    s.13(3) 232
    s.13(7) 232
    s.13(7) 232
    s.14 228
    s.15 228
    sch.1 227
    sch. 223, 229, 238

Pensions Act 1990 118
Protection of Persons Reporting Child Abuse Act 1998 226
    s.1 226
Refugee Act 1996 226
    s.3 141
Safety, Health and Welfare at Work Act 2005 .... 3, 47 *et seq.*, 190 *et seq.*
    s.2(6) 50
    s.12 48
    s.13(1) 48, 49, 52
    s.13(1)(a) 49, 50
    s.13(1)(b) 49, 50

Table of Legislation xxix

Safety, Health and Welfare at Work Act 2005—*contd.*
    s.13(1)(e) 49, 50
    s.13(1)(h) 49, 50
Schools Attendance Act 1926 .... 93, 100, 103
School Attendance Acts 1926–1967 .... 97, 98
    s.22 180
Sexual Offences (Jurisdiction) Act 1996 225
Social Welfare (No.2) Act 1985 118
VEC Acts 1930–2001 232

STATUTORY INSTRUMENTS

S.I. No.47 of 1999
    art.3(1) 257
S.I. No.239 of 1999 244
S.I. No.151 of 2002 226
S.I. No.264 of 2003 243
S.I. No.527 of 2003 226
S.I. No.468 of 2004 226
S.I. No.507 of 2005 .... 108, 185
S.I. No.508 of 2005 .... 108, 123, 185
S.I. No.509 of 2005 .... 108, 123, 186
S.I. No. 548 of 2005 180
S.I. No.636 of 2005 108

ENGLAND

Anti-Social Behaviour Act 2003 217
    s.19 218
    s.19(5)(b) 218
    s.19(6)(b) 218
    s.19(8) 218
    s.23 217
Care Standards Act 2000(Wales) 223
Care Standards Act (England) 2000 223
Children's Commissioners Act 2001 223
Children Act 1989 215
    s.36 215
    sch.3, para.9 216
    sch.3, para.12 216
Children Act 2004 216
Commissioner for Children and Young People (Scotland)
    Act 2003 234

Crime and Disorder act 1998 216
    s. 8 218
    s.9(7) 219
    s.16 ....216 et seq.
Criminal Justice and Court Services Act 2000 209
Education Act 1993
    s.298(1) 116
Education Act 1996 200
    s.7 205
    s.8 205
    s.13 206
    s.14 206
    s.19 .... 197, 206
    s.437 .... 203, 205
    s.443 205
    s.443(A) 209, 218
    s.444 .... 209, 211 et seq., 215,218
    s.444(1) 208
    s.444A 217
    s.444B 217
    s.444(3) 212
    s.444(3)(b) 210
    s.444(3)(c) 212
    s.444(5) 212
    s.444(8A) 209
    s.444(8B) 209
    s.444ZA 207
    s,444ZA(6) 207
    s.447 215
    s.509(4) 212
Education Act 1997 200
    s.18(1) 200
Education Act 2002 202
    s.53 203
Education Act 2005 202
Education (Schools) Act 1997 202
Elementary Education Act (Scotland) 1872 93
Elementary Education Acts (England) 1879–1909 93
Higher Education Act 2004 202
Humans Rights Act 1988 207
    s. 8 197
Learning and Skills Act 2000 202
Schools Standards and Framework Act 1998 .... 191, 192, 196, 202
    s.63 203
    ss.64–68 195

Special Educational Needs and Disability Act 2001 202
Teaching and Higher Education Act 1998 202
Trade Union and Labour Relations (Consolidation) Act 1992
    s.219 .... 192, 193
    ss.226–234 192
    s.235A 193

STATUTORY INSTRUMENTS

Commissioner for Children and Young People (Northern Ireland) Order
    2003 (S.I. No.439 of 2003 (N.I. 11) 223, 235
Education (Pupil Registration) Regulations 1995 (S.I. No.1995/2089)
    reg.(3) 209
    reg (4). 209
Education (Pupil Exclusions and Appeals) (Maintained Schools)
(England) Regulations 2002 (S.I. No.2002/3178)
    reg.7(2) 206
Education (Penalty Notices) (England) Regulations 2004
(S.I. No.2004/181) 217

INTERNATIONAL COVENANTS, DECLARATIONS AND DIRECTIVES

Council Directive 1997/80/EC 119
Council Directive 2000/43/EC 119
Council Directive 2000/78/EC 119
    art.4(2) 133
Council Directive 2004/113 119
Declaration of the Rights of the Child 1959 224
Equal Pay Directive 1975 139
Equal Treatment Directive 1976 139
European Convention on Human Rights .... 57, 128 *et seq.*, 196 *et seq.*, 207
    art.2 .... 196, 204
    art.8 211
    art. 8 (2) 211
    art.9(1) 128
    art.9(2) 129
Framework Directive 51
    art.5 51
    art.5(1) 51
    art.5(4) 51
    art.6(2) 208
Geneva Declaration of the Rights of the Child 1924 224

International Covenant of Civil and Political Rights
  art.23 224
  art.24 224
International Covenant on Economic, Social and Cultural Rights 1966 (ICESC) 99
  art.10 224
UN Covenant on the Rights of the Child (UNCHR) .... 224 *et seq.*
  art.2(1) .... 224 *et seq.*
  art.12 237
  art.12(1) 61, 237
  art.13(1) 61
  art.13(2) 61
  art.28(2) 61, 237
  art.28 .... 92, 204
  art.37 234
UN International Covenant on Economic, Social and Cultural Rights 1966
  art.13.2 92
UN Universal Declaration of Human Rights, 1948 and UN Convention on the Rights of the Child
  art.28 99

THE SCHOOL'S DUTY OF CARE TO ITS PUPILS: RECENT DEVELOPMENTS IN THE LAW

WILLIAM BINCHY*

THE SCHOOL'S DUTY OF CARE TO ITS PUPILS

One can feel fairly confident about discussing the main principles of the school's duty of care to its pupils since there have been several judicial decisions on the subject over many years. We are considering here the law of negligence which requires of us all that we act in a careful way towards each other so as to avoid causing injury, damage or loss. The crucial test applied by the courts is that of the reasonable person placed in the defendant's circumstances. If the defendant has acted with due care so as to try to avoid causing an unreasonable risk of injury to others, he or she will not be found to have been negligent even where injury results from that conduct. We are not required to ensure that our acts (or omissions) never result in injury: all that we must do is take reasonable care.

Of course what constitutes reasonable care in any case depends on the particular circumstances. The court makes a value-judgment, taking into account the likelihood of injury resulting from the defendant's conduct, the gravity of the threatened injury, the social utility of the conduct and the cost – economic, social, physical or psychological – of preventing the injury. Sometimes this value-judgment is easy: a drunken driver, for example, is clearly risking serious injury to others, his or her conduct has no social utility and the risk could be prevented simply by not driving. In other cases, the competing factors can be more evenly balanced.

When it comes to assessing the question of the negligence of schools, the courts have shown themselves to be very aware of the importance of giving children space to grow, to take some risks and not to be subjected to mollycoddling supervision. Perhaps the English judge who expressed the

---

*Regius Professor of Laws, Trinity College, Dublin.

view that it was better that a pupil's neck be broken than that his spirit be broken went a bit far but the need for schools to give their pupils an awareness of managing risk in their own lives is nonetheless a real one.

It should, however, be emphasised that the courts have made it clear that pupils need to be protected from avoidable dangers. What precisely must be done will depend on a number of factors, with the age of the pupil being of particular importance. Young children cannot be released onto the street during school hours. Their play must be closely supervised and they must be prevented from engaging in risky activity (such as sliding down banisters or opening windows) where their lack of maturity or experience makes them incapable of adequately measuring the danger. In this context, the discharge of a school's duty of care may require it to take interventionist decisions which, for older pupils, would be controversial. Thus, for example, a teacher would be perfectly entitled to confiscate matches from a very young pupil. Indeed, to fail to ensure that the matches were removed would probably be characterised as an act of negligence. The intervention is justified not because the youthfulness of the pupil deprives the pupil of rights but rather because the exercise of those rights has to be accommodated with the school's duty of care to the pupil.

The courts have made it perfectly plain that they appreciate the need to apply a standard of care that respects educational values and is sensitive to the realities of school life. In *Hosback v. Sacred Heart Boys' National School*,[1] Judge O'Leary said that it was in the public interest that children should be encouraged and supervised by teachers to compete in all field sports and be brought to swimming pools to learn to swim. Dismissing a claim for negligence where the plaintiff teenage student fell at a swimming pool when grabbing the poolside ladder after a false start to a race, Judge O'Leary said:

> "It is in the interest of the public in the widest sense that teachers and others in charge of children should not be hamstrung by the unnecessary fear of being sued to the extent that they would not be able to do anything."

In *Foran v. Caherleheen National School*,[2] where a pupil claimed that he had been lining up to go back into the school building after a break when one of two boys who were fighting hit him in the face with his elbow, Judge O'Hagan dismissed the claim, asking "What can a teacher do to stop that?"

---

[1] Circuit Court, May 24, 2000, *The Irish Times*, May 25, 2000.
[2] Circuit Court, Tralee, March 3, 2004.

The "careful parent" test

A very general guiding principle was expressed by Lord Esher in *Williams v. Eady*, that:

> "the schoolmaster [is] bound to take such care of his boys as a careful father would take of his boys ...".[3]

Although this statement has been quoted widely with approval in several decisions in this country and abroad, it has been criticised for being "unrealistic, if not unhelpful",[4] especially where the number of pupils in the school is high. The problems of care and control in a school bear *some* resemblance to those confronting a parent in the home but they are far from identical. It is possible that in a future decision an Irish court will drop the reference to the "careful parent" and stress the fact that it is the standard of the reasonable school teacher or manager which should prevail. The degree of care required of the teacher, naturally, will vary with the circumstances and especially the age of the child. As Costello J. observed in *Kelly v. Gilhooley*[5]:

> "the duty of care which school authorities owe to children differs from moment to moment and from place to place and the duty is different in different times of the day and in different places in the school."

This chapter will consider aspects of the duty to take reasonable care in supervising pupils. Next it addresses the position of schools under the Occupiers' Liability Act 1995 and under the Safety, Health and Welfare at Work Act 2005. It goes on to examine other ways in which schools may be held to fall under a duty of care. Finally it briefly discusses some other acts of negligence and some emerging issues: Pupils with disabilities and Pupils, Autonomy and Privacy.

The duty of care in supervision

The matter of supervision may be considered from five standpoints:

(1) Supervision on school premises;

(2) Injuries sustained off the premises;

---

[3] 10 T.L.R. 14 at 42 (C.A., 1893).
[4] See *Beaumont v. Surrey Co. Co.*, 112 Sol. J. 704 at 704 (*per* Geoffrey Lane J., 1968).
[5] Doyle's Personal Injury Judgments, Trinity and Michaelmas Terms 1994, p.86 at 88 (High Court, November 1, 1994).

(3) Supervision outside hours;

(4) The position in regard to school transport;

(5) Supervision on school tours.

Supervision on school premises

It is beyond argument that some degree of supervision is necessary where pupils are playing in school playgrounds but the courts have been anxious to make it plain that too high a standard of care will not be demanded. As Ó Dálaigh C.J. said in *Lennon v. McCarthy*[6]:

> "When normally healthy children are in the playground it is not necessary that they should be under constant supervision."

Similarly, in the English decision of *Rawsthorne v. Ottley*,[7] Hilbery J. expressed the view that:

> "it is not the law, and never has been the law, that a schoolmaster should keep boys under supervision during every moment of their school lives."

The Irish cases present interesting examples of the range of cases that can arise under the general heading of supervision. We will look at them in some detail. It is of course worth bearing in mind that very young children need protection from dangers which they have not the capacity to appreciate; but it is also true that teenagers' willingness to experiment and take risks generates a separate need on the part of the post-primary school to provide appropriate supervision.

In *Ryan v. Madden*,[8] the failure of a national school teacher to supervise young pupils, including the plaintiff, aged five, when they were leaving the building at the end of school hours was held to be negligence where the child slid down the banisters from the upper floor (where the class-room was).

Ryan v. Madden may be contrasted with *O'Neill v. Tipperary S.R. V.E.C.*[9] Again the problem concerned an accident on the stairs. The plaintiff, aged

---

[6] Unreported, Supreme Court, July 13, 1966.
[7] [1937] 3 All E.R. 902 at 905 (K.B.D.).
[8] [1944] I.R. 154 (High Court, O'Byrne J.).
[9] [1996] *Irish Law Log Weekly* 369 (Circuit Court, Judge O'Donnell).

12, injured her ankle when struck by another student sliding down the banisters at the start of the lunch break. There was some degree of conflicting evidence as to whether there had been a significant incidence of pupils sliding down the banisters on previous occasions. Judge O'Donnell dismissed the action. He was not satisfied on the basis of the evidence that the school had been negligent or in breach of the standard of care imposed on it: "accidents do occur, but the evidence must be very clear as to the facts and breach of duty". While the plaintiff had contended that there had been a persistent problem in the school with students sliding down the banisters, there had been "very peremptory evidence" that there had been "no problem whatsoever"; the pupil who had collided with the plaintiff had been involved in only one previous incident relating to the banisters and it was therefore wrong to impose liability on the school.

In *Cahill v. St. John the Baptist School*,[10] Judge Devally dismissed a claim for negligence where a 12-year-old pupil broke her ankle when descending a staircase. She alleged that the supervision had been inadequate on the fateful day as staff numbers were down on account of the funeral of a senior teacher. She also claimed that the staircase was defective and unsafe. Judge Devally is reported as having stated that the plaintiff had obeyed a school rule which required pupils to proceed in pairs on stairways, but she had said her friend had gone on ahead and she was on her own when the accident occurred. The Judge observed:

> "I have to ask what the school authorities did that was wrong and I cannot find on the evidence that there was any wrong on their part."

Judge Devally believed that the girls had run down the stairs and that the plaintiff's ankle had gone from under her on the right angle turn on the staircase. He felt that the stairway was totally suited for its purposes and scientific tests had shown that there had been adequate adhesion on the steps. The short report of the case makes it hard to know the precise evidence on which the judgment was based.

In *Duffy v. St. Joseph's National School, Coolock*,[11] Judge Smyth, President of the Circuit Court, dismissed a claim for negligence taken by a pupil who, when aged 11, had broken his elbow in a playground fall, during a game of chasing. Judge Smyth observed that children's exuberance of running around was part of growing up. As there was no direction forbidding running in the school's grounds, he could not find it unreasonable for teachers

---

[10] Dublin Circuit Court, March 6, 2001, *The Irish Times*, March 7, 2001.
[11] Circuit Court Dublin, January 30, 2003, *Irish Independent*, January 31, 2003,

to allow children to run about. Not all accidents were caused through somebody's fault. Judge Smyth could not fault the school on the condition of the concrete playground or on the level of supervision provided. The newspaper report notes that Judge Smyth said that supervision of school children "would have to operate within the limitation of school resources." This appears to have been a general observation and should not be interpreted as affording an automatic defence to a school that pleaded lack of resources.

In *O'Gorman v. Crotty*,[12] a ten-year-old pupil, when being chased during play in the school playground, fell over one of the several wooden blocks which were lying in the playground. The blocks were sometimes used to support boards for use as seats, but appear to have served no positive function as play objects. Holding the school manager and principal teacher liable, O'Byrne J. stated:

> "In circumstances such as those in this case careful supervision is essential, and the persons having charge of the school are bound to see that there is supervision of the playground during play intervals. It was the duty of the principal teacher to see that the playground was clear and not a source of danger to boys playing there, who could not be expected to keep their eyes fixed."

The boy was held not to have been guilty of contributory negligence on the basis that "[b]oys naturally run in a playground" and that the accident had taken place during a period of recreation, in a place specially set apart for play which the boy "was entitled to assume ... was reasonably safe for this purpose."

In *Healy v. Dodd*,[13] an 11-year-old pupil was injured when he fell while using his handcuffs in a game known as "still" – where the "police" arrested "poteen makers". The use of handcuffs had been forbidden two years earlier and a pair of handcuffs had been confiscated. In order to keep up the deception of the game imaginary handcuffs were put on by the boys after the real handcuffs had been taken by the master. Two days before the accident the handcuffs made their way back to the school – being brought there by the son of the principal teacher, unknown to him.

O'Byrne J. in the High Court dismissed the action. The teacher had been supervising play at the time of the accident and there was "nothing to arouse his suspicion" that the real handcuffs had returned.

---

[12] [1946] Ir. Jur. Rep. 34 (High Court, O'Byrne J.).
[13] [1951] Ir. Jur. Rep. 22 (High Court, O'Byrne J.).

In *Flesk v. King*,[14] the plaintiff, a seven-year-old pupil, was injured by a toy boomerang, which another pupil threw at him in the school playground. The boomerang had been taken to school by a pupil in his schoolbag and released by him into the playground unknown to the teacher. It was thrown from person to person, as if it were a ball, for five or six minutes before the accident occurred. The school principal who was in charge of playground supervision had to patrol three separate areas where different groups of children played.

Laffoy J. dismissed the case. A proper system of supervision was in place "in that in general the small children were segregated from the older pupils and [they] played on the safer grassy area". The principal had been "constantly ... patrolling" the entire play area on foot so as to supervise all eighty-five pupils and he was not merely relying on observation through school windows.

A case which runs against this trend is *Mapp v. Gilhooley*.[15] There Barr J. imposed liability on a school manager where the plaintiff, aged five, was injured in the school playground. At the time there were over two hundred boys in the playground. The accident occurred when one "train", made up of about ten boys, holding each other by the waist, collided with another train, similarly composed. Two teachers were supervising the recreation period, supported by six eight-year-olds who acted as prefects. The school head was also in the yard at the time, though not in the vicinity where the accident happened.

The plaintiff, also aged eight at the time of trial, gave unsworn evidence, because he had not yet learned the meaning of the oath. He impressed Barr, J., who considered him "a remarkably bright and intelligent boy". He attested that the "trains" game was a well-established practice, with up to five trains operating at the same time. On the fateful day, the game had been in progress for some time before the accident took place. The teachers who were on duty gave evidence that they had no indication that the "trains" game was in progress before the plaintiff received his injury. Barr, J. imposed liability. He stated:

> "In measuring the duty of care owed by a school authority to a pupil or pupils in given circumstances, the court must take into account all the relevant factors, including the ages of the children in question, the activities in which they are or may be engaged, the degree of supervision

---

[14] Doyle's Personal Injury Judgments, Trinity and Michaelmas Terms 1996, p.87 (High Court Laffoy J., October 29, 1996).
[15] Unreported, High Court, Barr J., November 7, 1989.

(if any) required having regard to the prevailing circumstances and the opportunity (if any) which those in charge of the child had to prevent or minimise the mischief complained of. It goes without saying that the duty ought to be measured realistically and should take into account also that children, particularly small boys, are high spirited by nature and some are inclined to be mischievous. In the absence of a regime of draconian servitude, it is impossible to keep very young children under complete control when at play. Disciplinary and supervisory measures required of a school authority should be construed within reasonable bounds."

Barr J. considered that the statement in *Lennon v. McCarthy*, that the duty of a schoolmaster is to take such care of its pupils as a careful father would of his children, was not at variance with his own approach. The proposition approved in *Lennon v. McCarthy* that, where normally healthy children are in the playground it is not necessary for them to be under constant supervision, however, "clearly relate[d] to the circumstances of that particular case and [was] not intended to have general application." It was "not any authority that two hundred and twenty four boys from four to eight years of age do not require some continuous supervision when playing in a small schoolyard."

In the instant case, over a hundred and sixty small boys from four to six years had been running around in half the yard in an area measuring 30 paces by 15 paces. In these circumstances it was not surprising that the supervisors had failed to notice the "trains" forming and running about before the collision.

On what Barr J. characterised the "crucial aspect" of the case, as to whether the game had been in progress long enough to have given the supervisors the opportunity to stop it before the accident occurred, Barr J. concluded that it had: the boys in the junior section had been playing the game "for [a] significant period which was sufficiently long prior to the accident to allow one or other or both supervising teachers to see what was happening and to end it before the accident occurred if they had been keeping a reasonable watch." It followed that they had been negligent in not supervising the children adequately.

The conclusion is not easy to reconcile with Barr J.'s earlier explanation of the teachers' failure to see the "trains", not in terms of their neglect, but rather the large number of boys in such a small area. If that was the reason then the school might well still be held liable, either for having too many pupils in the yard at the time or too few supervisors, but the teachers themselves should not have to bear the opprobrium of having failed in their duty of supervision.

It is worth noting that the Supreme Court directed a new trial in the case (because the plaintiff's unsworn testimony had been admitted). The Circuit Court, which heard the case, found in favour of the school and the High Court affirmed the dismissal of the action.[16] It is a source of some relief for school management that this was the eventual outcome. Barr J.'s judgment was not easy to reconcile with most other High Court and Supreme Court decisions on the question of a school's duty of care to pupils.

Another case worth noting is *Coffee v. St Pius National School*,[17] where Judge Smyth imposed liability on a school for lack of a sufficient number of supervisors in a yard, slightly larger than that in *Mapp v. Gilhooley*, in which there were 144 pupils and only one supervisor. The plaintiff had been punched by another pupil, who broke his wrist. Judge Smyth appeared to make some concession to the particular resources available to schools since he noted that in the instant case it had "not been suggested that there could not have been an extra teacher supervising".

Clarke v. O'Gorman[18] seems to involve a somewhat stringent application of the legal principles. In that case a ten-year-old boy was injured when he was carried by some older boys across the playground, kicking and screaming, during playtime and deposited with no great ceremony, fracturing his forearm. The trial judge, Keane J., characterised this behaviour as "a dangerous side of horseplay". There was no conflict of evidence and the trial judge found that "it [was] an extremely well run school" and that it "operate[d] a system of supervision which [could] not seriously be criticised". With regard to the system he said:

> "... one's own common sense will tell [one that] to have one teacher looking after 35 lively and volatile children and the headmaster moving between the four playgrounds and keeping an eye on each one of them is really as much as one could expect and probably more than one would found in a great many schools. I have no doubt that [it] represented a perfectly adequate and proper system."

Keane J. also accepted the evidence of the teacher who was supervising the yard at the time. She gave evidence that at the time she was correcting another pupil who was in breach of school rules in running onto the grassy bank

---

[16] See Dympna Glendenning, *Education and the Law* (Butterworths, Dublin, 1999), p.290, n.69.
[17] Circuit Court, Dublin, October 18, 1999.
[18] Supreme Court, February 13, 1996.

next to the yard. The teacher was reprimanding "the recalcitrant boy" and was in fact entering his name in her notebook at the time the plaintiff was being carried away.

Keane J. took the view that the teacher had had a momentary lapse of attention. The system was fine but it had broken down on this occasion and for this he held the school liable. In an interesting passage the learned judge gave his reason in the following passage:

> "I accept fully her [the teacher's] evidence that she was not conscious and was not aware of this happening until the boy had actually fallen on the ground. That I am satisfied was so because her attention was distracted by the significantly less serious matter of disciplining the young man who was breaking the rule of going on to the grass. This was the sort of momentary loss of concentration that [can affect] people in responsible positions and in the ordinary course of life is bound to happen on occasions ... It was unfortunate that on this occasion her attention was distracted more than it should have been by the incident she was dealing with."

On appeal the Supreme Court upheld the trial judge's approach. A couple of comments are called for. First, the trial judge held that the system of supervision which allocated one teacher to 35 lively students in the playground was faultless. This necessarily involved some level of risk as being acceptable. It meant, of necessity, that, if one student got into difficulty, 34 students could lawfully be ignored for an appropriate amount of time. In normal circumstances in such a case the teacher would not be liable, for example, if, while one of the students was being attended for a stab wound, another pupil was hit by a third student out of the teacher's sight. That is what acceptance of a 35:1 student-teacher ratio means.

It would of course be different if an injury occurs while the teacher is not paying attention: if, for example, he or she is listening to a walkman or struggling with a Sudoku. But this is not what happened here. In this case, the teacher was carefully supervising the playground and attending to an infraction of the rules. There was no lapse of attention. She was carrying out her duties faithfully in the circumstances in a system that the judge found to be faultless. Surely, the injury to the plaintiff was due to the system (involving a 35:1 ratio) and not to the carelessness of the teacher? She was in fact, held liable for not comparing the infringement she was attending to with the infringement that occurred to the plaintiff, even though she was not aware of it, and then for not concluding that the plaintiff's incident was more serious, even though she did not know of it.

It seems strange to impose liability in such a case. It would seem that liability should be imposed only in those circumstances if the teacher was aware of both incidents and did not attend to the more serious or threatening event, or if she was unaware of the second incident because she was not carrying out her supervisory role in a proper fashion.

Would any leeway be given to such a teacher if, in assessing two simultaneous incidents, she does not pick the more serious incident at the time? Perhaps the Supreme Court's holding can be based on a specific perception that the infraction that diverted the teacher's attention was so trivial that she should simply have ignored it, having regard to the more pressing demands of supervising potentially more serious situations of danger and dealt with the infringement at some later time when her attention was not diluted. The difficulty with this rationale is that the Court did not give any clear indication that this was the basis of its decision.

It may be noted that in several other cases, where a sudden danger arose during playtime, which resulted in injury to a child, but which was of its nature difficult for the school authorities to foresee or provide against, the courts have not imposed liability. These cases include *Clark v. Monmouthshire Co. Co.*[19] (unintended knife injury during scuffle), *Langham v. Wellingborough School*[20] (golf shot in playground), *Gow v. Glasgow Education Authority*[21] (boy unexpectedly jumped on back of another boy at school for blind children), *Chilvers v. L. C. C.*[22] (child injured eye when he fell on movable lance of a toy soldier). See also *Long v. Gardner*[23] (summer camp not liable for knife injury sustained by boy at camp during an argument with another boy; event held not foreseeable), *Durham v. Public School Bd. Of Township School Area of North Oxford*[24] (wire spring flew into boy's eye in playground: school not liable), *H v. Pennell*[25] (school not liable where piece of car radio aerial broke away on being violently flicked by pupil over his shoulder; aerial had been returned to pupil after confiscation; irresponsible use not foreseeable),

In *Kelly v. Gilhooley*,[26] Costello, P. held that the school authorities were not liable in negligence where a pupil was knocked down by two racing

---

[19] 52 L.G.R. 246 (C.A., 1954).
[20] 101 L.J.K.B. 513 (C.A., 1932).
[21] [1922] S.C. 260.
[22] 32 T.L.R. 363 (K.B. Div., Bailhache J. (with jury, 1916).
[23] 144 D.L.R. (3d) 73 (Ontario High Court Smith J., 1983).
[24] 23 D.L.R. (2d) 711 (Ontario C.A., 1960).
[25] 46 S.A.S.R. 158 (Sup. Court of South Australia, 1987).
[26] Doyle's Personal Injury Judgments, Trinity and Michaelmas Terms 1994, p.86 (High Court, Costello P., November 1, 1994).

dogs as he was walking down a path on the school premises on his way to class. The school gates were open at the time. Costello, P. rejected the plaintiff's contention that the gates should have been kept closed:

> "[T]here is very large traffic going into schools such as this in the morning time [and] it would be impossible to keep the gates closed even if such a duty were to be placed upon [the authorities], and in order to ensure that, if that duty did exist, ... it was fulfilled, it would mean putting a teacher or other employee on every gate. This seems too high a standard of care in the circumstances."

Costello, P. did not consider that an analogy could be drawn from the position where children were hurt by other children in the playground. There was simply no duty on school authorities to keep stray dogs from getting onto the school premises.

Costello P.'s approach may be contrasted with that of Judge McMahon in *Greene v. Mundow*,[27] considered later in this chapter.

In the Australian case of *The Commonwealth v. Introvigne*,[28] where a 15-year-old pupil was injured by a flagpole in the school grounds which fell on him when other pupils swung on it, liability was imposed on the basis of negligent lack of supervision. Only one teacher was that morning supervising nine hundred pupils. There was a somewhat stark explanation for there being only one: the Principal had died in the early hours of that morning and almost all of the staff were at a meeting, which lasted no more than a few minutes, at which the funeral arrangements were being announced.

Normally there would be at least five, and sometimes as many as twenty, teachers involved in the task of supervision. In the Full Court of the Federal Court, it was stated:

> "Children are in need of supervision. Their parents cannot provide this when the children are at school. The teachers must provide it. It was unfortunate that the death of the principal led to the brief staff meeting and only one member of staff being made available to perform supervision duties in the grounds; but this neither diminishes the scope of the duty of care nor operates to prevent the conclusion that the duty was breached, as it was on that occasion."

---

[27] Circuit Court, Judge McMahon, January 20, 2000.
[28] 150 C.L.R. 258 (High Court of Australia, 1982), affirming, 48 F.L.R. 161 (Fed. Court A.C.T. Dist. Reg. Gen. Div., 1980).

On further appeal, the High Court of Australia affirmed this holding. Brennan J. observed:

> "The calling of the meeting that morning did not preclude the discharge of the duty, though it explains why the teachers did not take the necessary steps to supervise the boys playing around the flagpole."

This might be regarded as a fairly tough decision for school management but the moral is nonetheless clear. Even humanitarian considerations should not be allowed to divert attention from the constant need for adequate supervision. Whether an Irish court would take quite such a stern view on the particular facts of the case is debatable.

Let us now consider the decision of the Supreme Court in *Murphy v. County Wexford VEC*.[29] It is very much concerned with a narrow legal question relating to how a court should set a test for determining the scope of the standard of care owed by schools to their pupils. This means that it offers only the most general guidance to school management on how to formulate and administer policies that discharge the school's duty of care.

The facts were simple enough. The plaintiff was injured in an accident during the lunch recess when attending the defendants' school. He was 16 years old at the time. He was in the company of other 5th year and 6th year students – about fifty all told. One of them produced a bag of chocolate bars which he offered to share. The bag burst and "a good deal of horseplay then ensued during which a number of pupils, put by the plaintiff as about nine, started throwing bars around the room at each other. The plaintiff estimated the duration of this disturbance to be about ten minutes, though this was considered by the trial judge, de Valera J., to be probably an overestimate. In the course of the horseplay, one of the bars struck the plaintiff in his eye, causing him serious injury. The plaintiff sued the school for negligence in the supervision that day.

There was uncontradicted evidence that there was no supervision that day, although normally supervision was provided. Documents discovered during the litigation showed that there were four teachers who were to be on supervision duty rota at four different areas in the school during the lunch break, one of whom was allocated to the area where the plaintiff and his fellow-pupils were having lunch. It appeared that the rota system had been introduced two years previously, after serious incidents had occurred resulting in the expulsion of 20 pupils.

---

[29] Unreported, Supreme Court, July 29, 2004.

Apart from giving evidence himself and calling a fellow-pupil to give evidence as to what had occurred, the plaintiff called no other evidence. Counsel for the defendant applied for a dismissal of the claim at the close of the plaintiff's case, having made it clear that he would not adduce any evidence. He argued that the defendant had no case to answer on the basis of what the plaintiff had put forward. He quoted some legal authorities in support of this submission.

De Valera J. held against the defendant. He stated:

> "In this matter what concerns me, what I take note of, is that the school authorities themselves obviously had come to the conclusion, because of the schedule that has been discovered, that it was necessary to have lunchtime supervision for this area and they scheduled a teacher to look after that supervision.
>
> The incident that occurred, and I have to say that things have changed since my time, if there was a packet of chocolate biscuits brought into my school the fight would have been to get them not to throw them away, but if there had been a teacher supervising, if there had been a supervisor, I have no doubt that they would have at least taken steps to control the situation.
>
> I accept that 10 minutes is probably an exaggeration but it is probably an exaggeration of the length of time this was taking place, but is a perfectly understandable, perfectly normal sort of situation, other than my comment about fighting to get them rather than to give them away. It is a perfectly understandable situation which could be controlled by a teacher and probably would have been controlled by a teacher. I am told that the school took the view that there should be supervision by a teacher.
>
> Now, in the absence of any explanation it may well be that the school could explain the situation and could explain it to my satisfaction, but there is nobody here from the school and I wasn't asked for an adjournment. Had I been asked to adjourn this matter because teachers were not in a position to attend in the circumstances I would have given it sympathetic consideration, subject to anything Mr Doyle might have said.
>
> In the absence of any explanation and in the presence of this schedule I have to take the view that the school decided – the school is of the opinion that there should be supervision, that there was not supervision, that had there been supervision this incident would not have taken place. In those circumstances, and again I say in the absence of – this would have been a circumstance in which the school could

have explained and possibly explained to my satisfaction, but in the absence of such explanation I have to find in favour of the plaintiff."

This represented the entirety of de Valera J.'s ruling on the legal issues which had been addressed to him. He did not refer to the legal submissions which counsel for the defendant had addressed to him. Nor did he identify the nature of the duty of or the standard of care.

The defendant school appealed to the Supreme Court. Its argument, in essence, was that de Valera J. had determined the standard of care by a yardstick which the school had itself created. If this were to be the test, it would result in the injustice that, the higher the standard a school set itself, the greater its duty of care would be. The standard of care should be a constant one, applied to all schools, and certainly not affected – to the detriment of particular schools – by the fact that they might have set a particularly high standard for themselves.

What the appeal involved – and a matter that divided the Supreme Court – was a question of interpretation: had de Valera J. really meant to let the schools determine their own standard of care or should his reference to the defendant's regime of supervision merely be regarded as incidental to the application by him – albeit not in so many words – of an objective standard of care?

The majority favoured the latter interpretation. McCracken J. (with whom McGuinness J. concurred) stated:

> "Quite clearly, school authorities are not insurers of the pupils under their care. However, they do owe a duty to those pupils to take reasonable care to ensure that the pupils do not suffer injury. To do this, some degree of supervision is clearly required. The extent of such supervision will depend on a number of factors, for example, the age of the pupils involved, the location of the places where the pupils congregate, the number of pupils which may be present at any one time, and the general propensity of pupils at that particular school to act dangerously.
>
> The evidence shows that in the appellants' school there had been serious disciplinary problems, following which the appellants considered it necessary to ensure that a teacher was present in certain specific areas, including the area where this incident took place, during lunch hour. It must be made clear that the question is not what the appellants considered necessary, but what is objectively necessary to comply with the appellant's duty of care. However, the undisputed evidence of this case is that there had been problems which had resulted

in twenty pupils being expelled, that following the introduction of the rota system the supervision was reasonable, and that for some unexplained reason the rota system did not operate on the day in question, and there was no supervision. It is also the undisputed evidence of the respondent that, had a teacher been present, the horseplay which resulted in his injury, would not have been allowed to take place ...

While the learned trial Judge can certainly be criticised for emphasising what the school had decided, the fact remains in my view that the undisputed evidence before him could only lead to one conclusion, namely that there had been a need for supervision, supervision had taken place on a consistent basis with considerable success, but that on this occasion, such supervision was not present and this unfortunate incident took place. The learned trial Judge was perfectly entitled to reach the conclusion, which was supported by the [plaintiff]'s own evidence, that the incident would not have taken place had there been proper supervision. I am of the view that the particular circumstances of this case, and the history of indiscipline in the school, imposed a duty of care on the appellant to provide supervision at lunch time in accordance with its rota system, and that the failure to do so constituted negligence on the part of the appellant."

Fennelly J. dissented. He stated:

"In one sense, counsel for the appellant took somewhat of a risk in not going into evidence. That aspect of the case, as counsel conceded, was something for which responsibility lies entirely on the appellant, which cannot now complain of its failure to call witnesses who could have been made available. However, the appellant was entitled, in my view, to expect that the learned trial judge would give a ruling based on the authorities cited to him and on the applicable legal principles. The learned trial judge chose, instead, to decide the case exclusively, as he was invited by counsel for the plaintiff, on the basis that, since, the school had adopted a roster for supervision, adherence to that standard had to be taken as the appropriate standard of care for the purpose of deciding the case. In my view, that was a mistaken approach. It substituted a new subjective approach test for that ordained by the law. The implication is that, if a schoolmaster takes an excessively cautious view, and makes provision for total and absolute supervision of pupils during every moment of the school day, the school will be liable for any departure from that standard. I do not think the school

The School's Duty of Care to its Pupils 17

should, in law, be liable for departure from a standard not required by the law. Yet, that seems to be the consequence of the decision of the learned trial judge in this case.

Because of his reliance on the school's own roster, the learned trial judge failed entirely to address the appropriate legal standard of care. He not only made no reference to the cases cited to him but he failed to identify any objective standard of care.

Counsel for the appellant argued at the hearing of the appeal that the learned trial judge took a leap by applying the roster and that the result was that he applied a standard which was contrary to the authorities and which required constant supervision. I agree with this submission."

Accordingly, Fennelly J. would have ordered a retrial.

So the outcome of the case was that the Supreme Court, by a majority, imposed liability on the school for negligent lack of supervision. Is this a source of concern for school managers? Does it represent a hardening of judicial attitude towards schools or a change in what constitutes reasonable care? It does not seem so. The case was, after all, concerned only with an issue of interpretation of the trial judge's remarks. Had de Valera J. set a test for liability based on the school's own standard, he would undoubtedly have been mistaken; but, the majority held, surely more plausibly, this was not what de Valera had intended to do. If one looks at what the majority had to say on the question of what constitutes reasonable care in supervision, all one finds is a statement of absolutely conventional law: the extent of the supervision will depend on a number of factors, including (but not limited to):

- the age of the pupils;
- the location of the places where they congregate;
- the number of pupils present at any one time; and
- the general propensity of pupils at the particular school to act dangerously.

In the instant case, the school had adopted a high risk strategy in not going into evidence, hoping to convince the trial judge that the plaintiff had not produced sufficient evidence, through what he and his fellow-pupil had said, together with the documentary material that had been discovered prior to the hearing. That documentary evidence established a problem with violence in the school: several incidents two years previously, resulting in twenty expulsions The rota system had been a direct response to these incidents and, according to the plaintiff, had worked efficiently providing reasonably good supervision, but had not prevented fights completely. If – without explanation from the school – supervision was not provided on the fateful day, what was the trial judge to infer? The necessity for fairly close supervision had been established, its absence unexplained.

Another recent case is *Maher v. The Board of Management of Presentation Junior School*.[30] The plaintiff, when attending school at the age of six, received an injury to his eye when another boy of the same age, who was sitting at the classroom table opposite him, used a rubber-band as a catapult and propelled his pencil in the direction of his face. The action came to trial five years later.

In the classroom there were three rows of tables, rather than individual desks, at which about five pupils sat on each side facing each other. The plaintiff habitually occupied a seat which was second in from the left of the table closest to the classroom door. He therefore had a classmate on his left, and another to his right, and others further down to his right. Others were seated at the opposite side of the table. The boy who caused the injury was sitting immediately opposite him. Each table was about four feet in wide.

After a detailed review of the conflicting evidence Peart J. concluded that the case concerned a normal class of six year olds whose known behaviour prior to the incident did not involve "any particular or unusual or special difficulty" He was satisfied that it had been "entirely appropriate" for the teacher to be in charge of the class of between 25 and 30 children: he observed that it was normal for much larger numbers of pupils to be in the charge of a single teacher. The incident had occurred " 'out of the blue', so to speak." The boy who used the catapult had not previously been known to be difficult to any special or abnormal extent: this was the first and only time that his conduct had warranted a reprimand from the principal. The incident had occurred when the teacher in charge of the class was speaking briefly with the Special Needs teacher who had come to collect pupils from the classroom. During the conversation, the boy had taken a pencil from his pencil case and used a rubber-band, " which he had somewhere either on his person or in his pencil case" to serve as a catapult.

Peart J. was satisfied that the teacher in charge of the class had no warning that this might happen. Even though it was a school rule that rubber-bands were not to be brought into school, Peart J. considered it not to be a reasonable imposition on teachers to search thoroughly the pupils of a class to ensure that no object such as a rubber-band was secreted either in their clothing or

---

[30] Unreported, High Court, Peart J., October 22, 2004.

in their schoolbags. The incident "was just something which happened without warning and suddenly while the teacher's attention was elsewhere".

Peart J. was satisfied that:

> "this classroom was conducted in a perfectly normal way, and a way which does not fall short of reasonable standards for such classrooms, and I believe that this is the view of [an expert witness] also, who accepted that this teacher would have needed eyes in the back of her head if this incident was to be prevented. She also said that it was not unusual for the remedial teacher to call into the classroom for the purpose of taking out pupils in need of tuition. I am satisfied that while she stated that it was also the practice that pupils would leave the classroom and go to the remedial teacher, it was normal and usual for the reverse to occur. She expressed no actual criticism of that practice happening."

Counsel for the plaintiff had highlighted the fact that the classroom teacher had not seen the rubber-band in question before the incident took place, even though it is clear that it must have been there. He said that the evidence was that this boy had taken his pencil and the rubber-band out of his pencil case and that she ought to have seen it. She had said that she did not. Counsel submitted that therefore that her level of supervision had not been adequate in the circumstances of the case, and that had she seen the rubber-band, it would have been confiscated and the injury would not have occurred.

Counsel for the defendant submitted that the standard of care to be imposed on a school teacher was that of the prudent parent, and that it was a duty to take reasonable care. The class was a well behaved one and the presence of the Special Needs teacher in the classroom for the time she was there was not relevant. The evidence showed that there had been no suggestion of misbehaviour in the classroom, what had happened was simply a sudden act which could not have been anticipated.

Counsel for the plaintiff invoked McCracken J.'s observations in the Supreme Court in *Murphy v. County Wexford VEC*,[31] which we have already considered, to the effect that:

> "[q]uite clearly, school authorities are not insurers of the pupils under their care. However, they do owe a duty to those pupils to take reasonable care to ensure to ensure that the pupils do not suffer injury.

---

[31] Unreported, Supreme Court, July 29, 2004.

To do this, some degree of supervision is clearly required. The extent of such supervision will depend on a number of factors, for example, the age of the pupils involved, the location of the places where the pupils congregate, the number of pupils which may be present at any one time, and the general propensity of pupils at that particular school to act dangerously."

Counsel argued that this passage supported his submission that the vigilance required in respect of a class of six year olds was a heightened one given their young age, and that in the case of older children, the degree of supervision required would be somewhat lower. Peart J. responded as follows:

"In the present case, I believe one must look at the actual situation in this classroom on this morning. [the classroom teacher] had been teaching these children for a couple of months by the time this incident occurred. No doubt she had got to know those in her care. She says in particular that the boy who hurt [the plaintiff] was a normal child and that she had not had to send him to [the principal] to be reprehended on any occasion before or after this incident. One has to ask what [the classroom teacher], or the school itself, could have done to ensure to any absolute extent that this incident would not occur. I am of the view ... that in order to provide any additional insurance against such an occurrence, it would be necessary to search each child's person and schoolbag upon arrival, and that is an unreasonable burden and one not required in my opinion in discharge of the duty of care owed by the school to its pupils.

It goes without saying that there is a duty to be vigilant to an extent that is within the bounds of reasonableness. That involves a measure of supervision appropriate to the needs of any particular situation, and some factors to be taken into account in the passage appear in the judgment of McCracken J. above. But for a breach of that duty of care to occur, there must exist in addition to the relationship of proximity (which clearly exists in the case of a school and pupil) the requirement of foreseeability. In the present case that means that before the defendant school can be liable, the Court would have to be satisfied that it is reasonable that [the classroom teacher] should be expected to anticipate that the moment she turned her back (not literally) on the class in order to have a very short conversation with [the Special Needs teacher] at the door of the classroom, it was probable or likely that some behaviour would occur which would cause injury to one or more of the pupils in her charge. I do not believe that the evidence supports the submission that she ought to have foreseen that this might happen. There can of course be situations in any school where the school is well aware of potential dangers, where for example there has been a history of disruptive and even violent behaviour on the part of a pupil or a group of pupils. Bullying would be a case in point. The duty of care on a school in such circumstances would extend to taking appropriate account of these known circumstances when deciding on the appropriate level of supervision in the school, perhaps particularly during break or recreation periods when pupils are outside the more controlled environment of the classroom."

Proceeding to dismiss the claim, Peart J. went on to observe:

"It has been said that the standard of care required in school is that of a prudent parent. The school is said to be *'in loco parentis'* In other words, the school is expected to be no more and no less vigilant of those in its care than a prudent parent would be in his or her own home. In any normal child, if there be such a creature, there is always a certain propensity for horseplay and high spirits. Indeed, if it were not so, there might be some cause for concern. It is inevitable that in the ordinary rough and tumble that is part and parcel of the daily life of a six year old child, cuts and bruises will occur. I am not equating what happened to [the plaintiff] as coming within the category of unblameworthy conduct on the part of his assailant. But I am asking, albeit rhetorically, if it can be reasonably said that if a group of children are playing at home in the garden and a neighbour's child falls while being chased by the others in a game of 'tig' while the supervising parent is in the kitchen boiling a kettle, that parent has been negligent in a way that renders him/her liable in damages for the injury? I do not think such a situation can amount to negligence. Again, I ask rhetorically, is there any reason why if the same situation occurred in school as opposed to at home, the school should be any more liable if there is supervision provided which reasonably meets the needs of the particular situation? I think not.

It is perfectly understandable that a parent of an injured child should wish to seek redress for the injury on his behalf. But it must be remembered that simply because an injury takes place in a school does not mean that the school management or any individual teacher has been negligent. Negligence must be established, and in this case I find no such evidence.

It is with great regret as far as the plaintiff is concerned that I must find that the case of negligence against the defendant school has not been proven, and in those circumstances I must dismiss the claim."

This holding is consistent with a number of earlier Irish decisions. It shows that courts are still willing to set the standard of care in a realistic way, which understands the demands of the classroom.

Let us now turn to consider the issue of bullying – a subject that Ciaran Craven also addresses in another chapter.[32] In *Mulvey v. McDonagh*,[33] the plaintiff claimed that she had been bullied by fellow pupils when she was attending the defendant's school at the age of four and that the school had been guilty of negligence in failing to have monitored the conduct of the pupils after having been informed of the problem. The plaintiff suffered from asthma and eczema and 'had an anaphylactic reaction to certain matters' This necessitated the principal and two other teachers receiving training in the use of injections of the plaintiff; the class teacher visited her in her home before the first term started to meet her and put her at her ease.

There was an incident in the school yard during the first term in which another 4-year-old pulled down the plaintiff's trousers. This was firmly dealt with by the school. Once the second term commenced, an extra teacher was placed on supervision duty in the yard. In February, the plaintiff's mother, uninvited, went to her daughter's classroom where she berated the pupils and said that if they did not stop bullying the plaintiff, she would "kick them up the backside" The plaintiff and her mother gave evidence that bullying continued until the end of the summer term. It was clear that another incident did take place on the last day of that term in which the plaintiff was struck. She was taken to hospital and released two days later.

The school staff denied that the plaintiff had been subjected to any bullying: the only incidents of which they were aware were the two that occurred in the first and third terms.

After a detailed review of the conflicting evidence, Johnson J. concluded on the factual issues as follows:

> "[W]here there was a dispute between the plaintiff and her mother and the defendants I am satisfied, having had the opportunity of watching both of them and listening to them, that the defendants version of the evidence of what took place is far more reliable and acceptable and I so find. Particularly I find as follows:
> 1. Only one complaint was made to [the class teacher] in the first term.

---

[32] See p.145 *infra*.
[33] Unreported, High Court, Johnson J., March 26, 2004.

The School's Duty of Care to its Pupils 23

2. I am satisfied that no request was made to [the class teacher] on February 3rd for liberty to address the class.
3. Despite the suggestion put to [the class teacher] that she had been given the names of other perpetrators of these alleged offences I am satisfied that no name other than the name in respect of the pulling down of the trousers incident was given to [the class teacher].
4. I am satisfied that the plaintiff was not covered in bruises as alleged by the plaintiff's mother, for had that been so I have no doubt that the examination in Crumlin Hospital would have revealed it."

Turning to the law, Johnson J. held that the school authorities were not guilty of negligence. His analysis is worth recording in full:

"The law in this case would appear to be accepted by both sides, namely that the degree of care to be taken is that of a prudent parent exercising reasonable care and I accept that that must be taken in context of a prudent parent behaving reasonably with a class of twenty eight 4 year olds having their first experience of mingling socially with other children.

I am satisfied that this care was taken. I think the suggestion that there should be a further and higher degree of liability, namely that of professional negligence, is a situation which has not yet been achieved in Irish law. I think that the principles as laid out in recent decisions in England and Scotland would appear to indicate more that the approach should be that of professional negligence. However I do not think we can adopt the principles laid down in *Scott v. The Lothian Regional Council* [Court of Session] Outer House, Scotland (September 29, 1998) 'where he applied the test as to whether it had been proved to be guilty of such a failure as no guidance teacher of ordinary skill would be guilty if acting with ordinary care'.

Messrs. McMahon and Binchy state 'the problems of care and control in a school bear some resemblance to those confronting a parent in the home but they are far from identical. It is possible that in a future decision in Irish court will drop the reference to careful parent and stress the fact that it is the standard of the reasonable school teacher or manager which should prevail'.

The definition of bullying which appears not to have been disputed between the parties to any great extent is contained in the guidelines on Encountering Bullying Behaviour in Primary and Post Primary

Schools, September 1993 and bullying is defined as:
'Bullying is repeated aggression, verbal, psychological or physical conducted by an individual or group against others. Isolated incidents of aggressive behaviour which should not be condoned can scarcely be described as bullying. However when the behaviour is systematic and ongoing it is bullying'.
I accept and adopt that definition of bullying.

The claim is brought in respect of a single incident which occurred on June 25, 1998 when the plaintiff was alleged to have been assaulted by fellow pupils in the school.

Having considered all the evidence in the matter I am quite satisfied that the incident did not take place as described by the plaintiff, that the injuries alleged to have been suffered, were not suffered. Any incident which may have taken place did not result in the personal injuries claimed by the plaintiff and certainly was not as a result of any negligence or breach of duty on the part of the defendants or any of them, under these circumstances I therefore dismiss the plaintiff's action."

A few points about this decision may be noted. First, it seems clear enough that this case was one in which the factual issues predominated. Johnson J.'s preference for the evidence of the defence witnesses is readily apparent. Secondly, there is no legal magic in the word "bullying", for the purposes of the law of negligence, since the scope of the duty of care is not defined in terms of it. Thus, a school (or other person or agency in charge of children) has a duty to take reasonable care to prevent the children from being assaulted or otherwise intimidated or cowed. That duty is not limited to preventing systematic and ongoing conduct of this character: it is possible to conceive of cases where liability will be imposed in respect of a single incident.

Of course, if the school has no reason to know of the violent or intimidatory characteristic of a particular person, it may well not be liable in negligence in respect of the first of a number of incidents simply because its ignorance was reasonable and the situation did not call for greater supervision than it provided; but there is no rule that the duty of care arises, or is breached, only in cases of systematic aggressive or intimidatory conduct.

Thirdly, *pace* Johnson J., it is hard to see how the professional negligence standard would involve "a further and higher degree of liability" than the general negligence standard. As is plain from the passage from *Scott v. Lothian Regional Council*,[34] which Johnson J. quoted, the professional

---

[34] [Court of Session] Outer House, Scotland, September 29, 1998.

negligence standard is *more deferential* to those to whom it applies than is the general negligence standard. A professional person will not be held negligent if he or she complied with a customary practice in the profession, even if that customary practice, however widely followed, was such as to involve inherent defects which ought to be obvious to anyone giving the matter consideration.[35]

Injuries sustained off the premises

Let us now turn to consider cases where a pupil is injured off the premises in circumstances where this is alleged to be the fault of the school management.

Perhaps the best starting point is the English Court of Appeal decision of *Bradford-Smart v. West Sussex County Council*,[36] where Judge, L.J. stated:

> "The school does not have the charge of its pupils all the time and so cannot protect them from harm all the time. At a day school that charge will usually end at the school gates, although the school will have a duty to take reasonable steps to ensure that young children who are not old enough to look after themselves do not leave the school premises unattended ... One can think of circumstances where it might go beyond that, for example if it were reasonable for a teacher to intervene when he saw one pupil attacking another immediately outside the school gates. It will clearly extend further afield if the pupils are on a school trip, educational, recreational or sporting. But the school cannot owe a general duty to its pupils, or anyone else, to police their activities once they have left its charge. That is principally the duty of parents and, where criminal offences are involved, the police. There was evidence from .... an educational consultant that some schools do patrol 'areas of concern' outside school to prevent incidents after children have left. But we agree with the [trial] judge that this is a matter of discretion rather than duty."

The first category of cases where injury is sustained off the premises concerns what might be called the negligent release of pupils from the school into a situation of danger. In *Hosty v. McDonagh*,[37] a ten-year-old child was injured by a car when she came through the school gate at lunch time and ran onto the road. Liability was imposed on the school manager for not having a

---

[35] See *Dunne v. National Maternity Hospital* [1989] I.R. 91.
[36] [2002] 1 F.C.R. 425.
[37] Unreported, Supreme Court, May 29, 1973.

suitable exit from the school, not having it supervised and allowing the plaintiff onto the road unattended. The judgment of Fitzgerald C.J. (for the Court) does not expressly state why the child went onto the road or what she should have been doing at the time.

The liability of a school in this context may extend to injuries sustained by third parties. In *Carmarthenshire County Council v. Lewis*,[38] a four-year-old pupil at a nursery school got out of the classroom when he was not being supervised and ran through an unlocked gate down a lane into a busy highway. He caused a driver of a lorry to make it swerve so that it struck a telegraph pole, as a result of which the driver was killed.

Liability was imposed on the school authorities by the English Court of Appeal, on the basis that the lack of supervision by the teacher had been negligent. The House of Lords held that the teacher had not been negligent but still imposed liability on the school authorities because they ought to have anticipated the danger of a child "escaping" in the absence of supervision, whatever the cause of that absence. Of course, in post-primary schools, pupils have a much greater ability to look after themselves and the scope of the school management's duty of care will reflect this factor.

Some other important cases dealing with injuries sustained off the premises also raise the issue of the scope of the school management's duty to supervise the pupils outside normal school hours. These cases will be addressed below.

Supervision outside hours

Clearly it would be wrong to impose on day schools a duty to supervise children day and night: there must be temporal limits to the scope of this duty. Equally clearly, it would seem legalistic and unjust to restrict the duty to the exact limits of school hours. The courts have therefore tried to strike a reasonable balance.

In the Scottish decision of *Hunter v. Perth and Kinross Council*,[39] a 12-year-old pupil hit her face against a bus in the area of the school grounds when she was pushed by another pupil, as she was about to get into the bus. She claimed that the school authorities had been negligent in failing to supervise their pupils between the final bell and the departure of the buses; there ought to have been an adult person constantly present and visible to the pupils. This argument was rejected by the Outer House of the Court of Session. Lord Essie stated:

---

[38] [1953] A.C. 549.
[39] (2001) S.C.L.R. 856.

"Given the extent of the area and the presence of the buses, it is difficult to see that this criterion could be satisfied except by the provision of a number of supervisors. Further, since there was no evidence that this particular time and area posed special problems not present at other times or locations in the school, ... the same duty of ever-present supervision would require to be performed elsewhere as the children were leaving the school through various exits. The cases to which I was referred do not support, but on the contrary rather negative, the existence of any duty on an education authority to provide such all-pervasive supervision. It is not suggested in the pleadings that there is any practice among secondary schools to make such provision nor can it, in my view, be said that the omission of such extensive supervision was obvious folly.

Further, ... it is evident that certain supervision was provided. The boarding of buses was supervised by the drivers. Teachers leaving the school passed across the area at (from the pupils' standpoint) unpredictable moments. The rector was there on rotation and, as he also pointed out in his evidence, a special care assistant would be present in the area to attend the transport arrangements of children with special needs.

Given that level of presence of adults in the relevant area of the playground, I do not consider that it can be said that the presence of another adult, even a teacher, somewhere in the area with supervisory duties would have made a difference in the present case. Even assuming a deliberate assault by the second defender on the pursuer, the consensus amongst the former schoolchildren was to the general effect that the presence of a teacher would have made little difference had a pupil been actively intent on attacking another. With that assessment I tend to agree. It follows even more so that on the facts as I have found them the presence of additional supervision could have had no role in preventing the incident, which did not take the form of a deliberate attack.

For all these reasons I consider that the case against the first defender is unsound."

It may be noted that a somewhat greater emphasis is placed in this Scottish decision than in the Irish or English cases on the relevance of the customary practice of schools in determining what constitutes due care. In the English Court of Appeal in *Kearn-Price v. Kent County Council*,[40] Dyson, L.J. stated:

---

[40] [2002] E.W.C.A. Civ. 1539, [2002] All E.R. (D.) 440, October 30, 2002.

"I accept that evidence of what is standard procedure at schools generally is highly material to a determination of what is reasonably required of a school. But it is no more than that. Sometimes, although probably rarely, a court may conclude that the standard generally applied is not sufficient to discharge the duty of care."

In *Kearn-Price v. Kent County Council*, the English Court of Appeal upheld a judgment in favour of its pupil who had lost the vision in his left eye when struck by a full size leather football in the playground some minutes before the school's doors opened. Pupils were permitted to be in the playground at 8.30 a.m. The doors opened a quarter of an hour later. Footballs of this type had been banned by the school authorities. Dyson L.J. addressed the issue of the pre-school-hours duty of the school as follows:

"I would unhesitatingly reject the proposition that, as a matter of law, no duty to supervise can be owed by a school to its pupils who are on school premises before or after school hours ... In my judgment, a school owes to all pupils who are lawfully on its premises the general duty to take such measures to care for their health and safety as are reasonable in all the circumstances. It is neither just nor reasonable to say that a school owes no duty of care at all to pupils who are at school before or after school hours ... It is inevitable and entirely reasonable that pupils will wish to arrive at school some time before school hours. In the present case, the claimant arrived at the school at about 8.30 am. That is typical of what happens in schools up and down the country. The real issue is what is the scope of the duty of care owed to pupils who are on school premises before and after school hours. It may be that it is not reasonable to expect a school to do as much to protect its pupils from injury outside school hours as during school hours. All will depend on the circumstances. The longer the period before the start of school hours, the more difficult it may be for a pupil who is injured to say that there was a breach of duty of care in failing to supervise. Moreover, it may be unreasonable to expect constant supervision during the pre-school period, but entirely reasonable to require constant supervision during the break periods ... But the governing principle is that the school is required to do what is reasonable in all the circumstances."

In *Greene v. Mundow*,[41] the plaintiff was bitten by a stray dog while playing

---

[41] Circuit Court, Judge McMahon, January 20, 2000.

with other children on school premises shortly before school commenced. School class began at 9:00 am, but the main gate was opened to admit teachers who drove to school early to avoid the traffic rush. At approximately 8:45, the gates for vehicular traffic were then closed and the pedestrian gates admitting pupils were opened at approximately 8:50. The children played in the yard until the whistle blew for class to commence, usually about 9:05. The plaintiff arrived at about 8:55 and went around the building to play with her friends. There were between fifty and sixty children in this area when a dog started to chase them. The dog first knocked the plaintiff's elder sister and then chased other children before biting the plaintiff.

Judge McMahon had no difficulty in holding that once on the property there was an obligation to supervise the children. The headmaster, in evidence, said that even though most of the teachers were on the premises since 8:30 he did not think it right that he should ask them to supervise before the official class began. (There was a suggestion that there might be a union problem). It was acknowledged that the school had a problem with straying dogs and used to ask individuals walking dogs not to come on the premises, the caretaker used to put the dogs out when he noticed them; and finally, the dog warden was called if a dog persisted or if there was more than one dog on the grounds before the children arrived was real.

Judge McMahon held that the duty to supervise commenced once the children were allowed onto the premises even if this was before official class time. In the present case this certainly commenced when the pedestrian gates were opened. By then, there were several teachers on the premises, and if there was union problem with them, the school should make alternative arrangements for that short period. He commented that the school had a caretaker and an assistant caretaker and the period in question, 10-15 minutes, was very short. He had no difficulty in concluding that, were the children supervised, the plaintiff would not have been bitten. The duty to supervise was not, according to Judge McMahon, confined to the "official" day, but spilled over to a short period before school when pupils were arriving and to a short period after school when pupils were dispersing. The length of those "spill-over" periods would depend on the facts of each case.

Let us now consider a crucial Irish decision of more than a decade ago. In *Dolan v. Keohane and Cunningham*,[42] the plaintiff, a nine-year-old pupil at a primary school was injured when swinging on the entrance gate of the defendant's secondary school which was across the road from the primary

---

[42] Unreported, Supreme Court, February 8, 1994, affirming High Court, February 14, 1992.

school at a distance of thirty yards. The accident happened at about 3 pm when the primary school pupils were going home. Children who lived near to the school walked or cycled home. Those who lived at a further distance were either collected by car or went home by bus under a private arrangement between their parents and the bus operator. The bus driver had formerly collected the pupils at a pre-arranged spot which had formerly been at the entrance to the primary school but, after consultation with the Gardaí, had recently move to a point close to the entrance to the secondary school.

On the day of the accident the pupils, including the plaintiff, had left their satchels at this collection point and gone to swing on the gate. It appeared from the evidence that, although the plaintiff and his friends had been swinging on the gate every day, no teacher from the defendant's school had been aware of this practice.

The plaintiff's case rested on two main planks. The first was that the defendant's duty of supervision did not end at the school gate and that the "pre-ordained system of collection" necessarily involved a continuing duty on the defendants' part to take reasonable care for the safety of the pupils until such time as they boarded the bus. Keane J. rejected this argument.

The degree of supervision required of school authorities obviously varied with the circumstances, including the age of the child. This duty, in the case of very young children, might include the obligation to ensure that they did not escape from the school on to a street where there was any significant volume of traffic, but no such considerations arose in the instant case. In Keane J.'s view, it would be unreasonable to treat the teachers in the primary school as being under any obligation to supervise the plaintiff at a stage when he had crossed to the other side of the rod and walked an appreciable distance to the gates of the secondary school. Manifestly, children of the plaintiff's age cold get into "mischief of various sorts" between the time they left the school grounds and arriving at their home.

In Keane J.'s opinion, the plaintiff was "well outside the ambit of any possible duty of supervision" on the part of the primary school teachers by the time he reached the gate. It was wholly immaterial that he was there because of an arrangement between the parents and the bus drivers that the boys would be collected at that particular point, since the uncontested evidence was that the defendants had not been involved in any way in making those arrangements. Equally, the teachers in the *secondary* school had not been under any duty to supervise the plaintiff at that point, their duty being confined to the secondary school pupils under their care.

The second basis of liability asserted by the plaintiff related to the defendants' duty, as owners and occupiers, to take reasonable care for the safety of children climbing on to a gate which they knew, or ought to have know, would be a source of danger to them. Keane J., held that the defendants should not be held liable. None of the teachers in either school had known of the children's practice of swinging on the gate; therefore, the only conceivable basis on which they could be found liable was that they ought to have foreseen that the absence of a stopping device of the type referred to by an expert witness of the plaintiff would be likely to cause injury to children who might be attracted to swinging on the gate. Keane J., thought that it would be "entirely unreasonable" to impose such a duty at the time the gate was installed.

The Supreme Court dismissed the plaintiff's appeal. O'Flaherty J., was unable to identify any distinction in principle between the respective positions of pupils from the town and those who were awaiting the arrival of the buses. While there were clearly cases where the duty to supervise did not end at the school gate, the present case was not one of them.

What is the best approach, therefore, for post-primary school management to take in relation to supervision before and after school hours? As may be seen from the decisions, there is no specific moment at which the duty of care starts or ends. It all depends on the circumstances of each case. The Department of Education's view that supervision should be provided for a period of at least twenty minutes before school begins is likely to be reflected, to some degree at least, in court decisions, not because there is any magic in twenty, as opposed to nineteen, minutes but because clearly the duty starts before the bell rings and twenty minutes is a reasonable enough estimate of the period when an effective system of supervision may be expected.

It must be emphasised that there can be cases where the duty to supervise goes well beyond twenty minutes. To a significant extent the existence and scope of this duty can be controlled by effective communication with the parents, involving written notes of acceptance by the parents that pupils are not to arrive before a certain time. These communications represent good management on the part of the school. One should not, however, regard them as magic exemptions from prospective liability. They can be overtaken by events. If all parents signed notes accepting that their children should not arrive before 9 a.m. yet the school playground is full every day at 8.45 a.m., the court could well hold that a duty to supervise arose because the management had acquiesced in a practice which contradicted the assurances given in the notes.

The school's duty of care to pupils *after* school hours seems from the cases to be far more constricted than the duty before the school opens. Pupils can be expected to go home as the business of the day is over. But again there will be instances where an extended duty of care falls on the school management – for example, where a parent has contacted the school to say that he or she will be late in collecting the pupil or where pupils are carrying out permitted activities on the school premises after school hours.

School transport

As a general principle, the school is not responsible for the transport system whereby the pupils are taken to and from the school. The responsibility for due care towards the children falls on those in charge of that system. We shall not here consider the question of how wide that net can be cast since it will not normally extend as far as the school authorities.

The general principle should not, however, be regarded as a universal rule. The courts will impose a duty of care on those on whom it is fair to place that burden. This is not always limited to the parties directly involved in providing the transportation system. A couple of examples may make this clear.

One can envisage a case where parents of a pupil reported to the school principal that their child had told them that he was being assaulted every day by other pupils on the school bus and the principal assured them that she would "get to the heart of the problem and resolve it immediately." If the principal fell down on that assurance and did nothing and the pupil was seriously injured during the next week, the principal could not rely on the primary responsibility resting on the transport providers to exempt her from the legal consequences of her promise to undertake a duty to intervene. (Of course, the transport providers might well also be liable but their liability does not automatically relieve the school of any liability.)

Another case might arise where the bus transport system is providing an unreliable service and the principal receives confidential information that the bus driver is drinking while on duty. A court could well consider that the principal falls under a duty to take *some* steps to protect the pupils from this hidden danger, even though the risk is created by the driver rather than the school. Sometimes the moral duty to protect others from a danger not of one's own making translates into a legal obligation. The exact scope of that duty is a matter for debate. In the present example, a court might consider that it should go no further than to communicate a concern to the transport authorities.

A third example may be found on Church & General's website:[43]

> "In situations where teachers voluntarily adopt the practice of escorting pupils to and from school or the bus, they could be held liable if, having

---

[43] http://www.allscoil.com/faqSupervPupils.htm.

established the practice, they miss out for some reason or another or fail to do so in a careful manner."

It should be stressed that these examples are very much the exception to the special rule of non-liability on the part of schools.

Supervision on school tours

School tours place a heavy burden on the teachers who are required to act as supervisors. Children lose their inhibitions when on the move. They experience a sudden range of new sights, sounds, tastes and smells. They find themselves relating to each other in new groupings, often making new friendships and discovering new aspects to the characters of their colleagues.

This novelty also extends to their relationships with their teachers whom they now see in unfamiliar contexts. The school classroom is a somewhat narrow stage: the school tour represents a far broader theatre of action in which, to some degree, the teachers play new roles. The old assumptions about the exercise of authority do not necessarily apply in this strange and exciting new environment.

Another complicating factor is that children in motion are very hard to control, not necessarily because they are unruly and disobedient but simply because streets are narrow and crowded, traffic is heavy and the teachers, like the pupils, may be unfamiliar about where precisely they are or should be going. Getting lost is part of the experience of being in a new place. With a group of excited pupils under one's supervision, getting lost can become a nightmare.

What does the law of negligence have to say about school trips, in Ireland or abroad? The answer is the same as for all other aspects of supervision: the school management must take reasonable care for the safety of the pupils. Let us try to add some degree of specificity to this very general criterion.

The first aspect that should be stressed is in relation to the planning that goes into the trip. Reasonable care should be exercised in the nature of the trip that is chosen, the venue, the means of transportation, the demands on the physical resources of the children, having regard to their age and capacity, and the dangers to which they may be exposed.

If, for example, a trip to a mountainous area were arranged for ten-year-olds, supervised even by a veritable army of teachers, it could still be negligence for the school to have exposed the children to the risk of injury if the trip, of its nature, involved too rigorous physical demands of them. None of the teachers on the trip would be guilty of negligence; their supervision might be of the first order. Yet the school would be liable because the whole idea of a venture of this kind was simply unreasonable. The negligence would lie in the plan, not in its execution.

Organising a trip to a notoriously dangerous location could well constitute negligence. In this context, it is worth noting the case of *McKenna v. Best Travel t/a Cypriano Holidays*,[44] where the Supreme Court, reversing the High Court judge, held that a travel agent and tour operator had not been guilty of negligence in failing to warn the plaintiff, who was contemplating visiting Israel, that a state of unrest existed in the Bethlehem area after the Iraqi invasion of Kuwait a few weeks previously. The plaintiff was injured by a stone thrown at the coach in which she was travelling. If a High Court judge could impose liability on these facts, albeit reversed on appeal, one can appreciate that it is far from fantastic to contemplate that a school management could be found negligent for a particularly imprudent choice of destination. One should not over-emphasise this risk but it should not be completely discounted either.

The other main area of potential liability, of course, is inadequate supervision. The fact that the children are in a new environment will increase the intensity of supervision that is required. In *MS Grewal v. Deep Chand Sood*,[45] the Supreme Court of India imposed liability on a school for the negligent supervision by its teachers of students when they were on a picnic trip to a riverbank. The teachers permitted 14 students to play in the area of a dangerous deep part of the river without warning them of the danger. This resulted in the death through drowning of all the children, which Banerjee J, with some understatement, described as "a rather unfortunate sad end and finale to the so-called extra curricular activities of the school."

Before any trip is contemplated, serious and detailed consideration, duly minuted, should be given to the question of supervision. There should be enough supervisors for all aspects of the trip. If at any stage, by virtue of the exigencies of travel, the pupils get broken up into groups that spread the supervisory resources too thinly, that is something for which the school management will carry responsibility. Again the problem can be traced to the drawing board rather than to the teachers who are doing their best.

Of course, if the teachers do not do their best – if they become diverted or if they drink too much or simply abandon their post – and a pupil is injured, liability will be imposed.

One should urge caution about using parents as supervisors on trips. They are not part of the school management system, nor directly subject to its organisational command structure. It would be imprudent to assume that

---

[44] Unreported, Supreme Court, November 18, 1997.
[45] [2001] 1289 L.R.I. 4.

all parents are necessarily effective and responsible supervisors. For consideration of this issue, see the very helpful analysis by Oliver Mahon, at pages 53 to 56, of his excellent work, *Negligence and the Teacher*, published by the Ennis Teachers' Centre in 1995.

THE OCCUPIERS' LIABILITY ACT 1995

Let us now turn to consider the position of schools, as *occupiers of premises*, under the Occupiers' Liability Act 1995. The 1995 Act has divided people who go onto property into three categories:

- visitors,
- trespassers, and
- recreational users.

Visitors are essentially all those entrants who come onto the school premises with your permission (such as the pupils, the teachers or parents) or under lawful authority (such as members of the Garda Síochána or postal workers).

Trespassers are not by any means all criminals. They are simply people who are on the premises without the occupier's consent. Some trespassers will, of course, be of criminal disposition but others will not. Anyone whom the occupier has barred from the premises will be a trespasser if he or she returns contrary to the terms of the exclusion. So a pupil who has been suspended but who comes back to school in circumstances where it must be obvious to him or her that this is contrary to the terms of the suspension will be characterised as a trespasser.

The duty that the Occupiers' Liability Act 1995 prescribes in relation to visitors is simply the duty to take due care – to take reasonable steps to protect the visitor and his or her property.

What is reasonable care naturally depends on all the circumstances of the case. The law does *not* require the school management to compensate an injured pupil simply because the pupil has been injured on the premises. It is essential for the injured plaintiff to establish that the injury was caused by the school management's carelessness. If this cannot be established, the claim must be dismissed.

Some guiding cases

It is useful to look at some of the cases decided on the basis of the common law because, for a number of years before the Occupiers' Liability Act 1995, the courts applied a test in relation to pupils in school which was in essence the same standard of reasonable care as that required by the 1995 Act.

In *Flynn v. O'Reilly*,[46] an 11-year-old pupil, in a race which required competitors to run backwards, fell on the ground in a field used for hurling and camogie which, Smith, J. found, "m[ight] have had a slight turfing or indentation" but was not "holed or rutted or so rough or uneven as to be ... hazardous or dangerous. ..." Smith, J. held that the school was not liable for the fall and the Supreme Court affirmed. O'Flaherty, J. (Keane and Murphy JJ. concurring) observed:

> "The history of the field was, everyone agrees, that it was not Wimbledon or Lansdowne Road or Wembley or some place like that [but] was for rather simple games and, to adopt the words of Chief Justice Ó Dálaigh [in *Lennon v. McCarthy*], it would be unreal to say that a parent would regard this field as dangerous. ...
>
> [E]ven accepting that there was some indentation or some unevenness and accepting that there is some risk attached to people running backwards as opposed to running forwards and that that is more hazardous, nonetheless, do we lay down that that should be forbidden in a way that would prevent children having due freedom to play and engage in sports? We think that would be too strict a rule. It would be to do what the law commands us in assessing negligence not to do, which is to impose standards which are unreasonable having regard to all the circumstances."

The Occupiers' Liability Act 1995 has had the following effect in relation to schools. Pupils are clearly "visitors", for the purposes of section 1(1). The school authorities owe "the common duty of care" towards pupils under section 3. In essence, as has been mentioned, this is the same duty as is imposed by the common law in negligence cases. A decision of Judge McMahon, in *Heaves v. Westmeath County Council*,[47] suggests that the duty under section 3 should not be regarded as being in any way greater than the former common law duty of care.

---

[46] [1999] 1 I.L.R.M. 158.
[47] 20 *Irish Law Times* (New Series) 236 (Circuit Court, Mullingar 2001).

In *Hall v. Meehan*,[48] the plaintiff, a six year old pupil at the defendants' school was injured when he fell against a concrete breeze block kerb in the playground after having collided with another pupil. He sued the school for negligence, arguing that it had breached its common law duty as occupier of the premises. The accident had taken place in 1992, three years before the Occupiers' Liability Act 1995 came into force. What is of interest for our purposes is that Gilligan J. proceeded on the basis that the common law duty owed to "invitees" (roughly equivalent to "visitors" under the 1995 Act) was to act with reasonable care. This is in essence the test specified by the 1995 Act in respect of visitors, to whom the occupier owes "the common duty of care".

There was a dispute between opposing expert witnesses as to whether blocks of the kind used were suitable for school playgrounds. This centred on whether their sharp edges were dangerous, in view of the likelihood of falls. Gilligan J. held in favour of the plaintiff on this issue. He stated:

"... I take the view that the kerbing that was in place was of a makeshift variety consisting of rough concrete breeze blocks with a sharp edge and broken in places.

I take the view that kerbing with sharp rough edges was inappropriate for installation in a school premises where, *inter alia*, 6 year old boys would be running and as would be normal falling. Quite clearly in my view the sharp rough edge of the kerbing presented an unusual danger to school children particularly of a tender age on the defendant's school premises and further I am satisfied that this was a danger of which the defendant knew or ought reasonably to have known as it appears self evident from the photographs that if a child was to fall against the sharp rough edge of the kerb stone an injury was likely to follow and the significance of that injury would be determined by the velocity involved in the impact against the sharp edge.

Accordingly I find that the defendant as the occupier of the school premises was guilty of negligence and breach of duty in failing to take reasonable care to prevent damage from an unusual danger of which he knew or ought to have known."

An interesting feature of the case was that relating to resources. The school in question was a two-teacher premises in need of repair. Gilligan J. noted that:

---

[48] Unreported, High Court, Gilligan J., December 17, 2004.

"unfortunately the school authorities were not in a position to obtain any funds from the Department of Education as a result of which various parents came together and brought in sand and soil in order to make a playing area and surrounded this area with concrete breeze blocks which were laid on their side to separate the path area immediately outside the school from the playing field area. This was voluntary work on behalf of the parents and ... who was the school principal at the time of this accident has given evidence that the breeze blocks would have been in position for approximately 4 – 5 years prior to the accident the subject matter of these proceedings. She accepted in evidence that the Department of Education were probably not even aware that this voluntary work had been carried out by the children's parents in order to better the school facilities in the absence of any funds being available."

Gilligan J., in his holding regarding liability, did not return to this aspect of the case. No doubt questions may arise in the future as to whether the State should be exposed to liability, exclusively or in conjunction with a school, where inadequate funding has been provided and the premises are clearly dangerous as a result.

Another issue may relate to work done by parents without the knowledge of the Department of Education. In the unlikely case where work is completed surreptitiously, without the knowledge or approval of the school principal, then it is possible that the school authorities will not be liable, provided, for course, that in the ordinary course of events, the school management, as reasonable occupier would not have discovered the work. Where as will surely be the position in the overwhelming majority of the cases, the school management is aware of the work, then its duty of care cannot be shuffled off onto the parents.

Occupiers/supervision/activity characterisation

There can sometimes be a difficulty in determining whether a claim should be regarded as one based on the principles of *occupier's liability* or instead or regarded as one of *negligent activity* not essentially related to the occupation of the premises or, thirdly, as one of *negligent lack of supervision*. Let us take the case where an extension is being added to a school premises. All kinds of interesting machinery are in action: steamrollers, pile drivers and drills, for example. If the school management does not take the greatest care to protect the pupils from the risk of injury resulting from their national curiosity, how should the default be characterised? A plausible argument can be made in favour of any of these three approaches.

In the Australian case of *The Commonwealth v. Introvigne*,[49] a 15-year-old pupil was injured in the school grounds where a flagpole fell on him. A group of his friends had been swinging on the halyard of flagpole at the time. In the Full Court of the Federal Court it was noted that:

> "[i]n some 'activity' cases there is a very fine line of distinction to be drawn to ascertain whether the only relationship is that of occupier/ entrant or whether the pursuit of the occupier or the permission he gives raises a general duty of care toward the [plaintiff]. ..."

The Court held that the school was *not* liable *as occupier*, since the injury was not foreseeable. It held, however, that the school *was* liable for negligent lack of supervision in failing to have had a rule that the pole was not to be used unless with the express authority of a teacher, in failing to have ensured that the halyard was secured by its padlock to the pole and in not having sufficient teachers on supervision duty on the fateful day. The High Court of Australia affirmed the holding in relation to liability for negligent lack of supervision.

The point is of some considerable practical importance because the 1995 Act replaces the former law in relation to occupiers' liability *only in respect of dangers existing on the premises*. A roof which is in a state of disrepair is an example of such a danger. Similarly a playground with loose bricks left scattered all around it. But what is the position where a teacher organises a game of football in the playground in the knowledge that these bricks are all over the playing area? A pupil who falls on one of the bricks could of course argue that it was a "danger existing on the premises" But, equally plausibly, he or she could claim that the injury was the result of negligent supervision by the teacher, which falls outside the scope of the act.

In truth, the difference between the two categories of claim will in most cases be entirely academic, since the essence of both is negligence. One can, however, envisage two principal contexts where the difference may have real practical implications. The first concerns the impact of section 5, which enables the occupier by express agreement or notice to restrict his or her or its duty arising under section 3 to visitors. This entitlement is subject to the requirement (*inter alia*) that the modification be "reasonable in all the circumstances": section 5(2)(b)(i).

No similar limitation attaches to an agreement between the school

---

[49] 150 C.L.R. 258 (High Court of Australia, 1980), affirming 48 F.L.R. 161 (Fed. Ct. Austr., A.C.T. Dist. Reg. Gen. Div., 1980).

authorities and pupils whereby the school authorities purport to restrict the scope of their potential liability in negligence under common law. It might be thought unlikely that the court would, under common law, give effect to an agreement between the school and the pupil which it regarded as unreasonable. Yet the common law imposes no function on the courts to police agreements for their reasonableness. The hallmark of contract theory is that the parties, and not the courts, carve out their respective entitlements. The whole question of the validity and enforcement of contracts with minors is, of course, relevant in this context.

The second context in which the difference may be important is where a pupil is a trespasser on the school premises. Under the legislation, the occupier owes no duty of care, in respect of dangers existing on the premises, to trespassers. The occupier is merely obliged not to injure the trespasser intentionally nor act with reckless disregard for the trespasser: section 4(1).

If we take a fairly common scenario: pupils are strictly instructed not to come to school until 15 minutes before the classes start. They and their parents are told in clear terms that the school playground is out of bounds before then. A particular pupil turns up twenty-five minutes before the start of the school day. If he is injured in the playground in the following couple of minutes, he may be characterised as a trespasser and thus unable to assert a duty of care on the part of the school so far as structural dangers are concerned but he will nonetheless be able to press a claim for negligent lack of supervision at common law. Whether that claim would succeed is, of course, a matter of uncertainty but the point to note here is that sometimes the facts of the case will enable a claim for negligent supervision to be made by a trespassing pupil where there is a danger on the premises in respect of which the pupil would have no claim under the 1995 Act.

Modifying the scope of liability

We now must consider the possibility that the school management can modify the scope of potential liability to pupils under the 1995 Act. Section 5(1) of the Act gives the occupier the power, by express agreement or notice, to *extend* the scope of his or her duty towards entrants (whether they be visitors or even trespassers). It seems unlikely that many occupiers will be taking advantage of this facility.

Section 5(2) gives the occupier power to *limit* the scope of liability towards visitors. It enables the occupier, again by express agreement or notice, to *restrict, modify* or *exclude* his or her duty towards visitors (most frequently, in our context, pupils) subject to certain qualifications. The visitor will not be bound unless the restriction, modification or exclusion is *reasonable in all circumstances*.⁵⁰ Moreover, where the occupier seeks to accomplish his or her goal by *notice* rather than by obtaining the visitor's express agreement, the occupier must take reasonable steps to bring the notice to the attention of the visitor.⁵¹ The occupier will be presumed, unless the contrary is shown, to have taken such reasonable steps if the notice is *prominently displayed at the normal means of access to the premises*.⁵²

There is a minimum level of obligation to visitors below which the occupier is not permitted to venture: the occupier may not exclude liability to injure a visitor (or damage the visitor's property) intentionally or to act with reckless disregard for a visitor (or the property of a visitor).⁵³

It may be worth considering briefly the question of when a restriction, modification or exclusion is "reasonable in all the circumstances" This is a matter of considerable practical importance for school management. Why should it ever be unreasonable for an occupier to restrict his or her liability? Clearly section 5(2) is premised on the acceptance of the judgment that there can be cases where a restriction of liability is unreasonable.

It seems likely that the courts will have regard to social factors, including the necessity of people to go on certain premises, such as schools, social welfare offices or hospitals. They have no real choice in entering these premises, so it may be considered unreasonable to reduce their rights on the false assumption that they freely accept the limitation.

Children are legally obliged to go to school. It is hard to envisage a stronger legal restriction on the right to choose one's location save that of imprisonment. There therefore is no real prospect of a school's reducing the scope of its liability by means of section 5. Even for pupils who are above the age where attendance at school is compulsory, it is most unlikely that a notice will have any efficacy. Similarly, one suspects that the courts would not look with favour on a notice on school premises purporting to restrict liability to "entrants as of right", such as the Gardaí, bailiffs or fire fighters, for example.

This does not mean, of course, that the school management will be acting with futility in communicating effectively with pupils and their parents regarding dangers on the property. A clear warning of a particular danger may have the effect of discharging the school's duty of care as occupier. It should be noted that the mere giving of a warning will not in itself suffice, unless, "in all the circumstances, it was enough to enable the visitor, by

---

⁵⁰ Occupiers Liability Act 1995, s.5(2)(b)(ii).
⁵¹ *Ibid.*, s.5(2)(b)(ii).
⁵² *Ibid.*, s.5(2)(c).
⁵³ *Ibid.*, s.5(3).

having regard to the warning, to avoid the injury or damage ... caused [by such a danger]".[54] So, for example, a warning to 15-year-old pupils not to pull heavily on a window blind that had seen better days might well discharge the school management's duty of care under the 1995 Act to those pupils, who would have little or no need in the first place to touch the blind. But a similar warning to five-year-olds would not. Nor would a warning to pupils that the seats on which they are sitting are unsafe suffice to discharge the school's duty of care to the pupils. They could hardly be expected to stand all day in the classroom.

The duty of school management to trespassers

We now must consider the duty that the school management owe to trespassers under the 1995 Act. It will be recalled that trespassers come in all shapes and sizes. In the present context, we are concerned with trespassers who are not on the premises with criminal intent or who do not succumb to the temptation to commit a crime while on the school premises.

The 1995 Act does not require the school management to avoid being negligent to non-criminal trespassers. All that it requires is that the school management neither acts with *reckless disregard* for them nor *intentionally* injure them.

It might seem clear from consideration of the several factors prescribed in the legislation that recklessness connotes *objective* default rather than necessarily requiring any subjective advertence on the part of the management to the risk of injury.

On this interpretation, a school principal or teacher who culpably failed to discover, or who forgot about, a particular danger would not on that account be relieved of liability. If an objective test were to be applied, a question would arise as the extent to which the courts would in practice set the standard at a lower level than the standard of reasonable care in actions for negligence.

The Act gives no guidance as to how much lower the level should be. The nine factors specified in section 4(2) contain no such yardstick; indeed, they might constitute a trap to an unwary judge who could easily seek to apply them without adverting to the fact that, although they are similar to criteria applicable for determining the issue of negligence, they have to be pitched at a level more indulgent to the defendant. The correct meaning of "recklessness", it may be suggested, is "very serious carelessness". This was how the Irish courts used to interpret the term when the common law

---

[54] *Ibid.*, s.5(5).

test of liability to trespassers was to avoid injuring them intentionally or recklessly.

Whether this is the correct answer must await judicial resolution. The Supreme Court, in the recent decision of *Weir Rodgers v. The SF Trust Ltd.*,[55] specifically declined to answer the question and indeed raised the real possibility that the test may be even more stringent, possibly incorporating (or consisting exclusively of) a subjective element. Geoghegan J. (with whom Murray C.J. and Denham J. concurred) stated:

> "I do not intend to express any view on the subjective/objective question. Such consideration should be left for a case where it properly arises. My concern in this regard arises from the fact that notwithstanding the recommendations contained in both the Consultation Paper and the ultimate report of the Law Reform Commission that the liability towards trespassers and recreational users should be one of 'gross negligence', the Oireachtas appears to have rejected this recommendation and adopted the phrase arising from the old case law namely "reckless disregard". It may well be, therefore, that the liability is something more than what might be described as 'gross negligence'."

Criminal entrants

The spectre of liability to a burglar or other law-breaker haunted the Oireachtas Debates. Non-lawyers have great difficulty in contemplating that an occupier could ever owe such unpleasant entrants *any* duty of care. The solution adopted by section 4(3)(a) of the 1995 Act is that the occupier should be relieved of the obligation not to act with reckless disregard for a person *who enters onto premises for the purpose of committing an offence or a person who, while present on premises, commits an offence there.* An "offence", either intended or actually committed, embraces an *attempted* offence.[56]

A couple of points about section 4(3) should be noted. *First,* the immunity is not absolute: it does not apply in a case where a court determines otherwise "in the interests of justice". It is impossible to predict with any degree of certainty how the court will exercise this discretion. One may anticipate that it would be disposed to hold occupiers to the recklessness standard where the offender was very young or the offence was relatively trivial – such as throwing a marble at a classroom window.

---

[53] [2005] 1 I.L.R.M. 471.
[54] Occupiers Liability Act 1995, s.4(3)(b).

Secondly, the occupier is relieved only of the duty not to act with reckless disregard for the entrant; he or she is still under the duty not to *injure* the entrant (or damage the entrant's property) *intentionally* In some cases, of course, that obligation will in turn be "trumped" by the occupier's entitlement to use proportionate force for his or her self-defence, the defence of others or the defence of property. Section 8(a) of the Act makes this clear. So if a vengeful pupil comes onto the premises, after having been suspended, with the intent of stabbing the principal, the principal is perfectly entitled to defend himself or herself without fear of legal sanction provided, of course, that only reasonable force is used.

Recreational users

Let us now consider the new category of "recreational users" which the 1995 Act introduced. It appears to have very limited relevance to schools. Section 1(1) of the Act defines "recreational activity" as:

> "any recreational activity conducted, whether alone or with others, in the open air (including any sporting activity), scientific research and nature study so conducted, exploring caves and visiting sites and buildings of historical, architectural, traditional, artistic, archaeological or scientific importance."

A "recreational user" is defined by section 1(1) as:

> "an entrant who, with or without the occupier's permission or at the occupier's implied invitation, is present on premises without a charge ... being imposed for the purpose of engaging in a recreational activity ..., but not including an entrant who is present and is—
> (a) a member of the occupier's family who is ordinarily resident on the premises,
> (b) an entrant who is present at the express invitation of the occupier or such member, or
> (c) an entrant who is present with the permission of the occupier or such a member for social reasons connected with the occupier or such member."

Recreational users are in a very disadvantaged position under the 1995 Act. The occupier of the premises does not owe them any duty of care in negligence in respect of dangers existing on the premises. All that the occupier is required to do is not injure them intentionally and not act with reckless disregard for them.[57] The only instance where a higher duty is imposed is where a structure on the premises is provided for use primarily by recreational users. The occupier must take reasonable care to maintain it in a safe condition: section 4(4). Recreational users, thus, are in virtually as bad a position as trespassers under the 1995 legislation.

Could it be argued that a pupil playing football during break at school is a "recreational user" who is not owed a duty of care in negligence by the school authorities in respect of dangers existing on the premises? It seems not. The pupil is on the premises, not "for the purpose of engaging in a recreational activity", but because the law requires him or her to be there, because his or her parents so ordain and because, so far as the pupil's own motivation determines the issue, school is where one receives an education. Even if we envisage the case of a sports-mad student with no academic interests, it seem inconceivable that a court would hold that his or her presence on the premises on a normal school day during school hours was "for the purpose of engaging in a recreational activity".

It may be useful to refer to the American case of *Bauer v. Minidoka School District No. 331*,[58] where a pupil tripped over sprinkler pipes while he was playing football in the school grounds a few minutes before classes commenced. The school obtained summary judgment in its favour by invoking a legislative provision regarding recreational users similar to our 1995 Act. The Supreme Court reversed. Johnson J., for the Court said:

> "Here, [the plaintiff] was a public school student participating in a game being played at school as the school day was getting under way. [He] was not merely a recreational user of the school premises; he was there as a student entitled to the protection of the district. This relationship is crucial to our decision in holding that the recreational use statute does not apply to this case ...
>
> This special relationship that a student has to a school district would be substantially impaired if the recreational use statute were applied to injuries children suffered while on school premises as students. Students would then bear the risk of defects in school premises.
>
> [The plaintiff] was not the type of recreational user contemplated in the recreational user statute. He was a public school student who came to the school early before classes began to play football with his classmates. If he had come to the school grounds to play a game of football that was not organised or sanctioned by the school on a day

---

[57] *Ibid.*, s.4(1).
[58] 116 Idaho 586, 778 P. 2d 336 (1989).

when school was not in session, we would have no trouble in applying the statute to limit the liability of the district. Nor would we have any difficulty in applying the statute, if he had come to the school grounds on a school day to play a game of football that was not organised or sanctioned by the school before the faculty and other students who were not involved in the game began arriving.

The problem we have in applying the recreational use statute to these facts is that [the plaintiff] arrived to play football at the very time that the school was beginning its operations for the day, although no classes had begun. He was not just a member of 'the public' referred to in the recreational use statute. He was there as a student to begin the school day with a game of football. Some students may come early to talk to their teachers, some to visit with their classmates, some to study and others to participate in informal activities such as football. All of these are legitimate activities within the scope of a student's special relationship with the school.

It would be entirely artificial to apply the recreational use statute to activities of students up to the moment the first bell rings and classes begin. No purpose would be served by drawing this line for application of the recreational use statute. When the principal is present some faculty members are on duty and students have arrived, the school day has begun and the recreational use statute has no application to a student who is injured on the school grounds."

This analysis is helpful but of course one should bear in mind the social, educational and legal differences between Idaho and Ireland. It seems certain that in Ireland, a pupil playing football on school grounds a few minutes before classes commence will be characterised as a visitor and not a recreational user.

It is not so clear whether the Irish courts will take the same view as was adopted in the *Bauer* case on the question whether there are some situations where the recreational user characterisation should be attached to pupils on school premises. It is likely that an Irish court would consider a pupil who arrives with a football at the school very early in the morning, before the time that supervision is scheduled to begin, as a visitor rather than a recreational user. He or she is still attending school as a pupil, for predominantly academic purposes.

Where the pupil comes onto school premises with the football on a day when no academic activities are taking place, he or she will still, probably be characterised as a visitor, if the sporting activity is, in the broad sense, part of the school programme. So a child who comes on a Saturday to play an organised match against a team from another school will seem certainly to be a visitor. If the school had no organisational input into the game, which was entirely informal and if the game took place on a day where absolutely no school activities were scheduled, the case for holding the child to be a recreational user is very much stronger.

It is interesting to note that, in *Byrne v. Dun Laoghaire County Council*,[59] Judge Smyth, President of the Circuit Court, held that an adult who fell when training an Under-15 soccer team at the playing fields in Sallynoggin at the end of July was a recreational user because he had not received the defendant's permission to use the playing fields at the time as it was off-season.

In practice, the school management can control the matter by a clear and effectively communicated policy as to whether, and if so when, pupils are permitted to use the school premises, even for informal games, outside specific times. A pupil who breaches the school's rules in this area will be a trespasser, whose legal position is marginally worse than that of a recreational user.

Concluding observations regarding the 1995 Act

The above analysis establishes that the courts do not set unreasonably onerous standards in relation to school management's duty as occupier of the premises. The standard is high, but that is no more than one would expect where pupils are in your care. The Occupiers' Liability Act 1995 does not really offer significant prospects of a reduction of liability in most cases. It was enacted for a social purpose unconnected with schools and it is safe to predict that judges will be very reluctant to apply its provisions over-enthusiastically where the school management has been careless and a pupil has been injured.

THE SAFETY, HEALTH AND WELFARE AT WORK ACT 2005

School management should be familiar with the provisions of the Safety, Health and Welfare at Work Act 2005, which enlarges the scope of obligations of employers and creates new duties for people who previously did not fall within the scope of the legislation.

The subject is a large one and ranges well beyond the context of litigation by pupils against schools. For a detailed analysis, see Raymond Byrne,

---

[59] 20 *Irish Law Times* (New Series) 16 (Circuit Court Dublin, Judge Smyth, November 13, 2001).

"Health and Safety Requirements for Schools: A 2005 Update", paper delivered at the Conference on Litigation Against Post-Primary Schools: Strategies to Reduce the Risk of Liability, Trinity College Dublin, Law School, on April 9, 2005. Although there has been health and safety legislation since 1989, supplemented by detailed Regulations in 1993, not all schools have managed to develop a satisfactory culture of protection and prevention. A survey of 270 second level schools conducted by ASTI in early 2005 revealed that 27% had not carried out a fire safety drill in the past year; 20% had no Safety Statement; and 82% of teachers had received no training or advice on stress management in the past year.[60] The 1995 Report of the Health and Safety Authority's Advisory Committee on Safety and Health at First and Second Levels in the Education Sector is a valuable source of information and analysis.

Although many of the provisions of the 2005 Act relate to duties owed by employers to employees, some are concerned with duties owed by employers, employees and others to people who are not employees. Thus school pupils are owed a range of obligations under the 2005 Act. Some of these are adumbrated below.

Section 12 provides as follows:

> "Every employer shall manage and conduct his or her undertaking in such a way as to ensure, so far as is reasonably practicable, that in the course of the work being carried on, individuals at the place of work (not being his or her employees) are not exposed to risks to their safety, health or welfare."

This obligation clearly extends to school pupils, as well as those visiting the school, including parents.

The duty prescribed in section 12 is to manage and conduct the undertaking in such a way as to "ensure, so far as is reasonably practicable," the result specified in the section. This duty is not discharged by doing one's best, even one's reasonable best. The employer must succeed in ensuring the result, so far as is "reasonably practicable".

Let us now turn to consider the obligations placed on employees which relate to pupils. Section 13(1) provides in part as follows:

> "An employee shall, while at work—
> (a) comply with the relevant statutory provisions, as appropriate,

---

[60] "Students and teachers at risk as schools breach health and safety legislation" – ASTI Press Release, March 21, 2005.

The School's Duty of Care to its Pupils 49

and take reasonable care to protect his or her safety, health and welfare and the safety, health and welfare of any other person who may be affected by the employee's acts or omissions at work,
(b) ensure that he or she is not under the influence of an intoxicant to the extent that he or she is in such a state as to endanger his or her own safety, health or welfare at work or that of any other person,
(c) if reasonably required by his or her employer, submit to any appropriate, reasonable and proportionate tests for intoxicants by, or under the supervision of, a registered medical practitioner who is a competent person, as may be prescribed,
(d) co-operate with his or her employer or any other person so far as is necessary to enable his or her employer or the other person to comply with the relevant statutory provisions, as appropriate,
(e) not engage in improper conduct or other behaviour that is likely to endanger his or her own safety, health and welfare at work or that of any other person,
(f) attend such training and, as appropriate, undergo such assessment as may reasonably be required by his or her employer or as may be prescribed relating to safety, health and welfare at work or relating to the work carried out by the employee,
(g) having regard to his or her training and the instructions given by his or her employer, make correct use of any article or substance provided for use by the employee at work or for the protection of his or her safety, health and welfare at work, including protective clothing or equipment,
(h) report to his or her employer or to any other appropriate person, as soon as practicable—
  (i) any work being carried on, or likely to be carried on, in a manner which may endanger the safety, health or welfare at work of the employee or that of any other person,
  (ii) any defect in the place of work, the systems of work, any article or substance which might endanger the safety, health or welfare at work of the employee or that of any other person, or
  (iii) any contravention of the relevant statutory provisions which may endanger the safety, health and welfare at work of the employee or that of any other person, of which he or she is aware."

The repeated references to "any other person" extend to pupils attending the school. If a teacher is careless in supervising a class, resulting in injury to a pupil, this involves a breach of section 13(1)(a). *A fortiori*, if this carelessness is attributable to intoxication on his or her part: section 13 (1)(b). If a teacher assaults or sexually abuses a pupil, it seems that this will constitute a breach of section 13(1)(e). Section 13(1)(h) appears to require one teacher to report to his or her employer the breach by another teacher of that other teacher's statutory obligations.

Let us now try to work out exactly what "reasonably practicable" means, since many of the employer's and the employee's duties are expressed as being subject to this qualification.

Section 2(6) provides as follows:

> "For the purposes of the relevant statutory provisions, 'reasonably practicable', in relation to the duties of an employer, means that an employer has exercised all due care by putting in place the necessary protective and preventive measures, having identified the hazards and assessed the risks to safety and health likely to result in accidents or injury to health at the place of work concerned and where the putting in place of any further measures is grossly disproportionate having regard to the unusual, unforeseeable and exceptional nature of any circumstance or occurrence that may result in an accident at work or injury to health at that place of work."

This definition has three elements. The first is that the employer must have "exercised all due care" by putting in place the necessary protective and preventive measures. This requirement is ambiguous in mixing what might appear to be a "due care" – negligence – standard with an obligation of strict liability: to put in place the necessary protective and preventive measures. Both cannot co-exist. Which of the two competing philosophies is to prevail?

It may be suggested that the strict liability philosophy is the winner and that the reference to "all due care" is merely an empty evocation of a negligence standard. The test does not require the employer to exercise all due care *to put* the measures in place: it requires the employer to exercise such care *by putting* them in place. If the employer, having exercised all due care, does not succeed in putting the measures in place, he or she will not have done what is required by the reasonable practicability test.

The second element in the definition is that the employer should have first identified the hazards and assessed the risks to health at the place of work concerned. If this historical fact has not occurred, the employer will not have done what is reasonably practicable even though the measures adopted by the employer are totally effective in providing the necessary protection and prevention.

The third element is that the putting in place of any further measures must be grossly disproportionate having regard to the unusual, unforeseeable and exceptional nature of any circumstance or occurrence that may result in an accident at work or injury to health at the place of work. This test bears some similarity to the test traditionally applied in determining whether the defendant's conduct was negligent. The court balances four factors: the *likelihood* of an accident occurring, the *gravity* of the threatened injury, the *social utility* of the defendant's actions and the *cost* of preventing the injury.

The test prescribed in respect of reasonable practicability is somewhat different. When answering the question whether putting in place any further measures is grossly disproportionate, the court is apparently not allowed to take into account the social utility of the employers' work, the lack of gravity of the threatened injury or the economic or social cost of preventing the injury. The only matter to which the court is permitted to have regard is the likelihood (or, more particularly, the lack of likelihood) of an accident or injury occurring.

This definition of "reasonably practicable" is Ireland's attempt to comply with Article 5 of the Framework Directive. Article 5(1) imposes on employers the duty "to ensure safety and health of workers in every aspect relating to the work". This is clearly a strict liability test: the employer will not discharge the duty by taking all due care to ensure such safety and health. Article 5(4) provides as follows:

> "This Directive shall not restrict the option of Member States to provide for the exclusion or the limitation of employers' responsibility where occurrences are due to unusual and unforeseeable circumstances, beyond the employers' control, or to exceptional events, the consequences of which could not have been avoided despite the exercise of all due care. Member States need not exercise the option referred to in the first subparagraph."

This option is similar to the defence of an "act of God" in tort law. It relieves the employer of liability only where the occurrence was extremely unlikely. It does not relieve the employer of liability where the taking of measures would be disproportionate, either in respect of the likelihood of such occurrence or in respect of social utility, the gravity of the threatened injury or the cost of prevention.

What practical implications does this have for school management? One possible implication, which would be unpalatable, is that the effect of this definition of "reasonably practicable" is to raise the bar too high for schools in relation to their duty to protect the safety, health and welfare of their pupils. We have seen that courts, in negligence claims against schools, are fully sensitive to the need to balance the risk of injury against the social utility of encouraging self-reliance. That calculus seems hard to reconcile with the definition of "reasonably practicable." It is one thing for legislation to require employers to be under a stringent duty towards their employees (including teachers); it is quite another for it to impose an obligation on schools relative to their pupils which is so stringent as to subvert other desirable social goals.

One should not overstate the problem. Judges are well aware of these social goals; they are the decision-makers and they are unlikely to set too demanding a standard under the 2005 Act in regard to claims against schools by pupils. In any event, there are questions yet to be resolved as to the extent to which the duties imposed by the various provisions of the Act, backed by criminal sanctions, may translate into civil liability and if so, the extent to which schools may be vicariously liable for breaches of section 13(1) by teachers employed by them. The recent decision of the English Court of Appeal in *Magrowski v Guy's & St. Thomas's NHS Trust*[61] adds support for the view that section 13(1) may involve the imposition of vicarious liability on schools, assuming that section 13(1) envisages civil liability in the first place.

OTHER ACTS OF NEGLIGENCE

Other acts of negligence may occur in the course of a school day. Two examples will suffice: a teacher or other school employee may leave dangerous things, such as a phosphorus,[62] within access of the pupils or a pupil may be sent on a risky task that is beyond his or her abilities.[63]

The extent to which schools owe a duty of care towards pupils (and their parents) outside the context of physical injury has yet to be litigated by our Courts. It is probable that at some stage they will have to consider whether a badly educated child has a right of action in negligence against the school on the basis of the school's poor teaching performance.

---

[61] [2005] E.W.C.A. Civ. 251 (March 16, 2005).
[62] *Williams v. Eady* (1893) 10 T.L.R. 11 (CA).
[63] *Smith v. Martin* [1911] 2 K.B. 775.

It is worth noting here that in the controversial decision of *Sinnott v. Minister for Education*,[64] Geoghegan J. made the following interesting observation:

> "While it does not fall to be determined in this case, I would be of the opinion that in the case of the vast majority of children in this State who are non-handicapped the constitutional duty is discharged simply by ensuring that there are schools providing the necessary minimum education available for every child and that the education therein will be provided free of charge. The Constitution must be interpreted in the light of the realities of life. One of those realities is that no matter how efficient an education system there may be, there cannot be a guarantee of high quality teaching. It may well be, therefore, that largely due to poor teaching in a particular school a child who has difficulty in learning to read and write may never acquire those skills. But apart from possibly exceptional circumstances, such as a child either at the time of schooling or in later life would not be entitled to bring an action based on an alleged breach of Article 42.4. Still less would some adult immigrant be entitled to invoke the Article, an idea which was mooted at the hearing of the appeal."

This passage is important as it appears to shut the door – almost completely – to claims of a constitutional nature taken against the State by badly educated children in respect of the deficiencies in their education. It is true that a crack of light remains in that Geoghegan J. envisages 'possibly exceptional circumstances' where such a claim could be sustained, but the overall tenor of his analysis is not receptive to claims of this kind.

One may hope that this question will be revisited. Clearly it is possible for there to be an infringement of the child's right to education warranting compensation by way of an award of damages. The rash of decisions resulting from Drimoleague disputes so attests.[65] These cases, of course, dealt with intentional wrongdoing rather than institutional neglect or managerial deficiency; but that difference is not necessarily one of principle.

If a plaintiff could establish that the "poor teaching in a particular school" was not merely some academic happenstance but was attributable to State neglect or discrimination regarding the social environment in which it operated, there surely would be formidable constitutional issues that would

---

[64] [2001] 2 I.R. 505.
[65] See e.g., *Crowley v. Ireland* [1980] I.R. 102, *Hayes v. Ireland* [1987] I.L.R.M. 651 and *Conway v. Irish National Teachers Organisation* [1991] 1 I.R. 305

need to be addressed. It is true that they could not, and should not, be considered in the context of an isolated analysis of Article 42.4, and thus Geoghegan J. is correct in saying that an action would not (save possibly in exceptional cases) be capable of being "based on an alleged breach of Article 42.5"; but the claim could plausibly be made in conjunction with Articles 40.1 and 40.3.

There would seem to be no reason in principle why a claim framed in common law negligence (or perhaps for breach of statutory duty) should not be successful in cases where the evidence is clear.[66]

EMERGING ISSUES

Let us now consider areas of law where new issues are coming to the centre of discussion.

Pupils with disabilities

Gerry Whyte deals with this general theme in detail. I will limit myself to a few observations.

If a school has on its rolls pupils with disabilities this naturally involves the school in a duty of care to those pupils, which takes account of their particular disability and to other pupils who may be affected by the disability. The school is not entitled to place on a disabled pupil the responsibility for protecting himself or herself, or others which it is the school's duty to discharge.

This broad duty may at times seem a challenging one for management since the needs of the pupil with the disability may on occasion appear to conflict, at least potentially, with the needs of other pupils. For example, the pupil's disability may have a tendency to make him or her disruptive in class or even aggressive towards other pupils. A delicate balance must be struck. The school management always has a duty of care towards all its pupils and, in discharging its duty to some pupils – even the majority – the school is not entitled to sacrifice its duty to other pupils – even a minority of one. The challenge is to get the best outcome, having regard to the equal entitlements of all to receive education. This clearly does not mean that any pupil should be exposed to an unwarranted risk of physical injury from another. It may

---

[66] This appears to be the message from such British decisions as *X (Minors) v. Bedfordshire Co. Co.* [1995] A.C. 766, *Phelps v. Hillington L.B.C.* [2000] 3 W.L.R. 776 and *Liennard v. Slough Borough Council* [2002] E.W.H.C. 398 (Q.B.).

mean some dilution of the academic attention that would be given to the most academically gifted students had the class been composed entirely of A-students.

It is not, and never was, the law that the school's duty of care to the brightest students should require it to neglect its duty of care to academically less gifted students.

In *Van Donselaar v. Central Coast Grammar School Ltd*,[67] the New South Wales Court of Appeal had to deal with an appeal from the dismissal of negligence claim against a school taken by a disabled student. The student was nearly 17 years old at the tie of the accident. He had recently injured his foot, the accident had occurred on a rainy day when the appellant was going up steps. The appellant described the rain at that stage as being "very very heavy". The appellant described the steps as having leaves and debris on them, washed down from the rain, as well as "pools of water" having formed on the steps. He described the steps as having "a lot" of rainwater on them "more than you'd expect to see on some steps". The appellant said that he ascended the steps by having his crutches on one step and then hopping to the next step with the crutches taking the full weight of his body as he moved up.

When the appellant commenced the school year, his House Master, Mr Boesenberg, had spoken to him, inquired how he was and said to him "If you need help to get to class we can arrange that". The appellant told him that he "should be able to get to class". Mr Boesenberg also advised the appellant that the School could "get someone to carry your books". The appellant again refused the offer, stating "No, I'll be okay". The appellant informed Mr Boesenberg that he wanted to attend classes. Mr Boesenberg also gave evidence that he told the appellant that he could do his school work in the library, saving him the necessity of moving from class to class but that he accepted the appellant's choice that he wished to attend the individual classes for his subjects. The appellant gave evidence that, for the purpose of attending his various classes, he would pack the books required for that class into a small backpack which he then wore on his back whilst he moved about the school. On the day of the accident he had two textbooks and a folder in the backpack.

It was accepted by the school that the appellant, being on crutches, had a disability. It said that the appellant was treated in accordance with the School's policy in respect of students with a disability, that is by offering assistance and checking to see if the student was managing. Mr Boesenberg said the appellant was offered the assistance, which I have referred to, and that he

---

[67] [2003] N.S.W. C.A. 241.

checked up on him every couple of days to see "that he was able to get on with his studies". It is common ground that the appellant did not complain or seek any assistance or seek to take up the offers of assistance which had been made.

Although two expert witnesses gave evidence in favour of the pupil the trial judge dismissed his claim for negligence and the New South Wales Court of Appeal affirmed. Beazley J.A. (for the Court) stated:

> "What ... was the magnitude of the risk? ... would seem as a matter of commonsense that, given the circumstances to which I have referred and the evidence as to the construction of the steps, the risk of the appellant falling was a real one, although not of a high magnitude. There is no doubt that it would have taken some effort to climb the steps using crutches, whether it was raining or dry. There is also no doubt that the appellant would have been extremely uncomfortable on the day of the accident given the heavy rain. However, that of itself would not have increased the risk of injury. In those circumstances, there was nothing which required the School to take steps beyond those already taken, that is, of offering assistance to the appellant. The appellant, whilst still a youth, must be taken at his age to be capable of making an appropriate decision as to whether he could move around the School, including negotiating the steps, on his crutches. He had done so for six days knowing that the offer of help was available. He had declined that help on more than one occasion, insisting that he was managing. There was nothing to indicate to the School that the position was otherwise. Likewise on this day, there was nothing to indicate to the School that he was not managing or would not be able to manage. He was keen to attend classes and, no doubt to him, confining him to the library was not a viable option. In my opinion, this challenge of the appellant makes to [the trial judge's dismissal of the claim] decision has not been made out."

Another challenge to the trial judge's verdict was that the School had been negligent in failing to have handrails on the flight of stairs, either on the side or up the middle. The New South Wales Court of Appeal was not impressed by this argument. Beazley J.A. stated.

> "Whilst [an expert witness] described the absence of a handrail as an inadequacy in the design and construction of the stairs there was no evidence that hopping up the stairs without the appellant using his crutches but leaving them tucked under his arm, would have been a

safer way of ascending them. Commonsense indicates that it would have been a difficult task to hop up 18 steps. Although the appellant said this was his preferred method on the steps where there was a handrail, there were only about a half dozen steps in the flight of stairs where the handrail was located. In my opinion, the appellant has not established any basis upon which the Court could conclude that a failure to provide a handrail was negligent."

It is by no means clear that an Irish court would necessarily have come to the same conclusion. Certainly, if the disability was of a more long-lasting character, the relative passivity of the school's approach might not be regarded so leniently.

Pupils, autonomy and privacy

Let us turn to consider briefly a broad issue yet to be addressed by our courts. To what extent are school pupils carriers of rights that formerly might have been widely considered to inhere only in adults, such as autonomy and privacy? What are the implications of changing norms in this area for schools and parents?

Undoubtedly, questions such as these will come to be considered judicially. Our Constitution is clearly relevant, since it protects rights of privacy, autonomy, dignity, expression, association and bodily integrity – all of which may have a bearing on the outcome – as well as recognising the rights and duties of parents in regard to the education of their children. In 2003, moreover, Ireland incorporated into Irish domestic law, albeit in an indirect, interpretive manner, the provisions of the European Convention on Human Rights.

It is worth examining the decision of the United States Supreme Court in *Tinker v. Des Moines Independent Community School District*,[68] where the Court held that the suspension of students for wearing black armbands in protest against the Vietnam War infringed the students' freedom of expression. Mr Justice Fortas, delivering the opinion of the Court, considered it to be:

> "relevant that the school authorities did not purport to prohibit the wearing of all symbols of political or controversial significance. The record shows that students in some of the schools wore buttons relating to national political campaigns, and some even wore the Iron Cross, traditionally a symbol of Nazism. The order prohibiting the wearing

---
[68] 393 US 503 (1969).

of armbands did not extend to these. Instead, a particular symbol – black armbands worn to exhibit opposition to this Nation's involvement in Vietnam – was singled out for prohibition. Clearly, the prohibition of expression of one particular opinion, at least without evidence that it is necessary to avoid material and substantial interference with schoolwork or discipline, is not constitutionally permissible.

In our system, state-operated schools may not be enclaves of totalitarianism. School officials do not possess absolute authority over their students. Students in school as well as out of school are 'persons' under our Constitution. They are possessed of fundamental rights which the State must respect, just as they themselves must respect their obligations to the State. In our system, students may not be regarded as closed circuit recipients of only that which the State chooses to communicate. They may not be confined to the expression of those sentiments that are officially approved. In the absence of a specific showing of constitutionally valid reasons to regulate their speech, students are entitled to freedom of expression of their views."

Subsequent decisions in the United States have made it clear that schools are perfectly entitled to abridge students' constitutional freedoms in the interests of discipline where this is necessary.

In *Bethel School District No 403 v. Fraser*,[69] a student delivered a lewd speech when nominating another student for an elective office in the school, in front of a group of 600 students, many of whom were 14-year-olds. The assembly was part of a school-sponsored educational programme in self-government. The speech included the use of what Chief Justice Burger described as "an elaborate, graphic, and explicit sexual metaphor" when describing the colleague. Two of the plaintiff's teachers, with whom he had discussed the contents of the speech in advance, had told him that the speech was inappropriate and that he probably should not deliver it and that doing so might have "severe consequences".

One of the school's disciplinary rules prohibited conduct that materially and substantially interfered with the educational process, including the use of obscene, profane language. After giving the plaintiff the opportunity to defend himself, the Assistant Principal suspended him for three days and told him that his name would be removed from the list of candidates for graduation speaker at the school's commencement exercises. After a further review procedure, the plaintiff served two days of the suspension, being permitted to return to the school on the third day.

---

[69] 478 US 675 (1986).

The plaintiff took his case to the Federal Courts, claiming that his right to freedom of speech under the First Amendment to the US Constitution had been violated. He succeeded at trial and on appeal to the Court of Appeals for the Ninth Circuit but lost in the United States Supreme Court. Chief Justice Burger stated:

> "The marked distinction between the political 'message' of the armbands in *Tinker* and the sexual content of the respondent's speech in this case seems to have been given little weight by the Court of Appeals. In upholding the students' right to engage in non-disruptive, passive expression of a political viewpoint in *Tinker*, this Court was careful to note that the case did not concern speech or action that intrudes upon the work of the schools or the rights of other students."

The Chief Justice went on to observe:

> "Surely it is a highly appropriate function of public school education to prohibit the use of vulgar and offensive terms in public discourse. Indeed, the 'fundamental values necessary for the maintenance of a democratic political system' disfavour the use of terms of debate highly offensive or highly threatening to others. Nothing in the Constitution prohibits the states from insisting that certain modes of expression are inappropriate and subject to sanctions. The inculcation of these values is truly the 'work of the schools'. The determination of what manner of speech in the classroom or in school assembly is inappropriate properly rests with the school board."

In *Hazelwood School District v. Kuhlmeier*,[70] the issue concerned the extent to which a school might exercise editorial control over the contents of a newspaper produced as part of the school's journalism curriculum. The newspaper was written and edited by the journalism students. The school principal objected to two stories scheduled to appear in an edition of the paper: one described three of the students' experience of pregnancy; the other discussed the impact of divorce on students at the school.

The principal was concerned that the identity of some of the students and their families might be identifiable. He also considered that the manner in which the themes were addressed – while completely devoid of salaciousness – might not be suitable for some of the younger readers of the papers.

---

[70] 484 US 260 (1988).

The students sought a declaration that their rights under the First Amendment had been violated. They lost at trial, won on appeal to the Court of Appeals for the Eight Circuit, only to lose again on ultimate appeal to the US Supreme Court. Justice White, for the majority, stated:

"A school must be able to set high standards for the student speech that is disseminated under its auspices – standards that may be higher than those demanded by some newspaper publishers or theatrical producers in the 'real' world – and may refuse to disseminate student speech that does not meet those standards. In addition, a school must be able to take into account the emotional maturity of the intended audience in determining whether to disseminate student speech or potentially sensitive topics, which might range from the existence of Santa Claus in an elementary school setting to the particulars of teenage sexual activity in a high school setting. A school must also retain the authority to refuse to sponsor student speech that might reasonably be perceived to advocate drug or alcohol use, irresponsible sex, or conduct otherwise inconsistent with 'the shared values of a civilized social order', or to associate the school with any position other than neutrality on matters of political controversy. Otherwise the schools would be unduly constrained from fulfilling their role as 'a principal instrument in awakening the child to cultural values, in preparing them for later professional training, and in helping him to adjust normally to his environment'."

As may be appreciated, *Fraser* and *Hazelwood* represent a significant modification of the broad libertarian principles articulated in *Tinker*. To a significant degree they reflect the changing values of the US Supreme Court judges over the period.

In the area of freedom of expression, where the Irish constitutional provision is somewhat less robust than its American equivalent, it seems likely that the courts would take the view that school authorities are legally entitled, in the interests of the welfare and safety of students, to have a policy controlling political expression in the context of school attire where the expression would be likely to provoke violence. Of course they would be so entitled – indeed legally obliged – where the expression involved incitement to hatred or threatened to violate or compromise human rights.

There is admittedly less legal clarity in cases where the expression lacks any such risks and merely communicates a political statement. If, for example, a student comes to school wearing a badge containing a robustly expressed rejection of US policy in Iraq, is this to be treated as a violation of the school's dress code or as involving something more important regarding freedom of expression? If the courts were to adopt the principles set out in *Tinker v. Des Moines Independent Community School District*, they could make such a distinction without undue difficulty. Making such a distinction does not, of course, necessarily protect the wearing of the badge. A court could will come to the conclusion that it is within a school's magisterial authority to restrict political expression of this kind and to channel it into particular contexts, such as debates and essays.

One should be conscious, in this context, of the UN Convention on the Rights of the Child of 1989. Under Article 28(2), states undertake to take "all appropriate measures to ensure that school discipline is administered in a manner consistent with the child's human dignity and in conformity with the present Convention".

Under Article 12(1), states assure to the child who is capable of forming his or her own views the right to express those views freely in all matters affecting the child, the views of the child being given due weight, in accordance with his or her age and maturity. Article 13(1) provides that the child has the right to freedom of expression. The exercise of this right may be subject only to necessary restrictions for respect of the rights or reputations of others or the protection of national security, public order, or public health or morals: Article 13(2). The narrow scope of these restrictions may be noted. A restriction inspired by paternalism would not seem to fall within Article 13(2).

Finally, we should consider briefly the difficult question of searches. No doubt, in former times teachers ordered pupils to empty their pockets without doubting for a moment that they had the legal authority to do so and searched pupils' lockers without asking their permission. One should counsel against any physical contact with the student's clothing, even where there is a suspicion of something serious, such as the presence of a weapon or drugs. Perhaps searches involving the student's own emptying of pockets can be justified on the basis of the "magisterial" function that Mr Justice Finlay mentioned in *State (Smullen) v. Duffy*,[71] backed by agreement between the school, the pupils and the parents as to a search policy. If this power exists, outside such agreement, it is certainly subject to strict limits.

As to searches of lockers, there are important unresolved legal issues regarding searches carried out by school authorities without the knowledge or consent of the pupil. Children, like adults, are entitled to their privacy. It may well be the case, however, that the courts would take the view that the

---

[71] [1980] I.L.R.M. 46.

"magisterial" function mentioned in *Smullen*, coupled with the school's duty of care to all its pupils, would justify searches in these circumstances for good reason based on reasonable grounds, such as concern for physical safety. The American Supreme Court has taken a somewhat more conservative stance on this question than on the issue of pupils' freedom of expression. A sensitive disciplinary policy can in any event deal with pupils who obstruct the management of the school without having to infringe pupils' rights. Consulting with parents and pupils and gaining their prior assent are the keys to a successful management policy in this area, as in so many other areas.

SECONDARY SCHOOL SPORTS AND THE LAW

Dr. Neville Cox*

INTRODUCTION

It is generally accepted that the presence on a school curriculum of some sort of sporting activity, be it a weekly physical education class, or an extra curricular option of rugby or hockey or GAA or whatever, is a good thing. Such activities after all promote health among students and introduce them to concepts like teamwork, motivation and indeed competition that may prove invaluable in later life. Indeed beyond this, school sport is quite simply something which is tremendously fulfilling and enjoyable. It is also something which exists in many schools simply by reason of the generosity of those teachers (and indeed parents or local volunteers) who, out of a sense of commitment which should be encouraged and commended, are prepared to give up their free time for painfully little financial reward to coach and supervise young and not so young children in the art of sport. More worryingly, it is something that can generate and has generated significant legal liabilities both for schools and indeed for individual teachers,[1] requiring them to face the difficult question as to whether they should continue to offer a sports element on their curriculum despite the fact that this could result in them being landed in legal hot water so to speak. Moreover, this applies both in the context of the updated PE curriculum and in the context of extra-curricular school sports. From the perspective of the courts there are two obvious competing policy concerns involving the needs of a potentially seriously injured schoolchild on the one hand, and those of the school which wishes to offer its pupils the opportunity to play sport despite resource based constraints on the other.

In this chapter, I will consider the principal aspects of school sports in

---

*Barrister at Law, Fellow Trinity College Dublin.

[1] Generally, see Cox and Schuter, *Sport and the Law* (First Law, 2004), at pp.235 *et seq.* and Grayson, *School Sports and the Law* (CCH Publication, Croner, 2001).

which legal liability may arise, namely in teaching or coaching sport, in supervision of sporting activities, in respect of sporting equipment and in respect of sports facilities, and I will further consider the best means of avoiding such liability. The message of the paper is largely positive for schools, namely that the courts are generally sympathetic to their situations, and especially that the application of simple common sense by teachers and administrators is a virtually impregnable guard against successful litigation.

THE GENERAL STANDARDS REQUIRED OF SPORTS TEACHERS

Teachers like all sports coaches are not insurers of their pupil's safety.[2] Thus for instance, the fact that a schoolboy rugby player is seriously injured in a schools' match does not automatically mean that the school is liable to compensate him and his family for such injuries, nor is it obliged to have an insurance policy in respect of such injuries or to advise sporting pupils to take out such a policy on their own behalf.[3] All that needs to be done by school and teacher as coach, supervisor, referee and facilitator is that which is reasonable in the circumstances, from the standpoint of a reasonable and prudent parent.[4] The pivotal question to be addressed therefore is what must a teacher do to act "reasonably in the circumstances" of any particular moment?

Perhaps unsurprisingly, there is no hard and fast answer to this question. Ultimately a common sense response is what is demanded, with the definition of "common sense" or perhaps more pertinently "*informed* common sense" being dependent on the circumstances of the moment. Again, however, this does not get us very far, in that the sports teacher, or more probably the teacher designated to teach sport could still benefit from some more concrete guidance as to how he or she should conduct his or her classes. Perhaps the best such guidance that can be offered is that the level of care that is needed tends to depend on three factors, namely :

- the foreseeability of harm arising out of the manner in which school sports are conducted,

- the severity of the consequences if such foreseeable harm should come to pass, and

---

[2] *Van Oppen v. Clerk of the Bedford Charity Trustees* [1989] 3 All E.R. 389 (CA); *Brady v. Sunderland FC*, unreported (Court of Appeal), November 17, 1998; but also see *Woodroffe-Hedley v. Cuthberston*, unreported (Queen's Bench), June 20, 1997.
[3] *Sweeney v. Duggan* [1997] 1 I.L.R.M. 21.
[4] *Kane v. Kennedy*, unreported, High Court (Budd J.), March 25, 1999.

- the extent to which it is reasonable to expect the injured party to have assumed the risk that led to the result.

Hence the teacher must act to avoid foreseeable risks, where it is not reasonable to expect the pupil to have assumed this risk for himself.

In practice for the school and the school teacher, these three factors may be broken down into one golden rule which applies to all the different elements of school sports, namely the more dangerous the activity and the more vulnerable the person undertaking the activity, the more care that must be taken by the teacher. In simple terms, we know that young children act in objectively unpredictable ways, and hence that they may be incapable of safely engaging in an activity that presents no problems whatsoever to adults or even older children. From a school perspective this means that a practice which a teacher follows (quite reasonably) when dealing with sixth year students may be unreasonable when dealing with first year students. Three cases indicate this principle in action.

Case One

In *Morrell v. Owen*,[5] the English Court of Appeal required that a higher level of supervision was required for a training session for disabled athletes than would be required for a training session for athletes who would perhaps be better able to take care of themselves.

Case Two

In *Smith v. Jolly*,[6] a High Court jury refused to find negligent supervision on the part of a teacher who allowed a group of 15 year olds to compete in a shot putt event (which included marking the distance of a throw with a peg) when one of the girls managed to throw the shot at another girl's head while the latter was close by and bending down to measure a third girl's throw. The point was that from the standpoint of a 15 year old, such an action was so unreasonable that it was objectively unforeseeable by a teacher.

Case Three

In *Comer v. Governors of St Patrick's RC Primary School*[7] the plaintiff took part in the "father's race" at a school sports day – a race in which he

---

[5] *The Times*, December 14, 1993.
[6] Unreported, High Court (O'Hanlon J.), May 18, 1984.
[7] Court of Appeal, November 13, 1997.

had competed on several previous occasions. This race was a sprint over approximately thirty yards, however only five feet beyond the finish line there was a brick wall. Mr. Comer had previously warned the relevant teachers of the dangerousness of the course in question and had suggested that there be a longer course allowing more of a stretch for deceleration. On this occasion, Mr. Comer competed with such vigour in the race that he was unable to stop in time, and so he collided with the wall seriously injuring his wrists and elbows. He sued the school as occupier and organiser claiming that it had exposed him to a foreseeable risk and hence should be liable in negligence and under the Occupiers' Liability Act. The Court of Appeal, however, rejected this claim on the grounds *inter alia* that the plaintiff was well aware of the existence of the wall, and hence should have taken steps to avoid colliding with it and it was legitimate for the teachers to expect the fathers competing in the race to do so taking into account the obvious danger at the end of the track.

In this paper I will consider how this general principle of duty applies to a number of aspects of school sports namely:

- the teaching of sport,
- sports equipment,
- supervision of sport,
- sports premises.

As mentioned above, whereas the picture of a seriously injured child is an emotional one, nonetheless courts are sympathetic to the circumstances in which schools operate, and tend not to give judgement against the school unless there is clear negligence (or colloquially, a clear absence of what we will term informed common sense). Equally this is obvious, and many of the cases that we will look at below focus on situations where the action or inaction of the teacher was simply and blatantly foolhardy.

DUTIES WHEN TEACHING OR COACHING SPORT

Sports teachers, like any coaches, have a duty of care to those under their charge and *in coaching* they must act reasonably in the circumstances. The key instruction for the teacher is to use informed common sense to avoid foreseeable risks. So what does this entail?

Ensuring that a pupil has adequate instruction in "injury avoidance" principles

In inherently dangerous sports such as rugby/Gaelic Football/Hurling or swimming, pupils should be instructed in both the techniques necessary to play the sport safely (for example how to dive,[8] or how to tackle or scrummage in a rugby match[9]), and also in "injury avoidance" principles. Plainly in order for this to happen, the teacher must be acquainted with such techniques and principles, and indeed with the basic "safety rules" of the sport that he or she is teaching. Thus in *Fowles v. Bedfordshire County Council*,[10] (a case not involving schools) the Court of Appeal in England concluded that:

> "Anyone who assumes the task of reaching the forward somersault [a difficult manoeuvre] is under a duty not only to teach the technique involved in the exercise and the dangers involved in its performance but to teach the steps which must be taken to prepare for it, including the laying of the crash mat, and to explain the danger of performing the exercise in an inappropriate environment. It matters not how obvious a danger may be, it should be pointed out. This is particularly the case where the danger of a minor accident (such as hitting an obstruction) may be obvious, but the risk of really serious injury is unlikely to be appreciated by the inexpert".

Linked in with this is, it is important that a sports teacher provide students with a programme of basic warm up exercises appropriate to the exercise that will be undertaken, on the basis that it is well known and hence foreseeable that failure to engage in some stretching exercises before a vigorous sporting exercise can lead to a risk of muscular injury, and therefore failure in this regard could constitute negligence. In *Hill v. Durham County Council*[11] a school staff meeting was replaced with a meeting in the school gymnasium where the teachers would be given a demonstration (in which they were required to participate) in the art of teaching 5–7 year olds how to dance. The expert co-ordinator of the session, required the said teachers to begin the session by traversing the gymnasium using long jump/hopscotch movements, during the course of which, the plaintiff teacher suffered a

---

[8] *Gannon v. Rotherham MBC*, Halsbury's Monthly Review (1991) 91/1717.
[9] *Van Oppen v. Clerk to the Bedford Charity Trustees* [1989] 1 All E.R. 273 (Q.B.); [1989] 3 All E.R. 389 (Court of Appeal).
[10] [1995] P.I.Q.R. 380.
[11] Court of Appeal, unreported, January 31, 2000.

rupture to the Achilles tendon. Her claim was that the activity was excessively vigorous and the expert should have prescribed a more gentle form of warm up. The court, while accepting that failure to provide some form of warm up would have been negligent, concluded that in this case, the hopscotch activity could have amounted to such warm up and the injury suffered was simple bad luck which could not have been blamed on anyone.

Finally, if a particular manoeuvre is an inherently dangerous one (the rugby tackle for example), then the school might simply ensure that a modified version of the sport is played where there is no need for this manoeuvre to be practiced – e.g. by only playing "tip rugby" with no tackles and no scrums – where the participants are incapable of participating safely in the unmodified game owing to their age or to any other factor.

Ensuring that a pupil is fit to engage in sporting activity

There are two important points to be made here. First, no matter how important a game, and no matter how inconvenient the alternative, the teacher/ coach should not require a pupil to play on a particular day if, owing to injury or ill health, participation might lead to harm. Depending on the sport, it is also important to stress that a player must be fit to play in the position in which he is selected.[12] This has arisen most notably in more senior rugby, where, rather than abandon the game, coaches have asked players with no previous scrummaging experience to play for a while in the front row of a scrum, leading to catastrophic injury and legal liability. Indeed recently in *Vowles v. WRFU*[13] a rugby referee was found to be negligent in allowing one team to replace a front row forward with another player who had no front row experience, despite the fact that both the player, the captain of the team and the coach of the team wished such replacement to occur. It appears that this practice is common in many schools rugby matches – particularly at young age levels where, ironically the concern for the well being of the pupil is greatest. Should injuries mean that for instance, a rugby team has no players left with front row scrummaging experience, then either the referee should insist that scrums be non-contested, or more appropriately, there should be no more scrums in the match, or the match should be abandoned.

Secondly, schools have to consider their policy in respect of a child who does not want to take part in physical education or sporting lessons. This is

---

[12] *Watson v. Haines*, unreported, Supreme Court of NSW (Allen J.), April 10, 1987. Generally, see Millane, "Neighbours in the Law" 4(2) *Sporting Traditions* (May 1988) 1.

[13] Court of Appeal, March, 2003.

hugely important. Typically after all, the reason why a player injured on the field of play cannot sue another player who injures him, or a school for which or in which he is playing, is because all players on a field can be taken to have consented to the ordinary risks associated with the game in which they are participating. But what of a student who does not want to play sport, and who has told the teacher this? More significantly still, what of a pupil who, owing to his or her build or other factors may be incapable of playing? On the one hand, there is merit in requiring compulsory participation in school sport – especially for children who by reason of their habitually sedentary nature frankly need the exercise. On the other hand, enforced participation may be legally imprudent. Thus in dealing with this matter the English Law Commission concluded that whereas as a matter of policy, the benefits from sport which could be derived in a school context outweighed the concern that some participants might be being required to act against their interests, nonetheless it was far from certain that teachers in extreme cases that forced unwilling students to participate in a dangerous sport, would thereby be immune from civil liability.

From an Irish perspective, it seems likely that the courts would have sympathy with a school policy that required participation in sport, provided that it was sufficiently flexible to allow exemptions for students who were manifestly physically incapable of participation. The question is once again one that requires a common sense approach – as teachers ask themselves how foreseeable is it, having regard to this students physical condition (for example where he or she is asthmatic) that participation might have unhappy consequences. Thus in *Williams v. Rotherham*,[14] where a pupil was required to join a PE class despite having previously injured his ankle, and his participation in the class aggravated the pre-existing condition, the teacher was deemed to be negligent for requiring participation in circumstances where there was a patent risk of injury. Within the limits of the school's resources the ideal situation would be to say that whereas participation in sport *is* mandatory, equally there is the option for pupils who cannot take part in say a boisterous game of football to engage in a more gentle form of exercise.

Having said all this, it is not the case that a teacher is negligent in allowing a child to take part in an endeavour which turns out to have a dangerous result. In *Delaney v. O'Dowd*,[15] the teacher had organised a handball exercise, in the course of which children had to run parallel to each other and about three meters apart. Two of the children collided and the claimant was injured.

---

[14] *The Times*, August 6, 1998.
[15] [1997] IR L Log W 157 (CC).

Carroll J. concluded that this was a safe exercise and the teacher was not negligent in not keeping focused on the children at all time. Similarly in *Murphy v. Jackson*,[16] a teacher was held not to be negligent in organizing a perfectly supervised piggy back race.

Appropriate matching of players

Similarly, in the organisation both of matches and of training sessions, it may be necessary (given the nature of the sport) to ensure that players are evenly matched, in terms of size, skill and experience.[17] This is particularly important in a contact sport like rugby or Gaelic football, but also in sports like hockey and cricket. It may simply be inappropriate, (no matter how necessary this is having regard to resources), that a small child is required to face up against other larger children where the difference in size, weight and experience between the two may pose a risk to him or her. In the Irish case of *Ward v. Donegal Vocational Education Committee*,[18] Keane J. refused to find a Gaelic football teacher negligent for failing to match players of equal sizes. Here the claimant and a much larger boy challenged for a ball together and the smaller boy was injured. Keane J. (as he then was) concluded essentially that the risk of injury was a hazard of the sport and that that was that. It is submitted that whereas this reasoning is of use in respect of adult sport, it may not be so when dealing with school children, where the fact that a small boy is likely for instance to be tackled by, or have to scrum against a much larger opponent, presents a foreseeable risk of injury that is not directly related to the playing of the game itself. In other words the foreseeable risk could be avoided without the cost of prohibiting the playing of sport. This will be of particular importance for schools where for instance a particularly talented young rugby player at under fourteen level is considered worthy of a place on the Junior Cup (under fifteen) team. Depending on his size and the position he plays, no matter how good he is, it might be advisable not to take the risk

Linked in with this is the case where, in order to enhance a training session, the teacher/coach himself participates as a player. This poses two risks; first that the teacher will not be able adequately to supervise the game, and secondly that the teacher might injure a much smaller player. Thus in *Affutu-Nartoy v. Clarke*,[19] a local club rugby player was coaching an under

---

[16] DPIJ Trinity and Michaelmas Terms 1993 (HC) 146.
[17] *Affutu-Nartoy v. Clarke, Times*, February 9, 1989.
[18] DPIJ Hilary and Easter Terms 1993 (IIC) 116.
[19] *The Times*, February 9, 1984.

15 team, and decided that he would himself play in a practice game. Tragically in the course of tackling one of the players on the opposing team he broke the young boy's back. The court held that he was negligent, not for playing himself, but for failing to take account of the foreseeable consequences of the fact that he was considerably heavier than the boys on the other team.

Weather permitting?

A further area of concern for a school teacher dealing with sporting events, is in deciding whether or not it is appropriate that a sporting fixture should go ahead in adverse weather conditions where such conditions pose a threat to the well being of participants. This ranges from bad light during a cricket match, to frost on a pitch in a rugby, soccer, hockey or GAA match, to a risk of lightening strikes, rain, sleet and hail in any outdoor sporting event. Obviously this does not mean that a teacher should regard every little shower of rain as justifying a break in play – especially in circumstances where there are no indoor PE facilities. Weather concerns should only arise where the conditions are such that they render an otherwise safe activity hazardous. Essentially it is again necessary for a coach to apply a common sense analysis and ask whether, in all the circumstances it is foreseeable that injury may be caused, and, if it is, to restrict that activity. Once again, reference must be made by the teacher to the vulnerability of his or her pupils and the dangerousness of the activity. Moreover, once again, prudence demands that the safety of the pupils be given the benefit of any doubt.

The coach as referee

In many sporting contests involving school children, the relevant games teacher will also referee the game. This itself generates risks for the teacher and the school as is indicated by two English cases.

In *Smoldon v. Whitworth*,[20] a rugby referee was found to be liable for injuries sustained by a young rugby player injured during the course of a colts rugby match. The Court of Appeal found that in controlling that most dangerous sporting event the rugby scrum, the referee had not applied appropriate rules, and especially had not dealt with constant and ongoing infractions of the rules, which caused the scrum to collapse. In *Vowles v. WRFU*,[21] the referee was deemed to be negligent in that he allowed a replacement with no scrummaging experience to play in the front row of the

---

[20] Court of Appeal, December 18, 1996.
[21] Queen's Bench, December 13, 2002.

scrum, which itself caused the scrum to collapse and another player to suffer horrific injury. Lest it be thought that this is purely a rugby issue, in *Leatherland v. Edwards*,[22] a player was held liable when, in violation of the rules of unihockey he raised his stick above his head and struck another player in the eye. Equally, it is entirely possible that had such infractions of safety rules been ongoing, and had the referee done nothing to stop this, then he himself might have been liable in negligence.

Once again, the moral of the story is clear. The referee no more than coach must ensure that he is familiar with the modern safety rules of the game and must apply the same strictly and with regard to the needs of the pupils for whom, at the time he has responsibility. Moreover, in the primary school context, he must ensure that his refereeing duties do not get in the way of his supervision of the event.

Coaching qualifications

At the end of the day, the ideal solution would be for all sports teachers in schools to attend courses in sports coaching run by the governing bodies of the relevant sports and to act on the basis of the instruction received at such courses, both as a way of ensuring best practice and also as a trusty defence in the event of a negligence action being taken against the school. The reality of the situation, (a reality which almost certainly the courts would bear in mind) is that for many schoolteachers this may be simply impossible, having regard to resources of time and money, given both the fact that most "sports teachers" are in fact teachers of other subjects who are voluntarily signing up to get involved in sport, and also the comparatively little dangerous sport that may be played. Nonetheless if it were possible that sports teachers could be afforded time and resources to go on such programmes this would be extremely useful.

Beyond this, it is necessary for a school to ensure that it is acting reasonably in appointing someone as a sports teacher – be it a "regular" teacher in the school, or an outside expert. This will also apply where for instance the school is facilitating or sponsoring or endorsing an out of school activity – for instance equestrian sport at a local equestrian centre, or more exotic sport overseen by an adventure activities operator. Two points arise; first obviously the appointment of such teacher as a teacher of the relevant sport should be disclosed to the relevant insurance company. Secondly (and especially if the school takes the step of endorsing an outside centre) the school must act prudently in checking out whether the teacher/expert is of

---

[22] Queen's Bench, November 28, 1998.

sufficient calibre that it is safe to appoint him to his job. Again much will depend on the age of the pupils and the nature of the sport. Thus it might be acceptable to appoint someone with no knowledge of the game of table tennis as a coach in that sport, but this would not be the case if we were dealing with boxing, or rugby. Similarly it might not be prudent to appoint a nineteen year old who is an excellent rugby player as the sole coach of a team of eighteen year olds, because of the former's lack of experience and maturity. The point is that, whereas it is accepted practice that not all schools sports coaches can be experts in their sport, the constraints of resources can never be a reason to put the health and well being of a pupil in jeopardy.

Some assistance in determining whether or not it is reasonable to transfer responsibility to an outside agency may shortly be forthcoming from the government. In 2001, the Adventure Standards Authority Act was enacted. Amongst various provisions, this Act provided that a new body, the Adventure Activities Standards Authority, would be created, to deal with a variety of "adventure activities" as defined. These included caving, orienteering in areas more than 300 feet above sea level, surfing, canoeing and so on. The objective of the authority is to promote, encourage, foster and facilitate the safe operation of such activities in the State. It will achieve this objective in a number of ways namely :

- By directing an investigation (and if necessary a more formal tribunal-like enquiry) into any accident at such a facility (other than a place of work) and the publication of a report following such investigation.

- By the establishment of a register of all adventure activities operators in the state – available for public viewing – and a requirement that no person act as an adventure activities operator unless he or she is entered in the register as an adventure activities operator in respect of that adventure activity.

- By the publishing of codes of practice for the purpose of providing guidance for the safe operation of such facilities, with which all adventure activities operators must comply

- By the creation of a scheme or schemes for the regulation of adventure activities in the State, outlining, *inter alia*, the circumstances in which inspections will be carried out by the authority and the circumstances in which an operator may be suspended from carrying out an activity, or have his name removed from the register of operators.

The net effect of this Act would seem to be that schools can rely on the fact that any body whose name appeared on the register was properly vetted by the authority and had, so to speak, its seal of approval. In other words, there is at least an argument that by selecting an operator on the register to co-ordinate and organise adventure activities for its pupils, the school was acting reasonably. Unfortunately, the Authority has not yet been established by the Minister. According to officials in the Department of the Marine and Natural Resources, there is some confusion (currently being resolved) as to whether the last Minister's statement that he intended to create a Marine safety body would mean that many of the functions of the Adventure Activities Authority would become void.

Equally, it is clear that once the decision to transfer supervisory/coaching duties to an outside agency (say a local swimming pool or leisure centre) is a reasonable one, and once the outside agency accepts such responsibility, then *it* will be the appropriate defendant should injury accrue to pupils on its property or under its care.

Use of drugs or dietary supplements

The statistics from the United States indicate that there is a high level of use among high school athletes of performance enhancing substances – notably stimulants and anabolic steroids. Increasingly, it is being reported that students are using these substances for three reasons, namely to enhance sporting prowess, as a recreational drug and in an attempt to build one's strength up so one can respond to a situation where one is being bullied.

It would be irresponsible to suppose that Irish school athletes have never and are nowhere using such substances.[23] To this end, it is hardly necessary to point out how unbelievably dangerous these substances are and others like them – notably androstenedione, genetically engineered testosterone, human growth hormone and ephedra. Much was made in recent years of the possibility of certain schools introducing random drug tests for students. In my view there is absolutely no constitutional difficulty with such an approach. And if a sports coach believes that a student *is* using anabolic steroids – as is indicated by sudden and inexplicable muscle development and mood swings, with heightened aggression, that coach should try to ensure that he or she talk to the student with a view to determining whether he or she is using a drug which, apart from its health risks, is also banned by all sports federations. Sports coaches should also be aware that from June 1. 2004 Irish Sports Council Rules provide that if a coach assists a minor to commit a doping offence then he himself is committing an offence which attracts a lifetime ban from all sport.

---

[23] See Cox and Schuster at Chap.3.

Linked to this is the use of lawful dietary supplements, and especially the supplement creatine. Indeed there is anecdotal evidence that some sports teachers have in the past actually prescribed this muscle building substance for use by members of school teams – although it appears that there is less evidence of this now. The problem is that whereas creatine is widely used throughout sport, and has no proven health risks, there are question marks over it. So for instance studies have suggested that at worst it may be carcinogenic and at best, it is dangerous for users with existing renal problems. Moreover, tests have also shown that many such supplements may be tainted with or contain traces of banned steroids. I would thus strongly advise all teachers and coaches to follow the advice of the Irish Sports Council and prohibit as far as possible students from using the substance. I would also suggest that if it did turn out to be harmful (and the problem is that it is not around long enough as a substance, nor do we know precisely in what dosage it is taken, for a definitive conclusion as to its safety or otherwise to be forthcoming), teachers who actively incite students to use it could face civil actions (as has happened in the US) or indeed, where the students are below the age of consent, criminal prosecution (as has happened in East Germany) for assault.

Duties in respect of equipment

Generally within sports law, if it is reasonable for a player to rely on the assertion of a coach that a particular piece of equipment is safe to use, then this should generate a duty on the part of the coach, and should there be some latent defect in the equipment then the coach should be liable if it causes harm to the said athlete.[24] In the case of schools, and especially primary schools because of the virtual inevitability of such reliance, if an injury arises out of defective sports equipment, then it is equally inevitable that liability will attach to the school who provided the equipment. The clear moral of the story is that there should be regular checks of sporting equipment. Indeed it is suggested that this entails more than simply the teacher in charge checking the equipment before a lesson. Rather it should also entail a regular independent audit of all sports equipment to ensure that it is safe.

Moreover, the school should ensure that the equipment, even if it is not defective, is adequate for the purpose for which it is intended and that there is sufficient equipment that the sport may be played safely by the relevant participants – that for instance where a school plays hurling all participants

---

[24] See Clancy, "Judo Mats, Climbing Walls, Trampolines and Pole Vaulters" 3(1) *Sport and the Law Journal* (1995) 28.

have protective headgear. This may of course mean that parents are required to supply such gear for their children, but the obligation is on the school to ensure that pupils without such gear do not participate in the sport. The key thing is that the pupils are able to compete safely. In *Harrison v. Shields*,[25] the claimant was a schoolgirl who had injured herself during a high jump competition. On the facts, the court concluded that her injuries were caused by her inexperience and lack of knowledge as to landing technique (and this might go the question of inadequate instruction) rather than the inadequate protection afforded by the landing mats, but, had the injury been caused by such inadequate protection, then liability would have been imposed irrespective of the fact that the positioning of the said mats complied with the International Athletics Federation rules in this regard.

Finally, it is also necessary for the school to ensure that the (non-defective) equipment is being used properly and that it is serving the desired purpose, and that pupils are properly instructed in the use thereof – which will again impose a responsibility on teachers to be aware of the procedures for using the same. This leads on to the next major area of responsibility, namely supervision.

Supervision

In theory the rule is easy to state; in supervising children's sports, the level of supervision must be reasonable in the circumstances. In practice once again, this does not get us very far; what after all is *reasonable* supervision in the circumstances? Again it comes back to the balance between foreseeability of risk and the degree to which a child can be expected to take care of him or herself, which will depend on the age of the child and the nature of the sport. Thus one can conclude that there would need to be a far higher level of supervision for an ultra hazardous activity like swimming, than for a more gentle activity like an egg and spoon race at a school sports day, but precisely how much supervision is necessary and to what extent is it acceptable to leave children to their own devices?

Four introductory points should be made:

(a) It is clear that such supervision is not confined to the field of play at the teacher's school. It will also include supervision of, for instance, peripheral areas where, following on from or preceding the actual sporting activity, injury might occur. This will include changing room and possibly shower areas. Naturally, the problems inherent in any

---

[25] Unreported, High Court (Carroll J.), November 15, 1996.

teacher in contemporary Ireland trying to "supervise" an area where young people are naked are huge.

(b) It is also clear that such supervision will extend to situations where the sporting event occurs in a different school or in a different country, and to the process of travelling to that other school or other country. Thus in *Chittock v. Woodbridge*,[26] the defendant school was (at first instance) held to be liable for injury to a pupil who had suffered a serious spinal injury while on a school skiing trip to Austria. On the other hand (and again provided that the decision was reasonable in the circumstances) it is legitimate to rely on: (a) a bus company, (b) public transport, and (c) parents to transport children to the relevant venue (although in the first two of these options there may be a need to have supervision of the children through the journey organised by the school.

(c) Once again, in supervising a sporting event, it has to be remembered that the teacher is only human, and more to the point is dealing with a large number of people, who, especially in the case of primary school children, are capable of doing surprising and unpredictable things. The courts bear this in mind, and, as before they refuse to make teachers insurers of pupils safety, imposing liability only where the action or inaction of the teacher defies common sense.

(d) Moreover, it is entirely possible that the court may deem the supervisor to be negligent but may also deem the injured party to have been guilty of contributory negligence and may reduce any award of damages accordingly.

At the risk of repetition, the point is that application of informed common sense should be the watchword for teachers here. To this end, an analysis of case law in this area is instructive.

The absence of supervision must cause the harm

The first point to be made is that in order for a plaintiff to succeed in a negligence action, he must show that the negligence actually caused the harm complained of. Thus for instance, if the injury suffered could not have been prevented by greater supervision, then the teacher and school will not be liable. So for instance in *Clark v. Bethnal Green Corporation*,[27] a child

---

[26] *The Times*, July 15, 2002.
[27] 55 T.L.R. 519 (1939).

at a swimming bath let go suddenly of a springboard that she had been holding, thereby causing another child who had been preparing to jump from the same to fall and suffer injury. Here the court held that the action of the first child was unpredictable and incapable of being anticipated, and would have occurred irrespective of the adequacy of supervision.

More recently in *Simonds v. Isle of Wight Council*[28] the plaintiff, a five year old child, was accompanied by his mother to a school sports day. The mother decided to do some shopping so she pointed to the teachers who were some distance away and told the child to go and rejoin them, saying "they will tell you what to do". On the way to the teachers, the child spotted some swings, and, like any self-respecting five year old, decided that it would be a good moment to play Superman, by climbing on the swing and then jumping off. He belatedly realised that he was unable to fly and broke his arm. At first instance the child successfully sued the school with the court saying that whereas greater supervision by the school would not have prevented the accident, nonetheless the swings should have been immobilized. On appeal, however, this finding was reversed, with the court finding that what had happened was an accident pure and simple. The sports day event itself was properly supervised and there was an air of unreality in the suggestion that further warnings attached to the swing or directed to the mother as to the danger of unsupervised playing on the swings, could have made any difference. Moreover, the court made two further statements to which we will return and which will be music to the ears of schools authorities, namely:

(1) School playing fields cannot be expected to be free from hazard, and the mere fact that the school had diagnosed a possible or potential hazard did not mean that it was duty bound to deal with it (in this case by immobilizing the swings).

(2) The danger with the type of decision made at first instance was that it would in all probability *not* lead to a situation where swings were immobilized but would most likely mean, in an era of high insurance premia, that sports days and other such events would have to be cancelled. This, as far as the court was concerned, would be a great shame, and hence judges should be slow to reach such decisions.

---

[28] [2003] E.W.H..C. 2303.

Mandatory supervision of potentially dangerous activity?

The next question is whether all sporting activity in which injury might occur *must* be supervised. This issue arose recently in the Irish Circuit Court case of *Doyle v. Little*.[29] Here the plaintiff schoolboy was playing unsupervised indoor football in a parish hall. The plaintiff apparently tripped while playing the ball and fell backwards onto the ground. He then stood up and walked to the wall of the hall where he fell again, this time as a result of dizziness or fainting. In falling he knocked two teeth out and sprained his neck. The plaintiffs alleged that the absence of supervision of this game constituted negligence, whereas the defence argued that any such supervision could not have prevented the first fall, and that it was the shock engendered by the same that caused the second fall. The court however, found for the plaintiff, concluding that whereas the presence of a supervisor would not have prevented the first fall, it could have prevented the second fall and hence the negligent failure to provide a supervisor or referee could be seen as the cause of the young boy's injuries. It is submitted that this is a somewhat harsh decision, and perhaps does not appreciate both the reality of the game of indoor soccer, and more especially the extent of what a supervisor of such a game can actually achieve.

Adequate supervision

It would be more appropriate to require that there be adequate supervision in the circumstances. In this respect we return again to first principles and say that the adequacy of supervision can be gauged from (a) the age/experience of the pupils and (b) the nature of the activity.

Appropriate levels of supervision in relation to the age and experience of the pupils

In *Mulligan v. Doherty*[30] a gymnastics teacher of 17 year old girls had demonstrated a particular exercise (involving a descent down wall bars) for students and had then supervised one girl in the exercise, before moving to another part of the gym to instruct another class. The claimant attempted the exercise, but claimed that she did not remember what the teacher had done in the demonstration and managed to let go of the bars and fall, injuring her back. She alleged that the teacher was negligent in that she should have

---

[29] Circuit Court, August 2, 2002.
[30] Unreported, Supreme Court, May 17, 1966.

supervised the entire class, so that all students would know the correct means of descent. The Supreme Court found for the defendants, but the reasoning is instructive from the school perspective. The exercise, according to the court was an easy one, and the technique needed to complete it successfully was obvious. Thus in the context *of 17 year olds*, there was no need for constant supervision. However, the Supreme Court expressly stated that had it been dealing with "young children", it might well have required such supervision.

So the age and experience of the students is pivotal. In *A (A Minor) v. Leeds City Council*[31] the 11 year old claimant was enjoying her first PE class in her new school's sports hall. The girls were given a talk on safety in the room next to the sports hall, and were then brought into the hall and told to move around the hall and to touch the four walls of the hall. The exercise was unstructured and somewhat competitive, and with a certain degree of inevitability the twenty-five children, who were keen to please a new teacher, and were in unfamiliar circumstances and with peers whom they did not know, ran extremely vigorously in a variety of directions. (There was some doubt as to whether they were told to run but the court accepted that that was the point of the exercise). Their paths crossed (they weren't told in which order they should touch the walls) the plaintiff collided with another girl and fell on her wrist breaking a bone. She sued the school for negligence, and the court awarded her four thousand pounds, holding that in as much as it was entirely foreseeable that injury would flow from the mêlée in question, the teacher was negligent in allowing it to proceed. According to the court, contact sports for young girls needed strict controls. Once again the court had regard to the circumstances of the case, and pointed out that some sports are by their nature hazardous, but this was a warm up exercise which did not have to be so. The court also stressed that this decision was not to be taken as a precedent that anyone who is injured following an accident thereby has a right to recovery.

Appropriate supervision in relation to the activity

The nature of the activity also goes to the question of reasonable supervision. In *Wright v. Cheshire County Council*[32] during a school gymnastics class, students were participating in a range of various exercises, with the teacher

---

[31] Unreported, March 2, 1999 (Leeds County Court). For comment see 2(3) *Sports Law Bulletin* (1999) 5.
[32] [1952] 2 All E.R. 789. See also *Wilson v. Governors of the Sacred Heart RC School* [1998] 1 F.L.R. 663.

moving from group to group, giving supervision as he went. One exercise involved the vaulting horse, where the students took it in turns to vault, aided by a group of standbys whose job was to ensure that the vaulter landed safely. Unhappily, one such stand by ran off upon hearing the school bell and the student who was in mid vault was unable to land properly as a result and suffered injuries. Legal action was taken against the school but was unsuccessful on the grounds that the procedure followed – allowing 11 and 12 year old boys who were fairly well trained in the area to look after each other – had been approved for years and had hitherto operated safely.[33] On the other hand in *Gibbs v. Barking Health Authority*,[34] a pupil during gymnastic training suffered injury when he jumped off a vaulting horse "in a stumble", but the teacher had not made any efforts to have anyone assist him in the landing. Here the teacher was deemed to be negligent, in that the activity was sufficiently dangerous that the absence of an assistant posed a foreseeable risk to the plaintiff.

In the United States in *Carabba v. School District*,[35] the defendants were organizing a wrestling competition and had hired a referee to supervise the competition. During the contest, the referee went to close a gap between mats and allowed the students to continue wrestling while his back was turned. During this time an illegal hold was applied on one student and as a result he suffered a broken neck. The court held that the defendant's owed a duty of care to the students and were liable in negligence for the inadequate supervision of the contest. The point here was that immediate and intense supervision of every moment of the match was necessary to protect the safety of the contestants, and it was eminently foreseeable that failure to have supervision of the event at all stages could lead to risk.

Similarly in Canada, in *MacCabe v. Westlock*,[36] during a gymnastics class, a student failed to complete an exercise properly and as a result sustained a spinal cord fracture and quadriplegia. At the time the teacher was supervising another exercise. The student was awarded $4m in damages, with the court setting out a fourfold standard of care test:

– the activity must be suited to the students' age and condition;

– the students must be properly coached;

---

[33] In Canada a similar result was given in the similar case *Myers v. Peel County Board of Education*, 123 D.L.R. (1981).
[34] [1936] All E.R. 115.
[35] See on this Drowatsky, "Assumption of Risk in Sport", 2(1) *Journal of Legal Aspects of Sport* (1992) p.92.
[36] (1998) 226 A.R. 1 (QB).

– the equipment must be adequate; and

– the performance should be properly supervised.

In this case, the duty was not met when a teacher sent students off to their own areas, thereby encouraging and not restricting dangerous activity.[37]

Does adequate supervision entail preventing irresponsible pupils from engaging in sporting activity?

A recent controversial case in this area is *Chittock v. Woodbridge*.[38] Here the 17- year-old claimant (who was a keen sportsman) was confined to a wheelchair following a skiing accident in Austria. For two successive days prior to the fateful accident he had skied "off piste" and had been reprimanded by the school teacher for doing so. However, his "ski pass" was not confiscated by the teachers on the trip, on the basis that they were trying to treat the boys as adults. The next day he duly went off piste again, and this time suffered the horrific injuries mentioned. At first instance the judge found the teachers 50% responsible, concluding that the inadequacy of their disciplinary measures in the face of evidence that the boys could not be trusted, constituted unreasonable supervision. In the circumstances, it is understandable why the court would want to balance out the financial cost to the unfortunate victim. Equally, it is submitted that the decision does not take adequate account of the nature of such trips, and indeed of the significance of allowing teachers discretion on the question of how to apply disciplinary sanctions. Indeed it was on this basis that the Court of Appeal in July 2002, upheld the appeal by the school, concluding that the reaction of the teachers was a reasonable response to the situation. Much was made in this case, however, of the fact that the claimant was a young adult and was being treated as such. It is still possible that a school might be under an obligation to prevent a pupil from engaging in any sporting activity if his or her level of irresponsibility was such that he could not be trusted to compete safely, having regard both to his own safety and to that of other participants.

---

[37] See also *Thornton v. Board of School Trustees of School District No. 57* (1976) 73 D.L.R. 3d. 35 (school liable when a student vaulted off a vaulting horse in summersault fashion and overshot the landing mat, landing on his head and as a result became quadriplegic), and also *Lunenburg (County) Dist. School Board v. Peircy*, (1998) 41 C.C.L.T. (2d.) 60 (N.S.C.A.) where a school was ordered to pay $2.3m in damages for not having supervised students properly at an adventure camp as a result of which one student was rendered quadriplegic when he fell head first from a rope line.
[38] *The Times*, July 15, 2002.

Appropriate supervision in the relevant location

The appropriate level of supervision will also depend on something that will be looked at shortly – namely the nature of the location where the event occurs. Thus in *Ralph v. LCC*,[39] a teacher organised a game of "tag" in a room which, in hindsight was insufficient in size for such an activity. In an attempt to avoid being tagged one of the boys put his hand through a glass door suffering injury. The court found that the teacher had not acted as would a "reasonably prudent father" – by not keeping the boys away from the glass door and indeed by allowing such event to go on at all in the circumstances. Again the case turned on the question of foreseeability of accident – and again, in hindsight application of common sense might have militated against allowing the games to go on in the facilities. Equally in *Cahill v. West Ham Corporation*,[40] the court found no negligence where a teacher organised a relay race in a classroom with a glass partition and where one pupil's arm went through the partition and was severely cut.

Failure to supervise owing to teacher participation/refereeing

Returning to an issue discussed earlier, if a teacher is participating in a sporting event/training session as player or referee, this may prevent him from adequately supervising the sporting event. In *Barfoot v. East Sussex CC*,[41] the cricket teacher in the school was also umpiring the match, and hence didn't notice that one of his pupils who was fielding had moved to within nine yards of the batsman, who struck the ball into the young boy's face. The court held that in the circumstances, the teacher's duties as umpire, prevented him from exercising the requisite supervisory attention, and upheld the claimant's negligence action against him.

Supervision of unauthorised sport – the "kickabout" before school starts

Professor Binchy discusses in more detail the issue of "out-of-hours supervision". For present purposes is it important to highlight one particular case. In *Kearn-Price v. Kent County Council*,[42] the fourteen year old claimant was hit in the eye by a full size leather football on school property and suffered serious injury. The incident occurred at 8.40 a.m. some three minutes before the school was due to be opened. There were a number of teachers in

---

[39] 63 T.L.R. 546.
[40] 81 Sol. J. 630 (1932).
[41] Unreported (Queen's Bench), August 16, 1939. See Grayson at p.14.
[42] [2002] E.W.C.A. Civ. 193.

the staff room at the time, but the point at which the incident occurred would not have been clearly visible from the staff room. It was school policy that such full size balls would not be permitted to be used on school property, and indeed this was communicated to teachers (in writing) and to pupils. Nonetheless the ban was not enforced and there were a number of reported incidents of pupils being hit by such balls, largely owing to the fact that the ban on the balls was simply not enforced. The Court of Appeal upheld the judgement against the school finding that it was negligent in not enforcing a policy which it had recognised as necessary to prevent injury to pupils. All that was needed in the court's view were random spot checks with confiscation of offending footballs and the pupils would have realised that the policy was to be taken seriously and would have acted accordingly.

Provision of appropriate medical care

This may seem out of place in a section on supervision, and indeed it possibly is. But it is increasingly necessary for a school that teaches sport or physical education to have some provision for how to deal with a medical emergency, ranging from a child who sprains his ankle, to a child who breaks his neck, to a child who, perhaps owing to a congenital condition has a heart attack while playing football. Again this can be a question of resources. However, medical research indicates that immediate and early management of injuries is key to recovery. Hence ideally the school should employ on whatever basis, someone competent in healthcare (and that person will obviously him or herself be exposed to liability in professional negligence) who can deal with emergencies arising out of sporting activity. Beyond this, teachers and medical staff should attempt to acquaint themselves with a basic knowledge of the attitude of the governing body of the relevant sport to certain injuries – for example the amount of time that a player should be rested following a concussion.

Premises

Significant liability may arise in the context of use of school premises for sporting purposes at common law and under the Occupiers' Liability Act 1995.[43] Essentially, it is incumbent on the school to ensure that latent defects/risks in the premises that might forseeably threaten the safety and well being of the pupils are remedied, and also that in all the circumstances the venue in question is suitable for, and guarded against foreseeable risks deriving

---

[43] Generally, see Grayson at p.41 *et seq*.

from the activity. Such defects/risks may arise in any number of circumstances, from a situation where a sporting field is 'boundaried' too closely by a patch of nettles or a wall, to where there are sprinkler heads at the side of the pitch that are not immediately obvious to players, to where there are hidden undulations in the ground that make it unsafe to play on.

It should again be stressed that the circumstances of the case will decide what must be done. So as a rule of thumb, the older and more experienced the pupil (and hence the more it is reasonable to expect him to take care of himself) and the more obvious the defect to anyone (and hence the less foreseeable it is that someone would be injured by it) the more reasonable it is for the school not to guard against such defect. So for instance it is unnecessary to warn a group of eighteen year old soccer players that it is inadvisable to collide with a goal post. On the other hand in assessing whether a risk of a defect resulting in an injury was foreseeable courts do look to "past history" to see how often the said defect resulted in the said injury in the past. Thus the obvious moral for the school is that if such risk does eventuate on one occasion it should be immediately remedied where this is possible, and this includes not only situations where sports players are injured but also where visitors to the school or even people outside school property are injured by for instance cricket balls flying out of the field of play.

Again analysis of the relevant case law is instructive.

General safety of sports facilities

In *Dibble v. Carmarthern Town*,[44] the defendant soccer club had drawn its pitch markings with hydrated lime. The plaintiff, a goalkeeper had on a number of occasions dived to make saves. When he removed his shirt after the game, he noticed that the pitch markings had burnt a four inch wide strip of flesh on his body from his shoulder to his hip. He recovered £20,000 in damages.

On the other hand in the Irish case *Lennon v. McCarthy*,[45] two pupils were playing "tag" in a hollow below a schoolyard where a number of trees and hawthorn bushes were growing. A branch of one tree projected out horizontally for seven feet from one of the hawthorn bushes. As one boy ran along, he bushed the said branch and it rebounded hitting the chasing boy in the eye. The court held first that a reasonably prudent parent would not deem it necessary to have children in a playground routinely supervised at every moment. Secondly, it refused to accept that the field in question was

---

[44] Unreported, Queen's Bench, 2001.
[45] Unreported, Supreme Court, July 13, 1966.

unsuitable for the game in question (or that a reasonably prudent parent would look into it and deem it to be so). To do so according to the court would be to proscribe the playing of "ordinary simple games like tig in rural Ireland". Essentially the court's point was that this was an accident pure and simple and was not attributable to any negligence on the part of a teacher.

In *Flynn v. O'Reilly*,[46] the claimant was an 11 year old girl who had been competing in her school sports day. The event included a "running backwards race", and the girl in question in running backwards caught her foot in some kind of hole or depression, fell on her wrist and fractured it. She claimed that the field was unsuitable for the event in question, and hence that the school was negligent in allowing the event to take place. The Supreme Court refused to make this finding, concluding instead that the field in question was not "... Wimbledon, or Lansdowne Road (a bad analogy!) or Wembley or some place like that". Rather in the circumstances of the sports day, the playing surface was adequate for simple games and sports, as was evidenced by the fact that there had been no previously recorded incidents of injuries of this nature. A rule that required that on a pitch of this nature there be no difficult events like running backwards would, according to the Supreme Court be excessively harsh, and would overly restrict the freedom of children to engage in sports.

Safety of areas peripheral to the sports arena

It should also be noted that apart from playing surfaces, a school will also be liable for peripheral areas such as viewing areas, changing rooms and shower/bath areas. Indeed the nature of wet tiles is such that this may be a key breeding ground for unwanted litigation. The advice to schools is to ensure that obviously slippy areas are kept as clean and as dry as possible through regular checks and immediate remedial action. Thus in *Taylor v. Bath & NE Somerset District Council*,[47] the claimant sued successfully when she fell on excessively slippery tiled floor having dropped her daughter off at swimming baths. She suggested that the excessively slippery nature of the tiles was caused by the fact that, not being properly cleaned there had been an accumulation of body fats thereon. The court accepted this proposition, noting that despite instructions from the manufacturer of the tiles, they had not been properly chemically cleaned and this caused the build up of fats which led to the injury.

---

[46] [1999] 1 I.L.R.M. 458.
[47] Unreported, Queen's Bench, January 27, 1999.

Swimming pools

The above should indicate that schools wherein swimming pools are located have another major concern – not just in terms of ensuring that pupils are properly supervised when engaged in this potentially hazardous activity, but also in ensuring that inherent and foreseeable risks connected with the pool are dealt with. In *Greening v. Stockton-on-tees BC*,[48] the defendant council operated a swimming pool, where the top of the water in the pool was at the same level as the edge of the pool, and the sides of the pool were light blue with a 20mm dark blue stripe at the top end of the tile. Moreover, on the day in question the water in the pool was murky, causing the claimant to swim into the edge of the pool and suffer injury. The Court of Appeal apportioned liability on a 50/50 basis between the defendant and the claimant, on the grounds that the state of the pool increased the risk of an accident occurring, but equally, *because* of the state of the pool the defendant swimmer ought to have been more careful. Equally, this was not a schoolchild, and had it been it is less likely that the court would have been so willing to find an assumption of risk on the part of the claimant.

Similarly in *Banks v. Bury Borough Council*,[49] the defendants were liable when they did not adequately display the depth of the shallow end of the pool with sufficient prominence. And in *O'Shea v. Royal Borough of Kingston Upon Thames Council*,[50] the Court of Appeal found 50/50 liability between defendant and claimant even when rules and regulations stated that diving at the pool was inadvisable because of the shallowness thereof. The Court of Appeal essentially concluded that the only safe approach was for the defendants completely to prohibit diving at the pool. Finally in *Farrant v. Thames District Council*,[51] a 17 year old was playing on a beach near what was termed a tidal pool, which was used for activities ranging from diving to rowing to swimming. The plaintiff and his friends had been diving in at the deep end of the pool, but he then dived into the middle of the pool, hit his head off the bottom and suffered serious spinal injuries. The court found that the occupier was negligent (with contributory negligence assessed at 20%), in that he had allowed the pool to fill up with silt, thereby making the depth levels of the pool uncertain, nor had he erected any signs warning people not to dive outside of the deep end. Because of this failure, it was foreseeable that people would suffer injuries of the type suffered by the plaintiff, and hence the defendant should be liable. On the other hand, it

---

[48] [1998] E.W.C.A. Civ. 1704 (November 6, 1998).
[49] [1990] C.L.Y. 384.
[50] Unreported, Court of Appeal, 1995.
[51] Unreported Queens' Bench Division, June 11, 1996.

should be noted that recent trends in both Ireland *and* England would seem to suggest that courts are becoming more resistant to the claims of injured plaintiffs in such situations.[52]

Equally the moral of the story is clear – that by their nature, swimming pools are venues filled with a potentially lethal substance (water) and in which there will be inevitable horseplay on the part of young children, and these factors should be borne in mind and accommodated in the design and maintenance of such pools and the supervision of activities carries on within them.

On the other hand and as mentioned earlier, if the school contracts with the owners of a local swimming pool that its pupils are taught swimming there, then (provided that the swimming pool was adequately checked out and the decision to have swimming classes there is a reasonable one) responsibility under the Occupiers' Liability Act 1995 for the safety of the premises passes to the owners of the pool.

Ensuring the facilities are safe for the relevant activity

Finally, as was mentioned, the two notions of supervision and location collide in that it is necessary for a teacher to exercise due caution in determining both whether a venue (including an indoor venue) is safe for a sporting event, and also what precautions are necessary to ensure such safety. In *Kane v. Kennedy*,[53] a class had been timetabled to have an outdoor game of rounders. The weather rendered this impossible so the teacher decided that the game would be held inside in the sports hall. Unhappily, the plaintiff was injured during the game, in that while running with great gusto towards the home base, she had collided with a wall, being unable to stop. After an extensive analysis of the game of rounders, Budd J concluded that whereas it was not necessarily negligent for a PE teacher to organise an indoor game of rounders – and the question of whether this is acceptable will always depend on the state and size of the particular individual facilities under discussion and the degree to which the students had been adequately instructed as to how to use the said facilities – nonetheless she was negligent in placing the home base cone too close to a wall, when it was foreseeable that an accident of the type at issue in this case would occur. Now there was considerable disagreement between witnesses as to where precisely the

---

[52] See, for example, *Tomlinson v. Congleton BC* [2003] All E.R. 1122; *Rhind v. Astbury Waterpark* [2004] E.W.C.A. (Civ.) 756 (June 16, 2004) and *Gorringe v. Calderdale MBC* [2004] 1 W.L.R. 1057.
[53] Unreported, High Court, March 25, 1999.

teacher had placed the final base. Equally, it has to be said that if the pupil's version of events was accurate, then the decision to place the home base that close to the wall was objectively foolhardy. Again simple application of common sense could have saved a lot of heartache.

Conclusion on premises

Finally, and as with equipment, it is necessary and advisable for schools to undertake regular independent checks on their sports facilities – both indoor and outdoor, and to act on any recommendations that might be forthcoming. This applies to indoor sports halls or gymnasia where, for instance, there will be a need to regularly clean the floor – especially if any wet substance gets spilled on it, and also to outdoor facilities. Nor does this mean that where the "sports facilities" consist of a bare field, this will automatically be deemed to be unsafe. The approach of the court in *Flynn v. O'Reilly* makes it clear that such facilities are valid. Moreover, even primary school children can be expected to notice certain obvious risks. What such a safety audit would do, is just to inform school authorities of unacceptable risks to which the children are being exposed and which they can then remedy.

Generally – the role of insurance

It goes without saying that a school can and must avoid many of the problems mentioned above by taking out appropriate insurance policies, particularly in the areas of public liability insurance, personal accident insurance, professional indemnity insurance, possibly legal expenses insurance and directors and officers insurance. Plainly in doing so the school should ensure that it has disclosed the full nature of the activities on school premises to the insurer (and also mentioned issues such as school trips, the fact that the school team played "away" matches and so on), and has checked the policy to ensure both that cover is sufficient and also that pupils are not engaged in any activity that is expressly not covered on the policy. Beyond this, it is necessary to ensure that actions by the school fit within the said policy – that for example a decision to appoint a sports coach, or indeed to appoint a "regular" teacher as a coach of a particular sport is reasonable. Ultimately the presence of insurance is a major source of security for a school and, increasingly a necessary one. Finally it seems certain that there is no obligation on the part of schools to advise pupils/parents to take out individual insurance policies.

Conclusion

Even with insurance policies, however, there may well be holes through which litigation can flow. Ultimately, and in conclusion, in attempting to avoid liability in respect of its sports; there are perhaps two basic rules of thumb for a school;

A. First, in seeking out best practice, schools would be well advised, (possibly in consultation with a solicitor) to draw up a policy document which can be inspected by all relevant parties, in respect of all areas of sports tuition and then to stick rigidly to that framework.[54] The terms of the document might be attached to the school's safety statement, should be displayed prominently at school property and should be conveyed to parents. The document should deal, *inter alia*, with:

- qualifications necessary for coaches/teachers of sport in that school,
- the extent to which individual pupils can be alone with individual teachers, and indeed the extent to which teachers can physically touch the students in demonstrating sporting exercises,
- the extent to which sport is compulsory,
- the degree to which sporting activities will be supervised,
- the policy of the school in respect of drug testing,
- the availability of medical assistance in the event of injury or illness,
- the existence and extent of safety checks on equipment and premises,
- the extent to which (if at all) a younger player may be selected for an older team,
- general safety precautions.

As mentioned, and as is clear from *Kearn Price v. Kent County Council*, moreover, if such a policy document is drawn up in whatever form, then it is vital that it be adhered to. Failing to spot a danger is one thing, but spotting it, noting it in a policy document and then failing to deal with it is almost worse.

In this regard all schools would be advised to get a copy of the Irish Sports Council *Code of Ethics for Good Practice in Children's Sport*, (2001) available at www.irishsportscouncil.ie. The code is a "non-legal"

---

[54] Brierly, "School Sports and the Law", 1 (1) *Sports Law Journal*, p.19.

document but provides excellent advise on how to ensure that sport is emotionally and physically profitable for children, while also ensuring that they are not subject to abuse, be it physical, mental or sexual. It also provides guidelines for supervision (including supervision of 'away' trips), disciplinary rules and so on. In all its aspects it sees respective roles for parents, clubs (or schools) and coaches (or teachers). Undoubtedly it represents best practice, and in this regard its importance for the school is twofold. First, it is a model for ensuring that sport flourishes and that pupils are happy in what they do. Secondly, and in as much as it represents best practice, failure to live up to its suggestions (which are themselves largely obvious) is a clear indicator that the school is acting negligently.

B. Secondly, and more importantly, it is vital (and in all probability the best of all legal defences) that teachers simply apply basic common sense and restraint – as distinct from some superhuman level of foresight – in dealing with a situation. So for example, it may be legitimate for a teacher to involve himself in a game, in order to make up numbers or to offer immediate tuition, but in doing so he should act in a responsible and reasonable fashion. In order to be able to apply such common sense, the teacher should be appropriately knowledgeable of relevant matters – for example the safety rules of the particular sport.

Finally, it is well to point out once again that school sport is a public service and the courts recognise this fact. It would be too strong to suggest that the courts draw a presumption in favour of schools – particularly when faced with gross negligence on the part of a teacher and a resultant horrific injury to a pupil. Equally, the courts have a significant sympathy for persons who quasi-voluntarily undertake what is undoubtedly a difficult task, for the good of the pupils in their charge.

THE DELIVERY OF MINIMUM EDUCATION AND THE COMMON GOOD

DYMPNA GLENDENNING[*1]

"Today, education is perhaps the most important function of state and local governments. ... It is the very foundation of good citizenship ... a principal instrument in helping to adjust normally to his environment. Such an opportunity, where the State has undertaken to provide it, is a right which must be available to all on equal terms."[1]

INTRODUCTION

Many human rights instruments have made the provision of elementary, fundamental, and second chance education mandatory on State Parties.[2] It is as though the state of childhood, with its inherent vulnerability, dependence and potential, establishes a principle that society must confer on children's basic needs a priority in competing claims and a first call on human and material resources.[3] Because education displaces ignorance, which is considered a hindrance to the development of individuals, the function of the law in ensuring school attendance is generally perceived as justified.[4] Not only is universal fundamental education seen as desirable, however, it

---

*B.A., M.Ed, Ph.D., Barrister.
[1] *Brown v. Board of Education* (1954) 347 US 483 at 493.
[2] U.N. Covenant on the Rights of the Child, Article 28: UN International Covenant on Economic, Social and Cultural Rights 1966 also states: "Fundamental education shall be encouraged or intensified as far as possible for those persons who have not received or completed the whole period of their primary education" (Art.13.2).
[3] See Declaration adopted by the first World Summit for Children held in New York in 1990.
[4] Ginsberg, *On Justice in Society* (Penguin, 1965), p.118 citing T.H. Green in *Lectures on the Principles of Political Obligation*, paras 208–209; see Amazon.com for current edition of this book by Thomas Hill Green edited by Paul Harris and John Morris.

The Delivery of Minimum Education and the Common Good

is so identified with the common good, that in certain countries, such as Ireland, the State has been appointed its constitutional guardian.[5] Most developed countries have accepted this fundamental principle and have incorporated it in statute law making basic education compulsory for all children and its provision an obligation falling on the State. As the late Professor John Kelly succinctly stated:

> "The state cannot allow its citizens to choose to remain ignorant, because for very good reasons it cannot afford to."[6]

At common law a parent was not legally obliged to educate his or her child. Scotland legislated for compulsory education in 1872,[7] and England made education compulsory in 1880.[8] In Ireland a minimalist form of compulsory education was introduced in 1892,[9] but this merely required parents in cities and large towns to send their children of 14–16 years to school for a minimum of 75 days annually. Under native government compulsory education was extended nationally in the School Attendance Act 1926 and, with certain minor amendments, that Act continued in operation until July 5, 2002. This chapter considers the provision made for minimum education and compulsory school attendance in the Republic of Ireland (Ireland) from July 5, 2002, when the Education (Welfare) Act 2000 was commenced, to November 2005.

MINIMUM EDUCATION AND EARLY SCHOOL LEAVING

The correlation between educational disadvantage and early school leaving, truancy and juvenile criminality is well established in Ireland.[10] Indeed,

---

[5] In the Irish Constitution of 1937, Art.42.3.2.
[6] When addressing a group of teachers in St. Patrick's College of Education in 1968, "Education and the Irish State", *Irish Jurist*, 1990–1992, p.83.
[7] Elementary Education Act (Scotland) (1872).
[8] A general system of public education was introduced in England in to the Elementary Education Acts (England) (1870–1909) and in Ireland informally by the Stanley Letter, 1831, see Glendenning, *Education and the Law* (Butterworth 1999), para.9.15.
[9] Education (Ireland) Act 1892.
[10] *The School Attendance/Truancy Report* (Department of Education, 1994); *Report of the Task Force on the Traveller Community* (Government Publications, 1995); Paul O'Mahony, *Crime and Punishment in Ireland* (Round Hall Press, 1995); I. Bacik and O'Connell, *Crime and Poverty in Ireland* (Round Hall Sweet and Maxwell, 1998); Gerry Whyte, *Social Inclusion and the Legal System* (Institute of Public Administration, 2001) and in particular Chapter 5 of Hannan, *Poverty Today*, July/Sept. 1992; Economic and Social Research Institute, School Leavers Survey, 1996.

there is a stark picture of educational failure at the base of the educational pyramid here which is reflected in prisons and places of detention.[11] Such persistent problems, which are not unique to Ireland, are inextricably bound up with poverty,[12] with the delivery of minimum education to children and with compulsory school attendance.

For example, the Report of the Task Force on the Traveller Community (1995) found that 800 Traveller children were not enrolled in any second level school and this was confirmed by the Early School Leavers and Youth Unemployment Report (1997). O'Mahony's research on prisoners, estimated that 89% of prisoners had left school before the age of 16 years and many of these were 14 or younger.[13]

In 1995, the OECD Economic Survey: Ireland considered that the quality of the education system, especially for pupils at the lower end of the ability scale, was not up to international standards.[14] One year later, the European Social Fund: Evaluation Report "Early School Leavers" (1996) confirmed that position and cautioned that if the Irish system of education did not alter so as to accommodate the long term education and training needs of early school leavers, this group would in all probability, resort to anti-social behaviour the ultimate cost of which would far outstrip pro-active investment in the shorter term.

Since the 1990s remarkable progress has been made in raising general educational standards in Ireland as the OECD PISA Survey (2002)[15] indicates. Yet, despite many initiatives in this sphere and despite significant financial interventions, the issue of educational disadvantage has remained an intractable problem as successive Ministers and educational policy-makers have acknowledged.[16] Arguably the most significant step in assisting the

---

[11] *Ibid.*
[12] The *OECD Economic Survey* (1995), at p.104, found that children from lower socio-economic backgrounds were almost five times as likely to leave school with low qualifications and face a 50% probability of being unemployed for one year after leaving school.
[13] *Crime and Punishment in Ireland* (Round Hall, Dublin, 1995)
[14] At p.90 of the Report.
[15] See Program for International Student Assessment (PISA)(2002) of the performance of 15 year-olds in 32 countries in which Ireland was rated 5th in literacy, 9th in Science and 16th in Mathematics.
[16] When speaking at an OECD conference on education policy on February 7, 2003, Noel Dempsey TD, who was then Minister for Education and Science, stated that the current priority in the Republic was the combating of educational disadvantage: "*I think we have a broadly successful education system, but in this area we need to do more.*": S. Flynn, "Education Policy Adrift IDA Chief, *Irish Times*, February 8, 2003, p.5.

educationally disadvantaged is to ensure their legal entitlement to a minimum education, at the very least, is discharged and this is normally achieved through the full implementation of school attendance legislation.

In their *Analysis of School Attendance at Primary and Post Primary Schools for 2003/2004 School Year*, the National Educational Welfare Board found that 1 in 10 students is absent for 20 days annually at post primary schools. This study concludes that there is a strong relationship between the levels of disadvantage and both the level of attendance and the number of students who miss 20 days or more. It also concluded that schools with larger numbers of children from disadvantaged backgrounds tend to experience greater problems with school attendance. As the right to a minimum education derives from a constitutional provision in this jurisdiction, I will first consider that context.

MINIMUM EDUCATION: A CONSTITUTIONAL RIGHT

The significance of the principle of universal minimum education was fully appreciated by De Valera, the chief architect of the Constitution of 1937, as the De Valera Papers demonstrate. In the penultimate draft of Article 42 (Education) of the Constitution,[17] De Valera altered the word "may"[18] to "shall" thereby ensuring that the provision of "a certain minimum education", *inter alia*, became a mandatory obligation on the State.[19] By the addition of the phrase "that the children receive..." the right [to a minimum education] was vested in children.[20] The final draft which was enacted and adopted by the people as Article 42.3.2 provides:

"The State shall, however, as guardian of the common good ensure

---

[17] Presented to him for approval on March 31, 1937, see File 1079/3, *De Valera Papers*, now available in the library of University College, Dublin.
[18] The use of permissive language such as "may" generally imports a discretionary power which is enabling or permissive, whereas mandatory language such a "shall" generally implies the existence of a statutory duty, but there are exceptions to this general rule, see *Julius v. Lord Bishop of Oxford* (1880) L.R. 5 Appeal Cases 214: see further Hogan and Morgan, *Administrative Law* (2nd ed., Sweet and Maxwell, 1991), p.358 *et seq*.
[19] Together with Articles 42.4 and 42.5.
[20] The revised phrase then read: "The State, however, as guardian of the common good, shall require in view of actual conditions that the children receive a certain minimum education, moral, intellectual, physical and social." This was typed up and headed "Article 42 (as revised on the instructions of the President on March 31, 1937) and this formula was incorporated in File 1079/3".

that the children receive a certain minimum education moral, intellectual and social".

The Supreme Court ruled in *Crowley v. Ireland and Others*[21] that this duty, cast upon the State, vests a constitutional right in children to receive "a certain minimum education ...". As Henchy J. stated, however, no single constitutional provision may be isolated and construed with undeviating literalness and any single constitutional right or power is but a component in an ensemble of interconnected and interacting provisions.[22] Accordingly the right to a minimum education needs to be read in the light of the general provisions for education in Article 42 but its link to the common good, nonetheless, seems to imply an overarching priority in the hierarchy of educational rights.[23]

As Professor Kelly, pointed out, the State like every Irish citizen is subject to the law:

> "This is particularly true in the case of the most solemn law we have, the law contained in our Constitution: because this Constitution was enacted not by any organ of the State, but by the people and it can be changed only by the People."[24]

Now the State figures centrally in the Constitution, he continues, generally where the People have laid a duty on their State or have conferred a right to it.[25] Almost every function of a democratic state involves a question of balancing the common good and the rights of the citizen and the right to a minimum education is no exception.[26] It is for the courts to decide the balance which must be struck between the common good and the interests of individuals when cases come before them. In *Director of Public Prosecutions v. Best* (the *Best* case), which dealt, *inter alia*, with the legality of home education, Denham J. in the Supreme Court considered that the common good confers a priority on the children's right to receive a certain minimum education[27] a principle which is now embodied in statute law.[28]

---

[21] [1980] I.R. 102.
[22] *People v. O'Shea* [1982] I.R. 384 at 426.
[23] A fact that is now established by virtue of the Education (Welfare) Act 2000.
[24] *Loc. cit.*
[25] *Ibid.*
[26] *Ibid.*
[27] [2000] 2 I.R. 17 78 at 49.
[28] In the provisions of the Education (Welfare) Act 2000.

Minimum Education: The Constitutional Standard

It was the *Best* case which cleared the way, so to speak, for the Oireachtas to pass new school attendance legislation, the Education (Welfare) Act 2000,[29] as it removed the unique restrictions imposed on State action in education by the Supreme Court in *Re Article 26 and the School Attendance Bill* 1942[30] (the 1942 case). The School Attendance Bill 1942 sought to regulate the manner in which parents might provide education for their children and it was referred by the President to the Supreme Court to test its constitutionality. A novel feature of the Bill of 1942 was that it conferred on the Minister the power to prescribe the content of "other suitable elementary education" together with the manner of imparting such education. The Supreme Court held that the State was entitled to require that the children receive a certain minimum education but once parents supply this general standard of education, the manner in which such education was being given and received was entirely a matter for the parents and was not a matter in respect of which the State under the Constitution was entitled to interfere. In other words, the Court ruled that the dominant rights in education were vested in parents and that the State could interfere only to the extent permitted by Article 42.3.2. As Professor Osborough indicates, the Dáil[31] and Seanad Debates[32] of the period present valuable insights into the singular nationalistic context in which the 1942 Bill was drafted and also to its covert objectives.[33] Whatever the intent of the proposed amendment, the Supreme Court in the 1942 decision imposed very substantial constraints on State action in education which appears to have impeded the enactment of substantive educational legislation until 1998[34] and any new school attendance legislation between 1926[35] and the year 2000.[36]

In the *Best* case, which came before the Supreme Court in 1998, it was established that the earlier Supreme Court finding in the 1942 case was wrong in law and that it rested on an unduly narrow construction of Article

---

[29] The *Best* case also buttressed the role of the State as enacted in the Education Act 1998, in this writer's opinion.
[30] [1942] I.R. 334.
[31] Dáil Debates, Vol. 88, cols.1605–1607, Nov 1942; also cols. 2136–2138, Nov. 1942: col.1573, 28 Oct. 1942: cols 1557–1560; cols. 2094–2098, November 18, 1942.
[32] Seanad Debates, Vol 27, Cols. 247–248, December 3, 1942
[33] W.N. Osborough, "Education in the Irish law and Constitution", *Irish Jurist*, 1978, n.s. 145–180 at 174.
[34] Education Act 1998.
[35] School Attendance Acts 1926–1967.
[36] Education (Welfare) Act 2000.

42.3.2 and should not be followed. If the State could not intervene although satisfied that teaching methods were patently inadequate, the Court considered, then the right of the child to be educated would be seriously violated.[37] In the B*est* case, the Court set down guidelines for the District Court Judge when assessing "a certain minimum education", for the purposes of school attendance prosecutions under the School Attendance Acts 1926–1967 since repealed.[38] It was the legality of home education, which was initially before the District Court in Listowel, Co. Kerry. A referral by way of Case Stated was made by the District Judge to the High Court for its opinion as to whether she could convict the parents of the Best children for failing to send them to school in view of the absence of a statutory definition of "a suitable elementary education" in the 1926 Act[39] and in the light of the meaning of "a certain minimum education" in Article 42.3.2 which had not been statutorily defined.

The High Court ruled that, in the absence of a statutory definition, or other formal definition of what was meant by "a certain minimum education", a District Judge trying a charge under the 1926 Act, and hearing evidence that a parent was doing his or her best to educate a child at home in basic subjects, and taking into account the moral and social aspects of education, should be very slow to convict a parent of an offence. Following an appeal by the prosecutor to the Supreme Court, five separate judgements were delivered indicating possibly a lack of judicial consensus on certain matters. The Court held, in a 4:1 decision, that the fact that "a certain minimum education…" had not been defined in legislation, did not prevent the District Judge from arriving at a fair and objective decision, since the Oireachtas had left it to the District Court to decide whether the constitutional minimum education was being given to the children in any particular case coming before it. Not only must the situation of the child and the family be considered, the Court stated, the actual situation must also be analysed in the light of the community ("toisc cor an lae") which includes the general educational standards of the time.[40] Thus, the requirements of the community (such as information technology), may now be one of elements comprising "a certain minimum education."[41] Moreover, the use of the word "minimum" did not indicate some lowest common denominator in education. Rather, the underlying objective is to provide young people with a basic education so

---

[37] *Ibid.*, p.62.
[38] By the Education (Welfare) Act 2000.
[39] Which is also absent from the Education (Welfare) Act 2000.
[40] *Director of Public Prosecutions v. Best* [2000] 2 I.R. 17 at 47 *per* Denham J.
[41] *Ibid.*

that they can communicate orally and in writing within society and record, organise and deal with ordinary social and business matters involving communication, enumeration and arithmetic, the Court considered. Furthermore, the common good also requires that children should be encouraged to develop a sense of responsibility and the capacity to live in a civilised society."[42] When commenting on the role of the State as guardian of the common good in Article 42.3.2, in her dissenting judgment, Ms Justice Denham stated:

> "The common good places the children's right to receive a certain minimum education, moral, intellectual and social as a priority. It does not require a high standard of education-but it is a mandatory minimum standard. The standard is a question of fact, which must be decided in view of factors including actual conditions in the community and having regard to, inter alia, the physical and intellectual capacity of the children. The minimum education must be conducive to the child achieving intellectual and social development and not such as to place the child in a discriminatory position."[43]

This finding is in line with human rights instruments[44] and in particular the International Covenant on Economic, Social and Cultural Rights 1966 (ICESC) which places a mandatory obligation on State Parties in regard to primary education and requires the buttressing of "fundamental education" for those who have not completed their primary education.[45]

In the *Best* case the Supreme Court held as follows:

- that parents may lawfully educate their children in their homes provided the constitutional minimum standard is met; that the parents' right in this regard is not absolute as it is balanced with a duty which includes a requirement to ensure that their child's personal potential is enhanced and not suppressed; that where parents elected to provide their children with "a certain minimum education"[46] in their own home, they assumed the burden of satisfying the District Justice that such education met the

---

[42] *Ibid.*, p.70 (SC).
[43] *Ibid.*, pp.49–50.
[44] See UN Universal Declaration of Human Rights, 1948 and UN Convention on the Rights of the Child, Art.28.
[45] Glendenning, *op. cit.*, pp.255–256.
[46] *Ibid.*, the Supreme Court was dealing here with the 1926 Act and the phrase "a suitable elementary education" was being considered.

constitutional standard and the onus falling on the parents was measured on the balance of probabilities;[47]

- that the minimum education was not necessarily to be equated with the primary school curriculum but that the curriculum could be used as a benchmark in analysing a home programme of education for children, but not inflexibly as circumstances may vary from child to child;[48] that the actual situation pertaining must be analysed in the light of the community[49] which includes the general educational standards of the times;[50]

- that the minimum constitutional standard [of education] is not a universal, uniform education for all children,[51] but must be balanced with other factors including, *inter alia*, the time the issue is determined, the family, the parents, their means, the child, the geographical situation, the actual circumstances, the common good and the expert evidence before the court;

- that having heard the evidence both of the parents and the inspector as to the nature of the education being received, as in any other case, the District Judge will then be in a position to bring to bear on the decision her experience of the world and her common sense;[52]

- that children with some degree of learning difficulties may be entitled to a form of education that takes account of those difficulties;[53]

- that, although the Irish language is not a mandatory part of the constitutional minimum education, it may be taken into account in determining whether the education of the child reaches the constitutional standard.[54]

The above principles, although considered in the context of the 1926 Act as amended, will prove useful in assessing the delivery of "a certain minimum education" under current legislation, the Education (Welfare) Act 2000. By legislating for minimum education in the 2000 Act, the State has sought to discharge its constitutional obligation, in its role as guardian of the common good, to require that the children receive "a certain minimum education, moral, intellectual and social".

---

[47] *Ibid.*, p.19.
[48] *Ibid.*
[49] "toisc cor an lae" in Art.42.3.3.
[50] *Director of Public Prosecutions v. Best* [2002] 2 I.R. 19 at 47.
[51] *Ibid.*
[52] *Ibid.*, p.60.
[53] *Ibid.*, p.61 *per* Keane C.J.
[54] *Ibid.*, p.60.

Limits to State's Obligations

Article 42.5 casts further serious obligations on the State in regard to children "in exceptional cases where the parents for physical or moral reasons fail in their duty towards their children ...". In the case of children of tender years, the courts have indicated that this obligation may only be discharged by the State assuming full responsibility, directly or vicariously for their care, shelter, health, education and general nurture.[55] In *T.D. v. Minister for Education*,[56] in which the applicants were children seeking the provision of secure, high support residential placements by the State, Hardiman J. stated that as young persons approach maturity, the State's obligations must necessarily be balanced with increasing levels of personal responsibility. As the child matures and passes the age of reason, and the age of criminal responsibility, the State's duties are complemented by a reciprocal obligation on the part of the child or young person to engage and co-operate with the facilities and services provided to him. It is neither realistic nor legally necessary, the learned judge continued, to treat a young person up to his eighteenth birthday as an entirely passive recipient of services whether provided by his parents or by the State without responsibility of any description for his own behaviour and formation. Indeed to regard a young person in that way, he indicated, would be quite inconsistent with the policy of the criminal law whereby criminal responsibility may be attached to him prior to his achieving his majority:[57]

> "But no matter what facilities are provided, and regardless of whether they are provided by public bodies or on the private initiative of parents, they will have no beneficial effect on a particular child or young person without his own co-operation. The fact that such co-operation is not forthcoming is not in itself evidence that the services provided are inadequate.
>
> Where a young person becomes unco-operative and unwilling to assist in his own education, difficult to accommodate in schools or institutions because he is felt to be a threat to other students and staff, and prone to taking drugs, a very difficult situation arises. This situation is acute whether the young person is being cared for by the State or by his parents."[58]

---

[55] *T.D. v. Minister for Education* [2001] 4 I.R. 259 at 343 (SC), *per* Hardiman J.
[56] *Ibid.*, p.344.
[57] *Ibid.*, p.343.
[58] *Ibid.*

In the *T.D.* case Hardiman J. noted that the Applicant had not sought to rely on any of the statutory provisions, such as the Education Act 1998, the Education (Welfare) Act 2000 or the Equal Status Act 2000 which may have had a bearing on the Applicants' position. Even if such legislative provisions had been relied upon by the applicants, he concluded that the obligations of the State must be viewed realistically and that there is a limit to the benefit that any service, statutory or voluntary, can afford the applicant in the absence of his own willing co-operation.[59]

MINIMUM EDUCATION: LEGISLATIVE PROVISION

The Education Act 1998

In the discharge of its constitutional obligations under Article 42 the State has enacted the Education Act 1998 (the 1998 Act), which makes provision in the interests of the common good for the education of every person in the State including those with a disability or other special educational needs.[60] Under the 1998 Act, the Minister has statutory responsibility, *inter alia*, for the level and quality of education[61] delivered to every person in the State and this also includes minimum education as Keane C.J. ruled in *Director of Public Prosecutions v. Best*:

"... the Minister in approving the form of education being given in those schools, and, for that purpose, inter alia, preparing and revising from time to time, as circumstances appear to him or her to require, the primary school curriculum, is clearly under a constitutional duty to ensure that the children receive that minimum standard of education."[62]

Accordingly, the Minister,[63] by virtue of ministerial powers of approval over the form or substance of education together with the ministerial powers in preparing and revising the curriculum, retains overall responsibility, *inter*

---

[59] *Ibid.*, p.345.
[60] The Education for Persons with Special Educational Needs Act 2004 has since been enacted and a number of provisions have been commenced. See further M. Meaney, N. Kiernan, and K. Monaghan, *Special Educational Needs and the Law* (Thomson Round Hall, Dublin, 2005).
[61] Ss.7, 10, 11, 12 and 30 (the Curriculum) of the 1998 Act: the Minister also has responsibility pursuant to the Vocational Education Acts 1930–2001.
[62] *Director of Public Prosecutions v. Best* [2000] 2 I.R. 17 at pp.58-59.
[63] For Education and Science.

alia, for the discharge of minimum education entitlements under the 1998 Act. Does the Minister also retain over-arching responsibility for the level, quality and delivery of minimum education under the Education (Welfare) Act 2000?

THE EDUCATION (WELFARE) ACT 2000

The constitutional obligation to provide "a certain minimum education" under 42.3.2 falls on the State acting as guardian of the common good in addition to the duties of provision in Articles 42.4 and 42.5. It is the specific duty under Article 42.3.2 that the Education (Welfare) Act 2000 (the 2000 Act) aims to discharge in view of the actual conditions in society[64] by providing for the entitlement of every child in the State to the constitutional minimum education either in recognised schools or in places other than in recognised schools.[65] With regard to the latter places, these include: the child's home, places of detention, prisons, in the care of the Health Services Executive (HSE), in special units, in Youthreach Centres etc.

On July 5, 2002[66] the 1926 Act was repealed by the 2000 Act and the system for enforcing school attendance under the 1926 Act as amended ceased. On the same date, the functions of the former School Attendance Officers in the cities of Dublin, Cork, and Waterford, together with the school enforcing function of the gardaí in the remainder of the country, ceased. No further prosecutions for failure to attend school could be brought under the 1926 Act and existing school attendance proceedings, normally dealt with in the Children's Court, were discontinued. The 2000 Act provides for the compulsory attendance of children of 6–16 years,[67] who are resident in the State, at recognised schools and for the registration of children who are receiving education in places other than recognised schools. The Act also provides for the amendment of the protection of Young Persons (Employment) Act 1996 and related matters.

With the commencement of the 2000 Act school attendance related services appeared to move from a strict disciplinary model to a more welfare based model in which court proceedings are used only as a final resort if at all. There is a risk inherent in this transition that the welfare model may be

---

[64] "toisc cor an lae".
[65] See long title of Act.
[66] And by operation of ss.37 and 40 of the 2000 Act.
[67] See definition of "child" in s.2 of the Act, note that the upper age limit for certain children may be the child's 18th birthday, e.g. where the child has nor completed 3 years of post-primary education.

unevenly resourced and patchily implemented. If the legislative sanctions are downgraded or ignored in this context, then certain vulnerable children, with constitutional and statutory entitlements to education, will inevitably fall out of the system [of education]. The main institutional change in the school attendance system under the 2000 Act is the establishment of the National Educational (Welfare) Board whose functions will now be considered.

The National Educational Welfare Board (NEWB)

A very onerous function, which is at the core of the common good, has been cast on the NEWB, *i.e.* to ensure that each child attends a recognised school or otherwise receives a certain minimum education. The Board is responsible for monitoring school attendance nationwide and for supporting the education and training of young people throughout the country. In addition to its other functions, the Board is required to research the underlying causes of truancy and to assist by early intervention and prevention children and their families who may be at risk of developing school attendance-related problems.

The NEWB is a body corporate [68] capable of suing and being sued in its own name. Its general functions are to ensure that each child attends a recognised school or otherwise receives a certain minimum education and to assist in the formulation and implementation of related Government policies and objectives.[69] While this Board has all such powers as it considers necessary for the performance of its functions under the 2000 Act,[70] it is subject to ministerial policy, ministerial written directions[71] and to financial[72] and resource limitations.[73] Even when giving advice or making recommendations to the Minister, the NEWB is required to "have regard to the cost of measures that would have to be taken if the Minister were to take such advice or implement such recommendations."[74] While the Board has a duty to appoint staff ("The Board shall appoint ..."), this duty is subject to the consent of the Minister for Education and Science and the Minister for Finance. Because the Act casts an obligation of such magnitude on the Board, one would expect this obligation to be balanced by a mandatory duty on the said Ministers in terms of financial provision so as to enable it to discharge

---

[68] *Ibid.*, s.41.
[69] *Ibid.*, s.10.
[70] *Ibid.*, s.10(2).
[71] *Ibid.*, s.13.
[72] *Ibid.*, see Pt IV of the 2000 Act and in particular ss.32 and 33.
[73] *Ibid*, s 10(3).
[74] *Ibid.*

its statutory functions in the discharge of the State's constitutional duty. However, section 32 merely casts a discretionary duty on the Ministers. Section 32 provides:

> "The Minister may, with the consent of the Minister for Finance, advance to the Board out of moneys provided by the Oireachtas such sums as the Minister may determine."

It is the Minister, who formulates policy, sets the curriculum, controls staff numbers, directs the NEWB, controls personnel and disburses Oireachtas grants but the latter grants are dependant on the consent of the Minister for Finance.

If analogous principles to those applied by Keane J. in the *Best* case[75] were applied in determining ministerial responsibility under the 2000 Act, the courts would be likely to read this issue harmoniously with the 1998 Act and conclude that by virtue of the ministerial powers over the form, substance, supervision and funding of minimum education, and the totality of ministerial powers in the Act, that the Minister retains overarching responsibility for the discharge of minimum education entitlements under both the 1998 Act and the 2000 Act.

While some of the NEWB's functions are of an advisory and research nature, it has a central role in:

- formulating and implementing Governmental policy and objectives;
- advising and assisting parents of children with school attendance problems;
- advising and assisting schools in meeting their obligations under the Act;
- assessing the adequacy of training and guidance provided to teachers in relating to school attendance matters;
- advising the National Council for Curriculum and Assessment (NCCA)[76] on curriculum matters;
- advising the Minister;
- enforcing school attendance[77] and
- in assessment of children. With parental consent, the Board may arrange

---

[75] Discussed above at pp.96 *et seq.* and 102.
[76] Established under Pt VII of the Education Act 1998.
[77] *Ibid.*, s.25; the Board may serve a School Attendance Notice on parents in accordance with s.25; failure to comply with that Notice constitutes an offence under the Act which is liable on summary conviction in the District Court and to a fine not exceeding £500 (€635 approx.).

for a child to be assessed[78] and where a parent refuses to give consent, the Board may apply to the Circuit Court[79] for an Order that the assessment be carried out.

Statutory duties are imposed on recognised schools to have a more proactive role in truancy issues and provision is made in the legislation for schools to be supported and assisted in meeting their statutory obligations. So as to avoid fragmentation and duplication of services, the Act provides for a mechanism to facilitate liaison and coordination between State-funded agencies[80] which have a role in school attendance matters. Central to the delivery of this provision nationwide are the "field officers", so to speak, of the NEWB *i.e.* the Educational Welfare Officers.

Educational Welfare Officers

The 2000 Act envisages that the NEWB, largely through its Education Welfare Officers (EWOs), would provide the services of the Board both at school level and at local level throughout the country. In their 2002 study, the National Economic and Social Forum (NESF) estimated that at least 210 EWOs were needed at national level to implement the Act on the basis that there are approximately 4,200 schools in the country. These numbers would provide one EWO for 20 schools.

The *Rochford Report* (2002) was of the view that 300 EWOs and Senior EWOs would be required to deliver the services of the NEWB to children throughout the country when the Act was fully operational.[81] Currently there are less than 100 EWOs employed nationwide.[82]

A recent report conducted by MORI Ireland for the NEWB (2005), confirms that absenteeism is prevalent throughout the country and is significantly worse in disadvantaged areas.[83] The report found that discipline

---

[78] Ss.10(4)–10(8).
[79] In the jurisdiction in which the child resides.
[80] The Minister or Health and Children, Health Boards, the Vocational Education Committees, the National Youth Advisory Committee, the NCCA etc., see s.12 of the Act.
[81] *Report on the Organisation and Staffing Needs of the National Education Welfare Board*, by Dermot Rochford, March 2002.
[82] In August 2005, the number of EWOs was 63 EWOs (these are Field Officers which include senior EWOs and Regional Managers). These 63 officers dealt with 17,000 new cases during 2004, the first fully operational year of the NEWB. This approximates to 267 cases per officer.
[83] John Walshe, education ed., "Unruly Student Crisis in Schools", *Irish Independent*, December 2005, p.1.

problems are frequently the outcome of non-attendance at school as students struggle to catch up and it confirms the link between poor school attendance and early school leaving which impacts economically, educationally, and socially on both the individual student and on society.

With its current allocation of EWOs, it is likely that the Board is capable of dealing only with the areas of greatest need, such as large cities and towns, and that significant entitlements under the Act are not being delivered to children and young persons in employment.

On commencement date (July 5, 2002), the former School Attendance Officers were transferred to the NEWB as staff members[84] but not as EWOS as the latter were appointed to deliver the services of the NEWB to children throughout the State until early March 2003 due to a dispute concerning the remuneration of the prospective EWOs.[85] It appears that for the first 8 months of the 2000 Act's operation, (between July 5, 2002 and early March 2003), basic minimum education services were not available to certain categories of children, despite the constitutional and statutory[86] guarantees provided. In view of the scope of the clearly identified problems associated with school attendance in Ireland for more that a decade,[87] this omission seems an indictment of Irish society. The *NESF Report* (2002) estimated that of the approximate 13,000 children who leave school annually before completing the Leaving Certificate, in or about 2,400 leave with no formal qualification while 1,000 do not transfer from primary to second level schooling annually thereby breaching the 2000 Act with impunity.

Prosecutions for failure to attend school

The 2000 Act imposes a duty on parents to cause their children to attend a recognised school on each school day,[88] unless they can establish that their children are receiving a minimum education in accordance with section 17(2). In 2004, the first year of full national service 80,000 children were absent for more than 20 school days. During this period, the NEWB took on 17,000 cases.[89] The Act requires the NEWB to serve a School Attendance Notice if it is of the opinion that a parent is failing or neglecting to cause his or her

---

[84] S.37, the remuneration of these staff members is governed by ss.37 and 38 of the Act.
[85] *Ibid.* Note that the NEWB may perform any of its functions through or by any member of the staff of the Board if duly authorised in that behalf by the Board, see s.39 of the Act.
[86] Both under the 1998 Act and the 2000 Act.
[87] See n.8 above.
[88] S.17 of the 2000 Act.
[89] NEWB website (www.newb.ie) citing Dr Ann Gilligan, Chairperson.

child to attend school in accordance with the Act. The first 28 such notices have now been served recently more than three years after the commencement date of the 2000 Act. Between July 5, 2002 and the date of writing (November 4, 2005) no school attendance prosecutions were taken under the 2000 Act. This contrasts with an estimated 7,500 prosecutions in England in 2004 some 80% of which resulted in a conviction.[90]

Many students with special needs appear to be unable to gain access to second level schools.[91] Recent figures indicate that certain schools carry an undue burden when it comes to special educational needs students while other schools cater for few such students. It has been alleged that some schools choose the more academic students and employ varying tactics to side-step, so to speak, their responsibilities in this regard.[92] In their defense schools frequently reply that they do not have the resources, financial or personnel, to cater for the needs of students with special educational needs. When fully in force, the Education for Persons with Special Educational Needs Act 2004, will address these issues[93] as the Council for Special Educational Needs established under the Act will designate the schools that such children will attend[94] and school boards may appeal that decision to the Appeals Board established under the Act.

Under the 2000 Act, it is a good defence for a parent if they can show that they are exempted from causing their child to attend a recognised school for any of the reasons set down in section 17(2). However, a person who contravenes a requirement in a School Attendance Notice shall be guilty of an offence and shall be liable on summary conviction (in the District Court) to a fine not exceeding £500 or to imprisonment for not more than one month or to both such fine and imprisonment. It is a defence for a parent under section 25(6) to show that he or she has made all reasonable efforts to

---

[90] National Audit Office, *Improving School Attendance in England*, HC 212 (London: The Stationery Office, 1998), para 1.8 cited in Neville Harris, *Making Parents Pay: The Legal Enforcement of School Attendance in England*.
[91] Sean Flynn, "Hanafin criticises secondary schools' record in special needs", *Irish Times*, October 15, 2005, p.7.
[92] S. Flynn, "Some schools duck duty to special-needs pupils", Education Today, *Irish Times* November 1, 2005. This edition contains recent figures supplied by the DES which indicate the extent of the problem. Some schools have a body of special needs students which comprise almost one third of their full enrolment and these figures range downwards to less than one per cent.
[93] Note the following: S.I. No.507 of 2005; S.I. No.508 of 2005; S.I. No.509 of 2005 and S.I. No.636 of 2005.
[94] S. 10 of the 2004 Act. The council may designate the school of its own volition or at the request of parents.

cause the child to whom the proceedings relate to attend a recognised school in accordance with the Act.[95]

Duties on Schools and Principals

Schools and Principals have duties under the 2000 Act, *inter alia*, to maintain school attendance records,[96] to admit students only in accordance with its admission policy,[97] to establish and maintain school registers,[98] to prepare and a Code of Behaviour[99] and to comply with section 24 of the Act when called upon to expel students. With regard to school attendance records, a supervisory framework of provision is laid down in section 21. This section may be viewed as the mechanism which would ensure, if implemented, that parents are complying with this obligation since July 5 last. Section 21(a) provides:

> "The principal of a recognised school shall cause to be maintained in respect of each school year a record of the attendance or non-attendance on each school day of each student registered at that school."

Each record thus maintained is required to specify, the fact of a student's attendance at school or, where a student fails to attend, the fact of such failure to attend and the reasons for such failure. Section 21 records are required to be maintained at the relevant school and are to be in such form as the NEWB specifies. Section 21(4) requires the Principal of a recognised school to inform, by notice in writing, an EWO in the following circumstances:

- where a student is suspended from a recognised school for 6 days or more;
- where the aggregate number of school days annually on which the student is absent is 20 or more;
- where the student's name is removed from the section 20 register by the Principal; or
- where a student is, in the opinion of the Principal of the recognised school at which he or she is registered, not attending school regularly.

---

[95] *Ibid.*, s.25(6).
[96] *Ibid.*, s.21.
[97] *Ibid.*, s.19 – to admit in accordance with its admission policy required by s.15(2)(d) of the 1998 Act.
[98] *Ibid.*, s.20.
[99] *Ibid.*, s.24.

On receipt of the section 21(4) notice, an EWO is required to;

(a) consult with the student concerned, his or her parents, the principal and such other persons as he or she considers appropriate, and

(b) make all reasonable efforts to ensure that provision is made for the continued education of the child and his or her full participation in school (section 21(5).

If there is no dedicated EWO for the area, Principals would be well advised to send their written notification to the NEWB. If section 21 is not implemented, then the system breaks down and the reasonable efforts at consultation with the parents and the Principal, provided for in the Act, do not take place. Even persistent failure on the part of parents to cause their child/children to attend school, in accordance with the Act, may go unpunished. No prosecutions of parents, for failing to cause their children to attend school in accordance with the Act, are taken. Furthermore, children at serious risk, (those whose parents would normally be convicted, or whose parents had established to the satisfaction of the Court, that they had made all reasonable efforts to cause their child to attend school), would be denied their right to be referred onward to the Health Services Executive[100] which can then exercise its statutory functions[101] in respect of these children's care, education and welfare.

Obligations to young persons in employment

The NEWB is obliged to establish and maintain a register ("the register") of young persons in employment.[102] Any "young person"[103] may apply to the Board to be registered in "the register". This group of persons will normally comprise 16-18 year-olds who have left school early having completed three years post-primary education, to commence employment. Sections 28, 29 and 30 are intended to address this situation and these sections, if fully implemented, would provide a mechanism to identify these young persons and, should they so wish, ensure the support and advice of the NEWB in

---

[100] S. 25(8).
[101] Under the Child Care Act 1991, under ss.26 and 27 of the 2000 Act and under the Education for Persons with Special Educational Needs Act 2004, s.39 (when commenced) and s.40 which amends s.7 of the Education Act 1998.
[102] See s.29(2)
[103] The term "young person" is defined as "a person (other than a child) who is of an age prescribed by the Minister but shall not include a person who has reached the age of 18 years.

regard to their future training/education. While section 29(2) indicates that the young person takes the initiative in making application to the NEWB to be registered, the Board have an important function is ensuring that students, their parents and employers are made aware of these provisions. Furthermore, any "child", who will, at the end of the school year, cease to be "a child" as defined in the Act may, during that school year, apply to the NEWB to be registered[104] with the NEWB. Once an application is made by the student to be registered, the NEWB is required to prepare a plan in order to assist these young persons to avail of education and/or training opportunities.[105] It is important that these significant provisions are publicised so that students can access their statutory entitlements and that they are fully implemented. Schools could also assist greatly by drawing these entitlements to the attention of relevant students and their parents.

Employers too have a significant role to play as they are required to employ only "young persons" who have a certificate to show that they are registered with the NEWB.[106] Employers are also required to inform the NEWB when they employ a "young person." There seems to be scant public awareness of these important statutory provisions which need urgently to be publicised and implemented in practice.

Clearly the NEWB is committed to building a national service to meet its obligations under the 2000 Act. If the Board is inadequately staffed, as it appears to be, will the courts vindicate the rights of individual children or groups of children whose minimum education entitlements have not been met?

THE SEPARATION OF POWERS DOCTRINE

The constitutional doctrine of the separation of powers,[107] guarantees to the main organs of the State specific powers and independence. The sole and exclusive power of making laws for the State is vested in the Oireachtas[108] while the executive power of the State is to be exercised by or on the authority of the Government[109] and the judicial powers are to be exercised by the Courts. While no one organ of State has paramountcy over another, it has

---

[104] S.29(3).
[105] S.29(5).
[106] S.29(9).
[107] See Article 15: see further M. de Blacam, "Children, Constitutional Rights and the Separation of Powers", *Irish Jurist* (2002), vol.37, p.113.
[108] Art. 15.2.1 of the Constitution
[109] *Ibid.*, Article 28.

been judicially acknowledged, that the separation of powers as enshrined in the Constitution is not a rigid separation of powers but a partial or functional separation[110] which can be departed from in rare and exceptional circumstances and that the Courts have the jurisdiction to do all things necessary to vindicate the personal rights of the citizen. In other words, the doctrine of the separation of powers must necessarily be balanced with the role and function conferred on the courts to guard constitutional rights and so it must be construed harmoniously. As Ó Dálaigh C.J. stated in *State (Quinn) v. Ryan*:

> "It was not the intention of the Constitution in guaranteeing the fundamental rights of the citizen that these rights should be set at nought or circumvented. The intention was that rights of substance were being assured to the individual and that the Courts were the custodians of these rights. As a necessary corollary, it follows that no one can with impunity set these rights at nought or circumvent them, and the Court's powers in this regard are as ample as the defence of the Constitution requires."[111]

It is well settled law that the courts are entitled to intervene if there has been a clear disregard by the Government of its rights and duties conferred on it by the Constitution[112] or to prevent the threatened or impending infringement of the guarantees given in the Constitution.[113]

In *Byrne v. Ireland* Walsh J. stated:

> "Where the People by the Constitution create rights against the State or impose duties upon the State, a remedy to enforce these must be deemed to be also available."[114]

Yet, recent case law demonstrates a marked reluctance by the Supreme Court

---

[110] See dictum of Kenny J. in *Abbey Films v. Attorney General* [1981] I.R. 158 at 171; see also judgement of Denham J. dissenting in *T.D. v. Minister for Education* [2001] I.R. 288 and 306.
[111] [1965] I.R. 70 at 122.
[112] *Boland v. an Taoiseach* [1974] I.R. 338 at 361–362 per Fitzgerald C.J.: *Crotty v. an Taoiseach* [1987] I.R. 713 at 775 per Finlay C.J.: *State (Quinn) v. Ryan* [1965] I.R. 70: *Murphy v. Dublin Corporation* [1972] I.R. 215.
[113] *East Donegal Co-Operative Livestock Mart Ltd v. Attorney General* [1970] I.R. 317 at 338 per Walsh J.
[114] [1972] I.R. 241 at 281.

to grant mandatory orders against the State.[115] When *Sinnott v. Minister for Education and Others*[116] came before the Supreme Court on appeal, Keane C.J. made it clear, that because of the separation of powers doctrine, the court would not make a mandatory order requiring the Oireachtas to provide funds for a particular purpose[117] in order to uphold the constitutional or purely legal rights of members of the public.[118] That is not to say, he continued, that where a plaintiff successfully claims that his constitutional rights have been violated by the State in the past and will continue to be so violated in the future unless the Court intervenes, the courts are impotent when it comes to the protection of those rights. Hardiman J. went on to clarify what he considered the constitutional position to be:

> "It seems to me that the constitutional requirements for the conduct of public business, and in particular the expenditure of public monies, as exemplified in this Article ... emphasise that the duty imposed by Article 42 must be discharged in a manner approved by the legislature on the recommendation of the executive. It is true that neither of these organs of government is in a position to disregard a constitutional duty and that the courts have powers and duties in the unlikely event of such disregard. But, excepting that extreme situation, the duty imposed by Article 42 is a duty to be discharged in the manner endorsed by the legislature and executive who must necessarily have a wide measure of discretion having regard to available resources and having regard to policy considerations of which they must be the judges."

Applying the above *dictum* to the school attendance/minimum education debate, the duty imposed by Article 42 on the State has been discharged in a manner approved by the legislature on the recommendation of the executive, so neither of these organs of government is in a position to disregard a constitutional duty and the courts have powers and duties in the event of such disregard. As the Supreme Court held in the *Best* case, if the State could not intervene, then the rights of certain children would be seriously violated. Furthermore, if this latter approach were to be adopted by the

---

[115] *O'Reilly v. Limerick Corporation* [1989] I.L.R.M. 181: *T.D. v. Minister for Education* [2001] I.R. 259: *Sinnott v. Minister for Education and Ors* [2001] 2 I.R. 545 at 598 (HC): 598–727 (SC).
[116] *Ibid.*, p.631.
[117] A mandatory order against the Minister directing him to provide for free education for the first named plaintiff appropriate to his needs for as long as he was capable of benefiting from same and damages.
[118] See *Brady v Cavan County Council* [1999] 4 I.R. 99.

Supreme Court in school attendance related issues, then statutory powers would be downgraded to the status of discretionary powers which could scarcely be in the interests of democracy.

The issue before the Supreme Court in *T.D. v. Minister for Education*[119] was whether the High Court had jurisdiction to make the form of order which it did, which was mandatory and addressing a number of persons' rights to secure detention in special units, rather than an individual's rights. Hardiman J. relied upon the distinction between two theories of justice, distributive justice and commutative justice,[120] advanced by Costello J., as he was then, in *O'Reilly v. Limerick Corporation*:

> "An obligation in distributive justice is placed on those administering the common stock of goods, the common resource and the wealth held in common which has been raised by taxation, to distribute them and the common wealth fairly and to determine what is due to each individual. But that distribution can only be made by reference to the common good and by those furthering the common good (the Government); it cannot be made by any individual who may claim a share in the common stock and no independent arbitrator, such as a court, can adjudicate on a claim by an individual that he has been deprived of what is his due. This situation is very different is a case of commutative justice. What is due to an individual from another individual (including a public authority) from a relationship arising from their mutual dealings can be ascertained and is due to him exclusively and the precepts of commutative justice will enable an arbitrator such as a court to decide what is properly due should the matter be disputed. This distinction explains why the court has jurisdiction to award damages against the State when a servant of the State for whose activity it is vicariously liable commits a wrong and why it may not get jurisdiction in cases where the claim is for damages based on a failure to distribute adequately in the plaintiff's favour a portion of the community's wealth."[121]

In her dissenting judgement[122] Denham J. considered, *inter alia*, the balance

---

[119] *T.D. v. Minister for Education* [2000] 3 I.R. 62 (HC); [2001] 4 I.R. 259 at 260 (SC).
[120] De Blacam, *op. cit.*, traces this concept, which is linked to a theory of justice, expounded by Aristotle in his *Nicomachean Ethics* and restated by St. Thomas Acquinas in his *Summa Theologiae*.
[121] [1898] I.L.R.M.181 at 194.
[122] This was a 4:1 decision.

to be determined between constitutional rights, obligations and principles, judicial adjudication and judicial discretion, the protection of fundamental rights in a modern democracy and the concept of the common good. She referred to the concept of the common good in the Preamble, to its particular relevance in Article 42.5, to the State's role as its guardian, and to the obligations falling on all three of the great institutions of the State to promote the common good in accordance with the Constitution. With reference to the separation of powers doctrine, Denham J. stated that the circumstances of the *T.D.* case were exceptional because of the on-going nature of the review of the situation by the High Court. She concluded that there are circumstances in which a court has a duty to intervene to protect constitutional rights and to make mandatory orders and that this was a proportionate response by the court to vindicate the applicants' constitutional rights in the interests of the common good.[123] Accordingly, Denham J. stated that she would not interfere with the exercise of discretion by Kelly J. in the High Court.

Turning to school attendance issues, if the Supreme Court decided that a balance needed to be struck between the delivery of a minimum education, the common good, equality and the protection of fundamental rights in a modern society on the one hand, and respecting the separation of powers doctrine on the other, this could conceivably permit mandatory orders to be granted in certain limited circumstances, for example where statutory and constitutional rights have not been discharged by the State to individuals.

Mandatory orders have been granted in two educational cases. In *Nagle v. South Western Health Board and the Minister for Education*[124] Herbert J. granted a mandatory injunction against the second named defendant, the Minister for Education and Science,[125] requiring that defendant to forthwith provide for appropriate free primary education and support services for the plaintiff who suffered from autism. It is notable that the *Nagle* decision was made after the commencement of the Education Act 1998. In *Cronin v. Minister for Education*[126] Laffoy J. also made a mandatory order against the Minister, at the interlocutory stage, directing the Minister to provide an appropriate programme for the plaintiff who was a four year-old boy who had been diagnosed as suffering from attention deficit hyperactivity and autism. But the Supreme Court has made it clear that it will not generally make mandatory orders against the Executive directing it how to distribute its public funds generally.

---

[123] *T.D. v. Minister for Education* [2001] 4 I.R. 259 at 315 (SC).
[124] Unreported, High Court, Herbert J., October 30, 2001.
[125] At the interlocutory stage.
[126] [2004] 3 I.R. 205 (HC).

What is the position in England where there is no written Constitution to safeguard educational rights? In *Regina v. East Sussex C.C. ex p. Tandy*[127] (House of Lords), a local authority contended that it lacked the resources to continue to maintain home tuition for a school girl, suffering from myalgic encephalomyelitis. The child was entitled to home tuition, under the Education Act 1993, section 298(1) and had been allocated five hours of home tuition per week. In 1996, because of a reduction in government funding, the local authority was faced with the need to reduce its spending and made a policy decision that the girl's tuition would be reduced to three hours. The girl's mother sought judicial review to quash that decision on the ground that the authority had taken into account an irrelevant consideration, *i.e.* the availability of resources. The House of Lords held that a local authority was not permitted to avoid performing a statutory duty on the ground that it preferred to use its available resources for other purposes and since Parliament had imposed on them a statutory duty, as opposed to a statutory power, to provide suitable education, the scarcity of resources was not a legitimate reason for the failure to perform that duty. Lord Browne-Wilkinson stated:

> "My Lords, I believe your lordships should resist this approach to statutory duties. First, the county council has as a matter of strict legality the resources necessary to perform its statutory duty under section 298. Very understandably it does not wish to bleed its other functions of resources so as to enable it to perform the statutory duty under section 298. But it can, if it wishes, divert money from other educational or other applications which are merely discretionary, so as to apply such diverted monies to discharge the statutory duty laid down by section 298 The argument is not one of insufficient resources to discharge the duty but a preference for other purposes. To permit a local authority to avoid performing a statutory duty on the grounds that it prefers to spend the money in other ways is to downgrade a statutory duty to a discretionary power."

In contemporary Ireland, which is still experiencing economic prosperity, the argument is certainly not one of insufficient resources to discharge the statutory duties in the 2000 Act but a preference for other purposes. If the Supreme Court determines that the funding of the NEWB is primarily a matter for the Executive, it is then incumbent on the People,[128] to press for

---

[127] [1998] A.C. 714 at 749.
[128] Art.6(1).

the full implementation of the 2000 Act. As a first step the Act could be amended to make the provision of public funds for the NEWB a mandatory duty falling on the two relevant Ministers.[129] If the statutory entitlements to a minimum education are not fully discharged both to children and young persons, parents will continue to vindicate their children's rights through litigation at considerable cost to the State and early school leavers will be at greater risk of unemployment, drugs, anti-social behaviour and crime. The ultimate cost to society will far outstrip pro-active investment in the delivery of minimum education to these children in the shorter term. The right to a minimum education, where the State has undertaken to provide it in its constitutional capacity as "guardian of the common good" is a singularly onerous duty which requires to be discharged to all children on equal terms and the Supreme Court has indicated the limitations to this obligation. The statutory framework for the delivery of these services to all children in the State has been in place for three and a half years but it awaits full implementation. Children's lives do not wait, however.

It is quite remarkable that a country which does not have a written Constitution can afford a greater measure of protection for its childrens' educational rights than Ireland which has an express Constitutional right to education.

---

[129] Art.32.

IMPLICATIONS FOR SCHOOLS OF IRISH EQUALITY LEGISLATION

Gerry Whyte*

INTRODUCTION

Prior to 1996, the only provisions in Irish law dealing with the concepts of equality and discrimination were Articles 40.1, 44.2 and 40.6.2 of the Constitution, the Anti-Discrimination (Pay) Act 1974, the Employment Equality Act 1977, the Social Welfare (No.2) Act 1985 and the Pensions Act 1990. Article 40.1 provides that:

"All citizens shall, as human persons, be held equal before the law.
    This shall not be held to mean that the State shall not in its enactments have due regard to differences of capacity, physical and moral, and of social function.

This constitutional provision has had relatively little impact on discriminatory practices in Ireland because for most of its history it was effectively sidelined by the judiciary. While there is evidence that the judicial attitude to Article 40.1 may be changing, it remains the case that the constitutional guarantee of equality is primarily applicable to action by the State and it is not yet clear whether it has any relevance to the actions of private individuals.
    Article 44.2 provides, among other things, that the State cannot discriminate on grounds of religious profession, belief or status, while Article 40.6.2 provides that laws regulating freedom of association and free assembly shall not contain any political, religious or class discrimination. These provisions are clearly addressed to the State and are not applicable to the actions of private bodies.

---

*Gerry Whyte is an Associate Professor at the Law School, Trinity College Dublin.

Implications for Schools of Irish Equality Legislation 119

All of the legislation in this area was enacted because of our obligations under EC law to prohibit gender discrimination in relation to employment, social welfare and occupational pensions. The prohibited grounds of discrimination were gender and marital status and (additionally in the case of pensions) family status.

Consequently outside of the context of employment, social welfare and occupational pensions, there was no statutory protection against discrimination of any sort. Moreover, even within the areas of employment, social welfare and occupational pensions, there was no statutory protection against discrimination on such grounds as disability, race or sexual orientation.

In 1996 and 1997, two Bills were introduced to remedy this situation. These were the Employment Equality Bill 1996 and the Equal Status Bill 1997. The former attempted to tackle discrimination on nine different substantive grounds in the context of employment. The nine substantive grounds were sex, marital status, family status, sexual orientation, religion, age, disability, race or membership of the Traveller community. The Equal Status Bill 1997 addressed the same grounds of discrimination in the context of the provision of goods, services and accommodation and the operation of educational establishments, clubs and partnerships. Neither Bill passed into law as both were declared to be repugnant to the Constitution by the Supreme Court.[1]

The Oireachtas subsequently returned to the fray, so to speak, enacting the Employment Equality Act 1998, which came into force in October 1999, and the Equal Status Act 2000, which came into force in October 2000.

Attention should also be drawn, in this context, to four European Directives, Council Directive 97/80/EC on the burden of proof in gender discrimination cases, Council Directive 2000/43/EC implementing the principle of equal treatment between persons irrespective of racial or ethnic origin in relation to, *inter alia*, education, Council Directive 2000/78/EC establishing a general framework for equal treatment in employment and occupation and Council Directive 2004/113 on equal treatment between men and women in the access to and supply of goods and services. The first three of these Directives have been implemented in Irish law by the Equality Act 2004.

---

[1] See *Art.26 and the Employment Equality Bill 1996* [1997] 2 I.R. 321 and *Art.26 and the Equal Status Bill 1996* [1997] 2 I.R. 387.

Equal Status Acts 2000–2004

I propose to consider the provisions of the Equal Status Acts 2000–2004 under the following headings:

(a) Grounds of discrimination.

(b) Contexts in which the Acts apply.

(c) Meaning of discrimination for the purposes of the Acts.

(d) Meaning of harassment for the purposes of the Acts.

(e) Consideration of section 7 of the Act.

(f) Enforcement procedures and remedies.

Grounds of discrimination

The Equal Status Acts prohibit, subject to certain qualifications, discrimination on ten different grounds in four different contexts. The prohibited grounds of discrimination are (sections 2 and 3):

- gender,
- marital status,
- family status, (*i.e.* being pregnant or having responsibility as a parent or person in *loco parentis* for a person under the age of 18 or as a parent or primary carer for a person over that age with a disability who requires care or support on a continuing, regular or frequent basis)
- sexual orientation,
- religion, (which includes absence of religious belief),
- age, (though this does not apply to persons under the age of 18 – section 3(3)),
- disability,
- race, (including colour, nationality, national or ethnic origins),
- membership of the Travelling Community (where Traveller Community is now defined for the purpose of these Acts as "the community of people who are commonly called Travellers and who are identified (both by themselves and others) as people with a shared history, culture and traditions, including, historically, a nomadic way of life on the island of Ireland"), or

- victimisation (where one has taken or is otherwise involved in proceedings taken under the legislation).

Context in which Acts are to apply

The Acts deal with discrimination outside the employment relationship and apply in four different contexts, namely:

- the disposal of goods and the provision of services (section 5);
- the disposal of premises and provision of accommodation (section 6);
- education (section 7); and
- clubs (sections 8–10).

Meaning of discrimination for the purposes of the Acts

According to section 3 of the 2000 Act, as amended, discrimination on most of the grounds identified in the Act can arise in any of three different ways.

First, it can occur where, on any of the discriminatory grounds listed in the Act, including a situation in which a ground is incorrectly believed to be applicable, a person is treated less favourably than another person.

Second, it can occur when a person who is associated with another person is treated, by virtue of that association, less favourably than another person and where similar treatment of the other person, with whom the first person is associated, would constitute discrimination under the Act.

Third, it can arise where a person who is able to invoke one of the nine substantive grounds of discrimination targeted by the Act is put at a particular disadvantage by an apparently neutral provision compared with other persons unless the provision is objectively justified by a legitimate aim and the means of achieving the aim are appropriate and necessary - section 3 as amended by section 48 of the Equality Act 2004.

Specifically in relation to disability, the Act additionally provides that discrimination includes a failure to do all that is reasonable to accommodate the needs of a person with a disability by providing special treatment or facilities if, without such treatment or facilities, it would be impossible or unduly difficult for the person to avail himself/herself of the service, accommodation, etc. – section 4. However, section 4(2) absolves the service provider from this obligation where the cost of providing such special treatment is more than nominal.[2] Section 4(3) provides a further limit to the

---

[2] For an example of where the provision of reasonable accommodation to a visually

obligation by providing that a failure to provide such special treatment or facilities for a person with a disability shall not constitute discrimination if, by virtue of another provision of the Act, a refusal to provide the service in question to that person would not constitute discrimination. Subsection 4 further provides that where a person has a disability that could cause harm to that person or to others, treating the person differently to the extent necessary to prevent such harm shall not constitute discrimination. In *Clare v. Minister for Education and Science*,[3] Smyth J. held that the making of special educational provision for a pupil with ADHD did not constitute discrimination, having regard to section 4(4). Section 4(5) provides that this section is without prejudice to the provisions of sections 7(2)(a), 9(a) and 15(2)(g) of the Education Act 1998 in so far as they relate to the functions of the Minister of Education and Science, recognised schools and boards of management in regard to students with a disability.

Section 4 is significantly different from its predecessor in the Equal Status Bill 1997. Under that Bill, the onus was on persons providing services, accommodation, etc. to do what was reasonably necessary to allow a person with a disability to avail of the service, accommodation, etc., unless what was reasonably necessary would give rise to undue difficulty. Section 4 of the former Bill also indicated the factors that were to be taken into account in determining whether "undue difficulty" existed in any particular case. Under the 2000 Act, however, the burden of proof has shifted in cases in which the alleged discrimination consists of failure to act to facilitate persons with disabilities. In such cases, the person with the disability must show that without the provision of special treatment or facilities in relation to the disposal of goods, the provision of a service or accommodation, the operation of an educational establishment or the operation of a club, it would be impossible or unduly difficult for that person to avail himself/herself of the service, accommodation, etc. Moreover, no definition of "undue difficulty" appears in the 2000 Act. However the principal change in that Act is that there is no obligation on a service provider to take action if that results in more than nominal costs. While it is the case that the Supreme Court held comparable provisions in the Employment Equality Bill 1996 to be unconstitutional because they imposed an unjust financial burden on the service providers, this constitutional objection could have been met by requiring the State to compensate the service providers for any significant cost incurred rather than, as here, simply diluting the obligation itself.

---

impaired student exceeded nominal cost, see *Kwiotek v. NUI Galway*, DEC-S2004–176.
[3] Unreported, High Court, July 30, 2004.

Before leaving this discussion of disability discrimination, it is worth noting that the *Education for Persons with Special Needs Act 2004* makes detailed provision for the education of children with special educational needs arising from disability. Some provisions of this Act have been brought into effect by Statutory Instrument Nos. 508 and 509 of 2005.

Meaning of harassment for the purposes of the Acts

In addition to tackling discrimination on any of the grounds prescribed in sections 2 and 3 of the 2000 Act, the Equal Status Acts also prohibit, in section 11(1)(c), sexual harassment or harassment on any of the discriminatory grounds, by a person in a position of authority, of a student or a person who has applied for admission to, or seeks to avail of services provided by, an educational establishment. Section 11(2) further provides, *inter alia*, that a person responsible for the operation of an educational establishment shall not permit another person who has a right to be present in, or to avail of any facilities, goods or services provided at, that place to suffer sexual or other harassment at that place. Where such harassment has taken place, the person in charge will have to show that s/he took such steps as were reasonably practicable to prevent it.

Section 11(5) (inserted by section 51 of the 2004 Act) defines "harassment" as:

> "any form of unwanted conduct related to any of the discriminatory grounds ... being conduct which ... has the purpose or effect of violating a person's dignity and creating an intimidating, hostile, degrading, humiliating or offensive environment for the person".

"Sexual harassment" is defined as:

> "any form of unwanted verbal, non-verbal or physical conduct of a sexual nature"

that has the same purpose or effect.

The Act further provides that "unwanted conduct" may consist of:

> "acts, requests, spoken words, gestures or the production, display or circulation of written words, pictures or other material."

Inasmuch as this definition covers conduct whose purpose is to violate a person's dignity and to create an intimidating, hostile, degrading, humiliating or offensive environment for the person, it may not be necessary for a complainant to establish that a defendant actually achieved this purpose in order to win his or her case. In determining whether unwanted conduct had the effect of violating a person's dignity and creating an intimidating, hostile, degrading, humiliating or offensive environment for the person, it is probable that an objective test would have to be used, *i.e.* would a reasonable person, under the circumstances, consider that her or his dignity had been violated or that an intimidating, hostile, degrading, humiliating or offensive environment had been created?[4]

Consideration of section 7 of the Act

Educational establishments are covered, as far as their principal activity is concerned, by section 7 of the 2000 Act as amended. (In any secondary capacity as service providers, educational establishments are subject to section 5 of the Act. For this purpose, service does not include any activity referred to in section 7(2) so that that activity is regulated only by section 7. The full text of sections 5 and 7 are set out in the schedule hereto.)

The definition of "educational establishment" in section 7(1) ranges from pre-school services to third level institutions (including institutions providing adult, continuing or further education) and covers both wholly private institutions and those supported by public funds.

Section 7(2) prohibits discrimination in relation to admission of a student or the terms or conditions of admission to an educational establishment; access of a student to any course, facility or benefit provided by such an establishment; any other term or condition of participation by a student in such an establishment; and the expulsion of a student, or imposition of any other sanction upon, a student.

The Acts do provide for some derogations from the principle of equal treatment. Subsections (3) and (4) of section 7 specifically permit educational establishments to discriminate in certain situations. As far as primary and secondary schools are concerned, subsection (3) protects:

---

[4] S.11 originally defined "harassment" as an act, request or conduct that, *inter alia*, "*could reasonably be regarded* as offensive, humiliating or intimidating to [the victim]". The italicised words, which clearly import an objective test for determining whether behaviour is offensive, humiliating or intimidating, do not feature in the new definition and that might suggest that the amendment to s.11 was intended, *inter alia*, to replace this objective test with a subjective test focusing on the effect of the behaviour on the actual victim in the particular case. However it is submitted that the new wording of s.11 is not sufficiently clear and explicit to achieve this result.

(a) first and second level institutions who wish to admit students of one gender only;

(b) first and second level institutions whose objective is to provide education in an environment which promotes certain religious values and who operate an admissions policy discriminating on grounds of religion. Where a school refuses to admit a student on grounds of religion, it must be shown that the refusal is essential to maintain the ethos of the school.

Section 7(4) permits:

(a) differences in the treatment of students on the grounds of gender, age or disability in relation to the provision or organisation of sporting facilities or events, to the extent that these differences are reasonably necessary (though bear in mind that students under the age of 18 cannot complain of age discrimination); and

(b) differences in treatment on the grounds of disability where compliance with the Act would make impossible, or have a seriously detrimental effect on, the provision by an educational establishment of its services to other students.

The effect of this last provision is to create a presumption in favour of the mainstreaming of children with disability that can only be rebutted if the school can establish that mainstreaming would render impossible, or seriously affect, the provision of education to the other children in the class. In *Clare v. Minister for Education and Science*,[5] Smyth J. held that, in the light of section 7(4)(b), a school did not discriminate within the meaning of the Act when it expelled a student suffering from ADHD whose behaviour interfered with the right of his fellow students to learn in an atmosphere conducive to learning.

In addition to these specific derogations from the principle of equal treatment in the context of education, regard should also be had to the more general terms of section 14 (b) which permit preferential treatment or the taking of positive measures *bona fide* intended to (a) promote equality of opportunity for persons who are, in relation to other persons, disadvantaged or who have been or are likely to be unable to avail themselves of the same opportunities as those other persons, or (b) cater for the special needs of persons who, because of their circumstances, may require facilities,

---

[5] Unreported, High Court, July 30, 2004.

arrangements, services or assistance not required by persons who do not have those special needs.

Enforcement procedures and remedies

The Acts are enforced, in the first instance, by the Director of the Equality Tribunal responding to:

(a) complaints taken by individuals; or

(b) a reference made by the Equality Authority.

Section 21(1) provides that a person who claims to have suffered discrimination may refer the case to the Director of the Equality Tribunal. The complainant must notify the respondent in writing of the nature of the allegation and indicate his/her intention, if not satisfied with the respondent's response, to refer the case to the Director within two months of the occurrence of the conduct and, in that notification, may put material questions to the respondent to which the latter may reply, is s/he so wishes. (Section 54 of the 2004 Act empowers the Director to extend this time-limit to four months wherever there is reasonable cause for such extension or, exceptionally, where it is fair and reasonable to do so, to direct that the aforementioned time limit and procedural requirements shall not apply to a particular complainant to the extent specified in the direction). The claim itself must be taken within six months of the date of the prohibited conduct (or the date of its most recent occurrence), though the Director may, for reasonable cause, extend the time-limit to twelve months. Section 21 as amended also provides that where a delay in complaining is due to any misrepresentation by the respondent, time will begin to run again from the date on which the misrepresentation came to the complainant's notice.

By virtue of section 23, the Equality Authority may refer a case to the Director where, *inter alia*, it appears that prohibited conduct is generally directed against persons, or is directed against someone and that person has not made a claim and it would not be reasonable for him to do so. If the Director finds that discrimination has occurred and if there is a likelihood of a further occurrence of this conduct, the Authority may apply to the Circuit or High Court for an injunction to prevent any such further occurrence – section 23(3).

The Director may refer any case received by her to an equality officer for mediation or, alternatively, she may investigate the complaint – sections 24 and 25. If either party objects to mediation, the Director is confined to investigating the complaint – section 24(2). If the equality officer believes that mediation will not work, the complainant can require an investigation by applying to the Director within 28 days of the officer's decision – sections 25(5) and (6).

The Director's investigation will be heard in private, though her decisions will be published, and she shall hear all persons who appear to be interested and who wish to be heard. Parties to such an investigation (or to mediation proceedings) may be represented by any individual or body that they wish. Section 64 of the Equality Act 2004 shifts the burden of proof to the respondent where facts are established by or on behalf of the complainant from which it may be presumed that prohibited conduct has occurred in relation to him or her. On conclusion of an investigation, the Director may order compensation of up to the maximum amount that could be awarded by the District Court in civil cases or direct a person to take a specified course of action – section 27.

An appeal may be taken against a decision of the Director to the Circuit Court within 42 days of the date of that decision – section 28. In addition, if a person fails to comply with a Director's decision or a mediated settlement, an application can be made to the Circuit Court for an order directing him/her to comply – section 31.

Caselaw

In 2003, the Equality Authority dealt with 78 legal case files under the Equal Status Act, 2000 relating to educational establishments.[6] These case files comprised 10% of the total Equality Authority's case files worked on during that year and they included issues of access by Travellers and students with disabilities to schools and to certain subjects, school uniform, access to non-denominational schooling, access by members of one religion to schools of another religious ethos, dress code on the gender ground, and harassment on the sexual orientation ground. Complaints against educational establishments were the second largest category after complaints against licensed premises. Many of the cases relating to educational establishments were settled.

In *A Parent v. A Primary School*,[7] the parent of a nine-year old girl was asked to remove her daughter from the school. The parent alleged, unsuccessfully, that the only reason for the school's request was that she had recently been divorced and so she complained of marital status

---

[6] A. Lodge and K. Lynch (eds.), *Diversity at School* (The Equality Authority, 2004, Foreword by Niall Crowley, CEO).
[7] DEC–S2003–135.

discrimination. However the Equality Officer held that the school acted as it did because of ongoing conflict between the mother and school management over the education of the child and that the mother's marital status formed no part of the reason for the school's decision. In DEC–S2004–028 an Equality Officer similarly held that the complainants had failed to establish a *prima facie* case of discrimination on the Traveller Community ground in relation to disciplinary action taken by a school against their son.

In Recommendation No. DEC–S2003–042/043, complaints made concerning nationality discrimination in relation to the Department of Education and Science's Post Leaving Certificate Maintenance Grant Scheme were dismissed because the applications were made before the Act came into force. The applicants did not hold EU nationality or have official refugee status.[8] However, the Equality Officer did suggest, in the interests of preventing future unlawful discrimination, that the Department annul the relevant clause completely. In what appears to be a response to this decision, section 50 of the Equality Act 2004 amended section 7 of the 2000 Act to permit the Minister to restrict grants in respect of third level education, including adult and continuing education, to persons who are nationals of a member state of the EU. In DEC–S2004–086, a local authority was held to have discriminated on grounds of marital status when it double checked signed declaration grant application forms made by single or separated parents but not those made by non-separated parents.

A recent UK case dealing with the wearing of Islamic dress by female students is worth noting, given its reliance on the European Convention on Human Rights which is now also applicable in Ireland. In *R. (S.B.) v. Denbeigh High School*,[9] a Muslim student was excluded from school because she would not comply with the school's uniform requirement. Holding that the school had not had proper regard to the student's rights under the Convention, the Court of Appeal said:

> "The decision-making structure should therefore go along the following lines:
>
> (1) Has the claimant established that she has a relevant Convention right which qualifies for protection under Article 9(1)?

---

[8] In DEC–S2004–162, an Equality Officer held that the imposition of a three-year residency requirement into Trinity College's definition of EU national for the purpose of determining fees constituted indirect discrimination against applicants holding official refugee status.

[9] [2005] 1 F.C.R. 530, March 2005.

(2) Subject to any justification that is established under Article 9(2), has that Convention right been violated?
(3) Was the interference with her Convention right prescribed by law in the Convention sense of that expression?
(4) Did the interference have a legitimate arm?
(5) What are the considerations that need to be balanced against each other when determining whether the interference was necessary in a democratic society for the purpose of achieving that aim?
(6) Was the interference justified under Article 9(2)?

The School did not approach the matter in this way at all. Nobody who considered the issues on its behalf started from the premise that the claimant had a right which is recognised by English law, and that the onus lay on the School to justify its interference with that right. Instead, it started from the premise that its uniform policy was there to be obeyed: if the claimant did not like it, she could go to a different school."

However, contrary to some media reports at the time, this did not necessarily mean that the student was entitled to insist on wearing her chosen form of garment for the Court later went on to say:

"Nothing in this judgment should be taken as meaning that it would be impossible for the School to justify its stance if it were to reconsider its uniform policy in the light of this judgment and were to determine not to alter it in any significant respect. Matters which it (and other schools facing a similar question) would no doubt need to consider include these:

(i) Whether the members of any further religious groups (other than very strict Muslims) might wish to be free to manifest their religion or beliefs by wearing clothing not currently permitted by the school's uniform policy, and the effect that a larger variety of different clothes being worn by students for religious reasons would have on the School's policy of inclusiveness;

(ii) Whether it is appropriate to override the beliefs of very strict Muslims given that liberal Muslims have been permitted the dress code of their choice and the School's uniform policy is not entirely secular;

(iii) Whether it is appropriate to take into account any, and if so which, of the concerns expressed by the School's three witnesses as good reasons for depriving a student like the claimant of her right to manifest her beliefs by the clothing she wears at school, and the weight which should be accorded to each of these concerns;

(iv) Whether there is any way in which the School can do more to reconcile its wish to retain something resembling its current uniform policy with the beliefs of those like the claimant who consider that it exposes more of their bodies than they are permitted by their beliefs to show."

EMPLOYMENT EQUALITY ACTS 1998–2004

I propose to consider the Employment Equality Acts 1998–2004 under the following headings:

(a) Grounds of discrimination.

(b) Contexts in which Act applies.

(c) Meaning of discrimination for the purposes of the Acts.

(d) Meaning of harassment for the purposes of the Acts.

(e) Enforcement procedures and remedies.

Grounds of discrimination

The Employment Equality Acts prohibit, subject to certain qualifications, discrimination by specified bodies on ten different grounds in relation to different aspects of work. The prohibited grounds of discrimination are (section 6):

- gender,
- marital status,
- family status, (*i.e.* being pregnant or having responsibility as a parent or person in *loco parentis* for a person under the age of 18 or as a parent or primary carer for a person over that age with a disability who requires care or support on a continuing, regular or frequent basis)
- sexual orientation,
- religion, (which includes absence of religious belief),

- age, (where complainant is aged between 18 and 65, though note that section 4 of the Equality Act 2004 replaces these age limits with specific provisions relating to school-leaving, recruitment ages and compulsory retirement ages),

- disability,

- race, (including colour, nationality, national or ethnic origins),

- membership of the Travelling Community, or

- victimisation (where one has taken or is otherwise involved in proceedings taken under the legislation).

Section 85A (inserted by section 38 of the Equality Act 2004) provides that, in establishing discrimination, the complainant must first establish primary facts from which it can be inferred that s/he has suffered discriminatory treatment. When such a *prima facie* case has been established, the onus then shifts to the employer to rebut the inference of discrimination.

Contexts in which Act applies

Employer and providers of agency work cannot discriminate, subject to qualifications permitted by the Act, in relation to access to employment, conditions of employment, training or experience for or in relation to employment, promotion or re-grading or classification of posts – section 8.

Employment agencies cannot discriminate, subject to qualifications permitted by the Act, against any person seeking the services of the agency to obtain employment with another person or seeking guidance as to a career or any other service (including training) related to the employment of that person – section 11.

Providers of vocational courses cannot discriminate against any person over the maximum age at which those persons are statutorily obliged to attend school in relation to the terms on which a course or related facility is offered, access to any such course or facility and the manner in which any such course or facility is provided – section 12. However, this prohibition on discrimination is also subject to certain qualifications such as permitting preferential treatment for EU citizens in relation to fees and allocation of places.

Trade unions, professional bodies or trade organisations cannot discriminate in relation to membership or the provision of benefits (other than pension rights) or in relation to entry to, or the carrying on of, a profession, vocation or occupation – section 13.

Meaning of discrimination for the purposes of the Acts

Section 6(1) provides that, for the purposes of this Act, discrimination occurs where, on any of the prohibited grounds of discrimination, one person is treated less favourably than another is, has been or would be treated. Discrimination may be direct or indirect. In this context, indirect discrimination refers to terms of a contract or employment practices which, on the face of it, are capable of being satisfied by members of different groups but which, in practice, place at a disadvantage a substantially higher proportion of members of one group than of others. Section 4 of the 2004 Act amends section 6 so as to align the definition of discrimination for the purposes of the 1998 Act with that in the Equal Status Acts 2000-2004 and to include, as discrimination, less favourable treatment on the grounds of pregnancy or maternity leave.

In the case of gender discrimination, section 19(4) as amended by section 12 of the Equality Act 2004 provides that, in relation to claims of equal pay, indirect discrimination occurs "where an apparently neutral provision puts persons of a particular gender ... at a particular disadvantage in respect of remuneration compared with other employees of their employer." The new provision goes on to provide that the employee suffering indirect discrimination shall be entitled to the higher rate of remuneration "unless the [apparently neutral] provision is objectively justified by a legitimate aim and the means of achieving the aim are appropriate and necessary."

In relation to gender discrimination and access to employment, conditions of employment, training or experience for or in relation to employment, promotion or re-grading, classification of posts or membership of a regulatory body, section 22(1) as amended by section 13 of the Equality Act 2004 effects a similar amendment to the definition of indirect discrimination in this context as that effected by section 12 in the context of equal pay.

In relation to grounds of discrimination other than gender, section 29(4) as amended by section 19 of the Equality Act 2004 provides, in relation to equal pay claims, a similar definition of indirect discrimination as that provided for by section 12 in the context of equal pay and gender discrimination.

In relation to other aspects of employment, section 31(1) as amended by section 20 of the Equality Act 2004 provides a similar definition of indirect discrimination in this context as that provided for by section 13 in the context of gender discrimination.

By virtue of section 16 as amended by section 9 of the 2004 Act, an employer is obliged to take effective and practical measures to adapt the workplace for persons with disabilities unless this would impose a disproportionate burden having regard to the circumstances of the employer.

Finally in this context, two provisions of the Act are of particular significance for our understanding of the concept of discrimination in the context of the employment of teachers. Section 36(3) authorises the application of provisions (whether in the nature of a requirement, practice or otherwise) in relation to proficiency in the Irish language with respect to teachers in primary and post-primary schools.

Section 37(1) of the Act provides that:

> "A religious, educational or medical institution which is under the direction or control of a body established for religious purposes or whose objectives include the provision of services in an environment which promotes certain religious values shall not be taken to discriminate against a person for the purposes of this Part or Part II if—
>
> (a) it gives more favourable treatment, on the religion ground, to an employee or a prospective employee over that person where it is reasonable to do so in order to maintain the religious ethos of the institution, or
>
> (b) it takes action which is reasonably necessary to prevent an employee or a prospective employee from undermining the religious ethos of the institution."

Note that this provision does not offer employers a defence against a claim of gender discrimination as section 37(1) does not apply in respect of Part III of the Act which deals with claims of that nature.

Much narrower protection for religious interests is provided for in Article 4(2) of EC Directive 2000/78/EC establishing a general framework for equal treatment in employment and occupation and which came into effect on 2 December 2003. It provides that:

> "Members States may maintain national legislation in force at the date of adoption of this Directive or provide for future legislation incorporating national practices existing at the date of adoption of this Directive pursuant to which, in the case of occupational activities within churches and other public or private organisations the ethos of which is based on religion or belief, a difference of treatment based on a person's religion or belief shall not constitute discrimination where, by reason of the nature of these activities or of the context in which they are carried out, a person's religion or belief constitute a genuine, legitimate and justified occupational requirement, having regard to the organisation's ethos. This difference of treatment shall be

implemented taking account of Member States' constitutional provisions and principles, as well as the general principles of Community law, and should not justify discrimination on another ground.

Provided that its provisions are otherwise complied with, this Directive shall thus not prejudice the right of churches and other public or private organisations, the ethos of which is based on religion or belief, acting in conformity with national constitutions and laws, to require individuals working for them to act in good faith and with loyalty to the organisation's ethos."

This would appear to be narrower than section 37 in two respects. First, one now has to show that, by virtue of the occupational activities of the employer or the context in which they are carried out, the employee's religion or belief constitutes a genuine, legitimate and justified occupational requirement, having regard to the employer's ethos. Thus Bolger argues that "it will be necessary to show that a person's religion is a determining factor in her actual ability to discharge the duties of her job, rather than simply showing the employer's perception that such religion or belief is fitting in light of the organisation's ethos."[10] Second, the religious discrimination will only be upheld provided that it does not also constitute discrimination on any one of the other prohibited grounds in addition to gender. Thus, the dismissal of an openly homosexual teacher could not be justified under this provision as the dismissal would constitute sexual orientation discrimination. Perhaps surprisingly, the 2004 Act does not appear to amend section 37(1) to reflect these differences.

Caselaw

A number of cases taken by teachers highlight different aspects of the Employment Equality Acts. For example, in *Nix v. Board of Management, Oola N.S.*,[11] an Equality Officer held that, in a competition for appointment as a principal, the requirement to have previous experience as a principal

---

[10] Marguerite Bolger, "Discrimination on the Grounds of Religion" in Costello and Barry (eds.), *The New Equality Directives* (ICEL, 2003) at p.384. Beaumont, however, disputes whether it is necessary to prove that religion is a "determining" factor in a person's ability to do a job – "Christian Perspective on the Law: What makes them distinctive" in O'Dair and Lenon, *Law and Religion* (Oxford, 2001), p.538. See also Whyte, "Protecting Religious Ethos in Employment Law: A Clash of Cultures" [2005] 27 D.U.L.J. 169.

[11] EE2/1999.

affected women more significantly than men and therefore could not be relied upon by an interview board as it was not an essential requirement for the position.

In *Crowley v. Co. Cork VEC*,[12] an unsuccessful candidate for the post of Assistant Principal was awarded IR£5,000 on grounds of unlawful discrimination. In making a finding of discrimination, the Equality Officer considered that the marking system used by the interview board for ranking candidates showed a gender bias. Criticism was also made of the lack of transparency in the selection process, the lack of interview notes[13] and the failure of the VEC to seek to achieve a more gender balanced interview board.

In *Riney v. Co. Donegal VEC*,[14] an Equality Officer held that the claimant's academic qualifications, which were superior to those of the successful candidate, were not reflected in the marks awarded by the selection panel. The Officer also criticised the panel's reliance on length of service as a 'tie-breaker' between these two candidates as this factor favoured male candidates who generally had longer service than female candidates. The Officer also recommended that the VEC make every effort, as far as is reasonably practicable, to ensure that selection boards reflect the gender mix of candidates.

In *Barry v. Board of Management (Aisling Project)*,[15] a claimant brought a successful action under the 1998 Act even though all of the applicants for the position were female. She had been asked at interview how she would cope with looking after her family and working full time outside the home. The Equality Officer was satisfied that a hypothetical male comparator would not have been asked the same question and so held that the interview board had discriminated against the claimant.

In *Lynskey v. Coolmine Community School*,[16] the Equality Officer concluded that both candidates for the position of Deputy Principal had reached the minimum academic standard, both had comparable further qualifications but the claimant, a man, had more extensive experience than

---

[12] Recommendation No. DEC–E/2000/10.
[13] In *Kenny v. Board of Management, Comprehensive School, Tallaght*, DEC–E2005/001, the Equality Officer disagreed with the suggestion that it is sufficient if the officer is supplied with the notes of only one member of the interview board. She also indicated that it was inappropriate for the principal to ring the candidates after the interviews to inform them of the outcome, stating that a standard letter would suffice. See also *Nic Fhlannchada v. Coláiste Mhuire*, DEC–E2004/058.
[14] Recommendation No. DEC–E2001/030.
[15] Recommendation No. DEC–E2001/031.
[16] Recommendation No. DEC–E2002/035.

the female appointee, both as a teacher and as the holder of a post of responsibility. She found that the Selection Committee had approached the interviews without any clear standards for the post being filled and without any specific, objective criteria against which to measure the candidates. She was also satisfied, *inter alia*, that the Committee had failed to give the claimant credit for certain qualities and experience he had and held that he had established a *prima facie* case of discrimination that the school failed to rebut.[17]

In *Bleach v. Our Lady Immaculate Senior School and the Department of Education and Science*,[18] the complainant claimed that the Board of Management and the Department of Education and Science discriminated against her on the gender ground in relation to the selection process for promotion to the post of Special Duties Teacher. She also claimed that by being ranked seventh in terms of Special Duties positions allocated, she was victimised in terms of section 74(2) of the Act for having appealed the results of previous competitions.

The Equality Officer confirmed that the employer of the complainant, a primary school teacher, is the Board of Management of the school. She considered that a serious question arose in relation to the authenticity of the documents and evidence presented, that the Board had failed to demonstrate transparency in the selection process and had not shown that the selection of candidates was based on objective non-discriminatory factors. She found that the employer discriminated against the complainant on the gender ground in the selection process for appointment to Special Duties teacher. The Equality Officer also found, on the balance of probability, that the complainant was singled out in relation to her treatment at the interview and that the employer failed to rebut the complainant's claim of victimisation in relation to her specific ranking in seventh position.

Accordingly, she ordered the Board to rank the complainant in the Special Duties No. 1 post with effect from May 4, 2000 and to arrange to pay her through the Department of Education the arrears of the allowance accruing. She also ordered the Board to draft an Equal Opportunities Policy and directed the Chairperson and the Principal to participate in a course on interviewing skills.

---

[17] In *Fosberry v. Roscommon VEC*, DEC–E2004/036, the Equality Officer held that the complainant's superior teaching and management teaching and management experience over that of the appointee raised an influence of gender discrimination, but that this was rebutted by evidence of the manner in which the interview process has been conducted.

[18] Decision No. DEC–E2003/028.

In *Glennon v. Board of Management, St Clare's Comprehensive School and the Minister for Education and Science*,[19] the Equality Officer noted that under the Education Act 1998 the role of the Minster in the appointment of teachers was confined to agreeing procedures, along with the patron, trade union and others. She was satisfied that the actual appointment was a function of the Board of Management and found that the Board was the correct respondent. On the facts, the Equality Officer held that the complainant had not established a *prima facie* case of discrimination.

In *Carroll v. Monaghan VEC*,[20] the Equality Officer recommended, in passing, that the employer take steps to ensure that the practice of destroying interview notes ceased immediately. In a subsequent case against the same employer, *Carroll v. Monaghan VEC*,[21] the complainant was able to raise an inference of unlawful discrimination on ground of age (she had been awarded fewer marks in the categories of experience of a professional nature in the field of education and capacity to meet the needs of the school than candidates with less teaching experience) and the fact that the interview board had failed to retain the notes of its members meant that the employer could not adduce any evidence to rebut this inference. The former practice of using date of birth for determining seniority among teachers is now contrary to the Employment Equality Act 1998 – *Dunbar v. Good Counsel College, New Ross*.[22]

In *Walsh v. Board of Management, Ballinrobe Community School*,[23] the Equality Officer held, *inter alia*, that where an unsuccessful female candidate in a competition demonstrates that she meets the advertised requirements for a position, has at least similar or superior qualifications and a considerably longer satisfactory service compared to a successful male candidate, a *prima facie* case of discrimination is established and the burden of proof shifts to the employer to show that there were reasons unrelated to gender for the outcome. He also noted that failure to retain notes as to how marks were awarded by the interview panel would make it extremely difficult for the employer to discharge this burden of proof. The Equality Officer further recommended that the Department of Education and Science should examine the extent and appropriateness of the apparent practice of interview boards to ask candidates if they were satisfied with their interviews.

In *Delaney v. Board of Management, Drumshanbo N.S.*,[24] the fact that

---

[19] Decision No. DEC–E2003/030.
[20] Decision No. DEC–E2003/060.
[21] Decision No. DEC–E2004/003.
[22] Decision No. DEC–E2003/051.
[23] Decision No. DEC–E2004/041.
[24] Decision No. DEC–E2004/067.

the claimant had been asked at interview whether she found it a problem to remain motivated as she had been teaching for so long was part of the evidence relied upon by the Equality Officer in concluding that a *prima facie* case of age discrimination had been established. The Equality Officer also indicated that a negative oral reference about the claimant should not have been given where the relevant issues had not been raised by the previous employer with the claimant and, moreover, that the Chairperson of the interview board should have requested that such a negative oral reference be reduced to writing.

In *O'Neill v. Board of Management, St. Gabriels' N.S*,[25] an Equality Officer held that the claimant had been discriminated against on ground of age when she was asked at interview, "Considering that you have been teaching for 27 years, why would you now be bothered with the hassle of the job of Deputy Principal?"

Infringing the Employment Equality Acts can prove expensive – in *McGinn v. Board of Management, St. Anthony's Boys N.S., Kilcoole*,[26] the Board of Management was ordered to pay the complainant 10,000 euro for infringing her right to equal treatment under the legislation, a further two years' salary for the victimisation she suffered as a result of bringing a claim under the legislation and interest on the above sums running from a date approximately three years before the date of the Equality Officer's ruling until payment was actually made.

Meaning of harassment for the purposes of the Acts

Harassment of employees on any of the prohibited grounds of discrimination is contrary to the Employment Equality Acts 1998-2004. Section 14A (inserted by section 8 of the Equality Act 2004), *inter alia*, defines "'harassment" as:

> "'any form of unwanted conduct related to any of the discriminatory grounds ... being conduct which ... has the purpose or effect of violating a person's dignity and creating an intimidating, hostile, degrading, humiliating or offensive environment for the person."

"Sexual harassment" is defined as

> "any form of unwanted verbal, non-verbal or physical conduct of a sexual nature,"

---

[25] Decision No. DEC–E2005/007.
[26] Decision No. DEC–E2004/032.

that has the same purpose or effect. This section further provides that "unwanted conduct" may consist of:

> "acts, requests, spoken words, gestures or the production, display or circulation of written words, pictures or other material."

Inasmuch as this definition covers conduct whose purpose is to violate a person's dignity and to create an intimidating, hostile, degrading, humiliating or offensive environment for the person, it may not be necessary for a complainant to establish that a defendant actually achieved this purpose in order to win his or her case. In determining whether unwanted conduct had the effect of violating a person's dignity and creating an intimidating, hostile, degrading, humiliating or offensive environment for the person, it is probable that an objective test would have to be used, *i.e.* would a reasonable person, under the circumstances, consider that her dignity had been violated or that an intimidating, hostile, degrading, humiliating or offensive environment had been created?

Employees are protected against harassment by an employer, a fellow employee or by a client, customer or other business contact of the employer where the circumstances of the harassment are such that the employer ought reasonably to have taken steps to prevent it – section 14A(1)(a).

In *Two Named Female Teachers v. A Boy's Secondary School*,[27] an Equality Officer held that a school could be held liable for the actions of pupils where they sexually harass teachers, though in that case the Equality Officer was satisfied that the school had taken all reasonable steps to deal with the problem of sexual harassment in the classroom and so held that the claim of discrimination in relation to sexual harassment was not made out. However the officer also held that the claimants had been penalised by the school for referring complaints to the Labour Court and awarded damages of IR£7,000 and IR£12,000 to the two complainants.

Enforcement procedures and remedies

Two different fora exist for dealing with claims under the 1998-2004 Acts. Most claims are lodged with the Director of the Equality Tribunal but where a dispute relates to discrimination on grounds of sex or is otherwise covered by the 1975 Equal Pay Directive or the 1976 Equal Treatment Directive, a claim may be initiated in the Circuit Court. Claims (other than claims for

---

[27] Recommendation No. DEC–E2001/05.

equal pay) must be lodged within six months of the date of occurrence of the discrimination or the date of its most recent occurrence, though this time limit may be extended to twelve months where there is reasonable cause. Where a delay in complaining is due to any misrepresentation by the employer, time will begin to run again from the date on which the misrepresentation came to the complainant's notice.

By virtue of sections 85 and 86, the Equality Authority may refer certain types of case to the Director. If the Director finds that discrimination has occurred and if there is a likelihood of a further occurrence of this conduct, the Authority may apply to the Circuit or High Court for an injunction to prevent any such further occurrence – section 85(4).

The Director may refer a case for mediation, provided neither party objects, or she (or more usually an Equality Officer acting on her behalf) may investigate and rule upon the claim. If the equality officer believes that mediation will not work, the complainant can require an investigation by applying to the Director within 28 days of the officer's decision – sections 78(6) and (7). Section 38 of the Equality Act 2004 shifts the burden of proof to the employer where facts are established by or on behalf of the complainant from which it may be presumed that prohibited conduct has occurred in relation to him or her.

The Director may award compensation or arrears of remuneration (subject, in both cases, to certain limits) or make an order for equal treatment or direct a party to take a specified course of action or order that the complainant be reinstated or re-engaged. The Circuit Court may also make any of the above orders and, in this case, the normal monetary limits that apply to Circuit Court awards do not apply to the amount of compensation or remuneration that may be awarded by the Court.

An appeal against the Director's decision lies to the Labour Court and an appeal against a Labour Court determination lies, on a point of law, to the High Court. A final decision of the Director or a final determination of the Labour Court is enforceable by the Circuit Court.

SCHEDULE

Section 7 of the Equal Status Act 2000 (as amended)

"(1) In this section "educational establishment" means a preschool service within the meaning of Part VII of the Child Care Act, 1991, a primary or post-primary school, an institution providing adult, continuing or further education, or a university or any other third-level or higher-level institution,

Implications for Schools of Irish Equality Legislation 141

whether or not supported by public funds.
(2) An educational establishment shall not discriminate in relation to—
   (a) the admission or the terms or conditions of admission of a person as a student to the establishment,
   (b) the access of a student to any course, facility or benefit provided by the establishment,
   (c) any other term or condition of participation in the establishment by a student, or
   (d) the expulsion of a student from the establishment or any other sanction against the student.
(3) An educational establishment does not discriminate under subsection (2) by reason only that—
   (a) where the establishment is not a third-level institution and admits students of one gender only, it refuses to admit as a student a person who is not of that gender,
   (b) where the establishment is an institution established for the purpose of providing training to ministers of religion and admits students of only one gender or religious belief, it refuses to admit as a student a person who is not of that gender or religious belief,
   (c) where the establishment is a school providing primary or post-primary education to students and the objective of the school is to provide education in an environment which promotes certain religious values, it admits persons of a particular religious denomination in preference to others or it refuses to admit as a student a person who is not of that denomination and, in the case of a refusal, it is proved that the refusal is essential to maintain the ethos of the school,
   (d) without prejudice to section 3 of the Refugee Act, 1996, where the establishment is an institution providing adult, continuing or further education or a university or other third-level institution—
      (i) it provides different treatment in relation to—
         (I) fees for admission or attendance by persons who are nationals of a member state of the European Union and persons who are not, or
         (II) the allocation of places at the establishment to those nationals and other nationals,
      or
      (ii) it offers assistance to particular categories of persons—
         (I) by way of sponsorships, scholarships, bursaries or other awards, being assistance which is justifiable, having regard to traditional and historical considerations, or

(II) in relation to the allocation of places at the establishment, where the allocation is made pursuant to an agreement concerning the exchange of students made between the establishment and an educational institution or authority in a jurisdiction other than the State,

or

(e) where the establishment is a university or other third-level institution, it provides different treatment in the allocation of places at the establishment to mature students (within the meaning of the Local Authorities (Higher Education Grants) Acts, 1968 to 1992).

(4) Subsection (2) does not apply—

(a) in respect of differences in the treatment of students on the gender, age or disability ground in relation to the provision or organisation of sporting facilities or sporting events, to the extent that the differences are reasonably necessary having regard to the nature of the facilities or events, or

(b) to the extent that compliance with any of its provisions in relation to a student with a disability would, by virtue of the disability, make impossible, or have a seriously detrimental effect on, the provision by an educational establishment of its services to other students.

(5)(a) In this subsection 'grants' mean grants to assist persons to attend or continue to attend—

(i) an institution providing adult, continuing or further education,

(ii) a university, or

(iii) any other third level or higher level institution,

whether or not supported by public funds.

(b) The Minister for Education and Science does not discriminate where he or she—

(i) requires grants to be restricted to persons who are nationals of a member state of the European Union, or

(ii) requires such nationals and other persons to be treated differently in relation to the making of grants.

Section 5 of the Equal Status Act 2000 (as amended)

(1) A person shall not discriminate in disposing of goods to the public generally or a section of the public or in providing a service, whether the

disposal or provision is for consideration or otherwise and whether the service provided can be availed of only by a section of the public.

(2) Subsection (1) does not apply in respect of—
   (a) an activity referred to in section 7(2),
   (b) a service related to a matter provided for under section 6, or a service offered to its members by a club in respect of which section 8 applies,
   (c) differences in the treatment of persons on the gender ground in relation to services of an aesthetic, cosmetic or similar nature, where the services require physical contact between the service provider and the recipient,
   (d) differences in the treatment of persons in relation to annuities, pensions, insurance policies or any other matters related to the assessment of risk where the treatment—
      (i) is effected by reference to—
         (I) actuarial or statistical data obtained from a source on which it is reasonable to rely, or
         (II) other relevant underwriting or commercial factors,
      and
      (ii) is reasonable having regard to the data or other relevant factors,
   (e) differences in the treatment of person on the religion ground in relation to goods or services provided for a religious purpose,
   (f) differences in the treatment of persons on the gender, age or disability ground or on the basis of nationality or national origin in relation to the provision or organisation of a sporting facility or sporting event to the extent that the differences are reasonably necessary having regard to the nature of the facility or event and are relevant to the purpose of the facility or event,
   (g) differences in the treatment of persons on the gender ground where embarrassment or infringement of privacy can reasonably be expected to result from the presence of a person of another gender,
   (h) differences in the treatment of persons in a category of persons in respect of services that are provided for the principal purpose of promoting, for a bona fide purpose and in a bona fide manner, the special interests of persons in that category to the extent that the differences in treatment are reasonably necessary to promote those special interests,
   (i) differences in the treatment of persons on the gender, age or disability ground or on the ground of race, reasonably required for reasons of authenticity, aesthetics, tradition or custom in

connection with a dramatic performance or other entertainment,
(j) an age requirement for a person to be an adoptive or foster parent, where the requirement is reasonable having regard to the needs of the child or children concerned,
(k) a disposal of goods by will or gift, or
(l) differences, not otherwise specifically provided for in this section, in the treatment of persons in respect of the disposal of goods, or the provision of a service, which can reasonably be regarded as goods or a service suitable only to the needs of certain persons.

BULLYING AND SCHOOL DISCIPLINE

Dr. Ciaran Craven[*]

Introduction

It is axiomatic that disruptive pupils and other pupils with challenging behaviours may cause problems, both of a particular and general nature, that pose acute and long-term difficulties for teachers and school management. However, having disruptive and troublesome pupils in any particular school is not just reasonably foreseeable: it is a virtual certainty. Against that background, a clear view and approach as to what is, and is not, appropriate – with a clear understanding of what the limits for intervention are – is not alone desirable but essential. The question to be addressed, therefore, is: what liability issues arise when responding to difficult pupil behaviour?[1]

Pupil Exclusion from Class

A common situation that may arise is this: having complied with the normal pedagogical advice in relation to a pupil, his or her behaviour is still such that exclusion from the classroom is necessary, not least for the sake of the other pupils. If a decision is made to exclude a pupil from a classroom, even for a short period of time, what liability issues arise?

---

[*] Dr Ciaran Craven is a Barrister. He lectures on medical law in the LL.M Degree Programme at Trinity College, Dublin. He is co-author of a textbook on Psychiatry and the Law and the co-author and co-editor of other texts and several articles on aspects of medical law and tort law. He is also a regular contributor to conferences organised by the Law School, Trinity College, Dublin, including conferences on the liability of primary and post-primary school management.

[1] Dealing with ordinary classroom behaviour is not considered in the discussion that follows; the issues arising there are principally of a human rather than a strictly legal nature.

The answer to this question is, of course, the classic lawyer's reply: it all depends. And it does depend, on a myriad of factors, all of which are relevant to an assessment of liability in negligence in relation to the supervision of, and discharge of the appropriate duty of care to, pupils. This is an issue dealt with, in general terms, elsewhere[2] and it would be otiose to repeat that discussion here. A more appropriate focus is on what might be considered to be egregious behaviour on the part of pupils.

VIOLENT AND AGGRESSIVE PUPILS IN THE SCHOOL[3]

As teachers are well aware, the old common law rule in relation to what used be termed "corporal punishment" was abolished – although in abeyance for years beforehand – by the Non-Fatal Offences Against the Person Act 1997. Section 24 provides as follows:

> "The rule of law under which teachers are immune from criminal liability in respect of physical chastisement of pupils is hereby abolished."

That is not to say, of course, that verbal chastisement and admonition is unlawful. But, what if such chastisement or admonition does not work and aggressive or violent behaviour either flares up, or continues, such that co-operative exclusion is not possible, because of the rapidity with which a situation develops? Here, two principal heads of liability arise for consideration, in relation both to criminal and civil liability. Each is considered in turn.

CRIMINAL LIABILITY

General

An intervention to prevent unlawful activities in a school setting, whether by way of acting in self defence or defence of a third party or property, or in assisting in a lawful arrest, may give rise to criminal liability. In essence, not alone is there potential civil liability arising from the manner in which a school or teacher deals (or fails to deal) with pupils whose conduct is violent,

---

[2] See *supra*, p.1 *et seq*.
[3] In this context, see, also, Department of Education and Science Circular M18/99.

criminal liability may arise from the manner in which they deal with the alleged assailant or wrongdoer. Liability for assault is at the centre of the discussion.

Assault

The Non-Fatal Offences Against the Person Act, 1997 abolished, *inter alia*, the common law offences of assault and battery, assault occasioning actual bodily harm and false imprisonment, and replaced them with new statutory offences. Thus, section 2 provides as follows:

> "A person shall be guilty of the offence of assault who, without lawful excuse, intentionally or recklessly—
> (a) directly or indirectly applies force to or causes an impact on the body of another, or
> (b) causes another to believe on reasonable grounds that he or she is likely immediately to be subjected to any such force or impact,
> without the consent of the other."

"Force" includes the application of heat, light, electric current, noise or any other form of energy and the application of solids, liquids or gases. However, no offence is committed if the force or impact, not being intended or likely to cause injury, is in the circumstances such as is generally acceptable in the ordinary conduct of daily life and the defendant does not know or believe that it is in fact unacceptable to the other person. Such an exception, for example, is applicable to persons jostling one into the other in a crowded corridor. Running amok with a weapon through such a crowd, however, does not fall within the exception!

On summary conviction for such an offence, a person is liable to imprisonment for a term not exceeding six months and/or to a fine.[4]

Assault causing harm

Where an assault causes harm – defined (somewhat opaquely) as "harm to the body or mind and including pain and unconsciousness" – section 3 of the Act of 1997 goes on to provide that the person is guilty of an offence, for which (s)he is liable on summary conviction to imprisonment for a term not

---

[4] The maximum fine is the Euro equivalent of IR£1,500 (€1,905).

exceeding twelve months and/or a fine not exceeding the maximum for a section 2 offence. On conviction on indictment, the person is liable to an unlimited fine and/or imprisonment for a term not exceeding five years.

Assault causing serious harm

Where a person intentionally or recklessly causes serious harm – meaning injury which creates a substantial risk of death or which causes serious disfigurement or substantial loss or impairment of the mobility of the body as a whole or of the function of any particular bodily member or organ – to another, section 4 of the Act of 1997 provides that (s)he is liable on conviction on indictment to imprisonment for life and/or an unlimited fine.

Other offences

Other criminal offences are also created and re-cast by the Act, e.g. threatening to kill or cause serious harm, offences in relation to syringes and syringe attacks, watching and besetting, harassment and demanding payments of debt causing alarm. To a greater or lesser extent, they are of variable relevance to schools; however, detailed consideration is beyond the scope of this discussion.

Defences

Of importance to any person who is minded to intervene in an escalating violent situation, the Act of 1997 also provides for a number of defences to charges of what would otherwise be assault in respect of the justifiable use of force in relation to the protection of the person or property and the prevention of crime. Although section 22 of the Act abolished the common law defences in respect of the use of force, they were replaced with new statutory rules at least insofar as the criminal law is concerned. Effectively these defences, which are discussed below, relate to self-defence, defence of one's property, the defence of others, the defence of the property of others and effecting and assisting in a lawful arrest. In this regard, it might be observed that there is no more definitional clarity regarding the lawful use of force than in the non-criminal (civil) law on trespass to the person, except insofar as the subjectivity of the belief of the actor is concerned.

"Use of force"

For the purposes of the defences, the definition of "use of force" is extended by section 20 of the Act of 1997. Thus, a person uses force in relation to another person or property not only when (s)he applies force to, but also where (s)he causes an impact on, the body of that person or that property. And, a person is treated as using force in relation to another person if:

(a) (s)he threatens that person with its use (this also applies in relation to property), or

(b) (s)he detains that person without actually using it.

Although a threat of force may be reasonable, the actual use of force may not be. Furthermore, the fact that a person had an opportunity to retreat before using force is to be taken into account, in conjunction with other relevant evidence, in determining whether the use of force was reasonable.

Self-defence and the defence of property

Section 18 of the Act of 1997 provides that the use of force (within its extended meaning)[5] by a person for any of the following reasons – if only such as is reasonable in the circumstances as (s)he believes them to be – does not constitute an offence:

(a) to protect him/herself or a member of that person's family or another from injury, assault or detention caused by a criminal act (or from its continuing); or

(b) to protect him/herself or (with the authority of that other) another from trespass to the person (or from its continuing); or

(c) to protect his or her property from appropriation, destruction or damage caused by a criminal act or from trespass or infringement (or from its continuing); or

(d) to protect property belonging to another from appropriation, destruction or damage caused by a criminal act or (with the authority of that other) from trespass or infringement (or from its continuing), or

(e) to prevent crime or a breach of the peace (or its continuing).

In this context, property is treated as belonging to a person, *inter alios*, who has the custody or control of it. Furthermore, an act involves a "crime" or is

---

[5] This also applies to acts preparatory to the use of force, see Non-Fatal Offences Against the Person Act 1997, s.20(2).

"criminal" notwithstanding that the person committing it, if charged with an offence in respect of it, would be acquitted on the ground that:

(a) (s)he was under the age of seven years;[6] or

(b) (s)he acted under duress, whether by threats or of circumstances; or

(c) his or her act was involuntary; or

(d) (s)he was in a state of intoxication; or

(e) (s)he was insane, so as not to be responsible according to law, for the act.

Whether the act against which force (within its extended meaning) is used is of one of the specified kinds is to be determined according to the circumstances as the person using the force believed them to be. However, the person using force has no defence if (s)he knows that the force is used against a member of the Garda Síochána acting in the course of the member's duty or a person so assisting such member, unless (s)he believes the force to be immediately necessary to prevent harm to him/herself or another. Furthermore, there is no defence where a person causes conduct or a state of affairs with a view to using force to resist or terminate it. That said, the defence may be availed of although the occasion for the use of force arises only because the person does something (s)he may lawfully do, knowing that such an occasion will arise.

Use of force in arrest

For its part, section 19 of the Act of 1997 provides that the use of force (within its extended meaning)[7] by a person in effecting or assisting in a lawful arrest,[8] if only such as is reasonable in the circumstances as (s)he believes them to be, does not constitute an offence. Furthermore, for this purpose, the question as to whether the arrest is lawful is to be determined

---

[6] The Children Act 2001, s.52, however, provides as follows:
"(1) It shall be conclusively presumed that no child under the age of 12 years is capable of committing an offence.
(2) There is a rebuttable presumption that a child who is not less than 12 but under 14 years of age is incapable of committing an offence because the child did not have the capacity to know that the act or omission concerned was wrong."

[7] This also applies to acts preparatory to the use of force, see: Non-Fatal Offences Against the Person Act 1997, s.20(2).

[8] See, however, the provisions of the Criminal Law Act 1997 in relation to arrest.

according to the circumstances as the person using the force believed them to be.

Reprise

It should be noted that these provisions are directed at the prevention of injuries to persons and damage to property, and the prevention of crime. They are not directed towards the arrest of an individual with the intention of initiating a criminal process. Nor do they address the issue of false arrest, for which a person might still be liable, in certain circumstances, under the civil law. In summary, they excuse acts that would otherwise amount to criminal assault in certain circumstances. Where force is used and criminal liability is excluded, it may be – although it is by no means certain – that civil liability may also be avoided. This apparent contradiction arises because of the different standards of proof required to determine civil as distinct from criminal liability, being on the balance of probabilities in the former and beyond a reasonable doubt in the latter.

CIVIL LIABILITY

General

Where a pupil sustains injury as a consequence of a battery or a criminal assault by another person in the classroom, or at school, the offending pupil is liable at common law – and, as has been set out in the preceding discussion, (s)he may also be liable under the criminal law too. Thus, where a person is injured – whether physically or psychologically – by another, whether intentionally or negligently, the appropriate defendant in civil proceedings is the actual wrongdoer, *i.e.* the person who actually caused the injury complained of. For example, where a person, knocked over on a footpath by a fourteen-year old on a skateboard, falls and sustains a fractured wrist, the appropriate person to name in any legal proceedings is the teenage skateboarder.

However, even if the person were to succeed in an action for damages against the teenager, recovery of those damages may simply not be possible: many people, including young teenagers do not, without insurance, have the financial wherewithal to pay damages awarded by a court. The damages could not be recovered from the teenager's parents either, in such circumstances: parents are not liable for the torts of their minor children.

Similarly, when one child or several children injure(s) another child in school, whether as a result of a one-off action, or as a result of a pattern of behaviour, such as is generally involved in bullying, the appropriate defendant(s) should, of course, be the child or children implicated in the wrongdoing. However, as, generally, they have no money for which it would be worthwhile suing them, and as their parents are not, insofar as the civil law is concerned, liable for their acts or omissions, aggrieved and injured children and their parents will inevitably look to the party against whom recovery will be possible, and who would be worth pursuing, *i.e.* an insured party. In the case of school injuries and bullying, this is the school and its board of management.

Basis of liability

This begs the question: why should a school or its board of management be liable in negligence for the intentional or criminal acts of others? Liability is imposed because certain relationships impose an obligation on one party to protect others from injury resulting from the intentional conduct of the other party. Thus, a psychiatrist in a mental hospital may be liable for injury caused by a patient who is negligently released from, or not committed to, appropriate medical care, or by a patient who is allowed to escape or otherwise cause injury. Similarly a prison or other custodial institution may be liable for damage or injury caused by an inmate who should not have been let out or who should otherwise have been kept under control. Also, liability may be imposed on landlords, employers, hoteliers, carriers and school managers where they fail to take reasonable steps to ensure that those in their charge do not injure others.[9]

Two related issues

In this regard, there are two related aspects that merit discussion. The first is in respect of the liability, in negligence, of a school, for injury caused to a pupil in the school by the bullying or other intentional acts of other pupils. Secondly, the issue of liability in respect of disciplinary or other procedures, instituted on foot of incidents of bullying or other injurious conduct requires consideration.

---

[9] See, B. McMahon & W. Binchy, *Law of Torts* (3rd ed., Butterworths, Dublin, 2000), para.8.25 and the footnotes thereto.

Liability in Negligence

The duty

Although the analogy is an unhappy one, cases involving assaults on prisoners by fellow prisoners, or drunks on other persons on licensed premises, provide an insight into matters that are likely to concern the courts on the question of bullying in school and the approach that is required to be taken to prevent injury to pupils as a result of such behaviour.

Thus, in *Muldoon v. Ireland & Attorney General*[10] the plaintiff, who was a prisoner in Arbour Hill Prison was attacked from behind by another prisoner, with what appears to have been a blade. The attack was sudden and unprovoked and the injury required 22 sutures to a neck wound. The plaintiff, because of the number of prisoners in the vicinity at the time and the direction of the attack, was unable to identify the assailant and he alleged negligence against the prison authorities on two grounds:

(1) that they did not have enough staff on duty in the recreation yard to exercise proper supervision; and

(2) that they were wanting in care in permitting a prisoner to get in to the recreation yard with some sharp instrument, be it a blade or knife or some other instrument of that kind.

Allegations of a similar nature are at the heart of school bullying complaints.

Having regard to the search regime which operated in the prison, and notwithstanding the submission that the prison authorities should have conducted a body search of the prisoners before going to the recreation yard, on the basis that similar searches took place before people entered football grounds and aeroplanes, because there was the potential for an assault taking place during recreation, particularly if there was a dispute simmering in the prison, Hamilton P. (as he then was), withdrew the case from the jury and dismissed the plaintiff's claim. As a matter of law, he considered that it would not be open to the jury to find that the prison authorities were in any way negligent on the occasion in question: the requisite standard of care of prison authorities to prisoners in this case was:

> "... to take all reasonable steps and reasonable care not to expose any of the prisoners to a risk of damage or injury. The law does not require them to guarantee that an incident like this could not occur or to

---

[10] [1988] I.L.R.M. 367 (HC).

guarantee that prisoners do not suffer injury during the course of their imprisonment."[11]

A slightly different approach to the duty issue was taken in *Walsh v. Ryan*[12] a case involving an assault on licensed premises, and which is also of relevance to schools and school management. Here, a female customer was seriously assaulted by another customer on the licensed premises where the publican knew the assailant and was aware of his violent or unruly propensity for some considerable time previously. The court was satisfied that the publican, as occupier, owed a duty to take reasonable care to ensure that his premises were "conducted without risk to his customers" – which duty had been breached in this case. This same principle of occupier's liability, substituting "pupils" for "customers" must be considered to apply to schools too.

Having said that, since July 1995 and the coming into force of the Occupiers Liability Act 1995 the basis of an occupier's liability, under the Act, is in relation to "dangers due to the state of the premises". As to whether or not an aggressive inebriate in a licensed premises who injures another patron or damages his/her property constitutes a "danger due to the state of the premises" as contemplated by the Act – although arguable – must be questionable. Similar considerations also apply in respect of a school playground where a bully is allowed to operate. However, that is not to say that a commercial occupier has no liability in respect of activities carried out on his/her premises, no more than a board of management, as occupier, has no liability in respect of activities carried out on school premises. The trial judge, in *Walsh*, was clearly of the view that there was a duty of care owed by the publican to his customers. Such a duty is also owed by a school's board of management to its pupils.

The New South Wales Court of Appeal in *Haines v. Warren*[13] noted that the duty of a school authority to its pupils is to take reasonable care to obviate risks of injury, which are reasonably foreseeable.[14] This is wholly consistent with the authorities in this jurisdiction.[15]

---

[11] A similar dictum is found in *Bolger v. Governor of Mountjoy Prison, Ireland & Attorney General*, unreported, High Court, O'Donovan J., November 12, 1997.
[12] Unreported, High Court, , Lavan J., February 12, 1993.
[13] NSW Court of Appeal (CA 85 of 1986, CL 348 of 1984) Glass, Samuels and Priestly JJ.A., December 23, 1986. This is discussed more fully at p.161, *infra*.
[14] Here, the court cited the relevant Australian authorities: *State of Victoria v. Bryer* (1970) 44 A.L.J.R. 174, *Geyer v. Downs* (1977) 138 C.L.R. 91, *The Commonwealth v. Introvigne* (1981–82) 150 C.L.R. 258.
[15] See, also, *Waters v. Commissioner of Police of the Metropolis* [1997] I.C.R. 1073,

The standard of care

What, then, of the standard of care which is owed and how is it to be assessed? In *Muldoon*, Hamilton P. held that as the incident in question happened suddenly, was unprovoked and there was no prior warning, it could not have been prevented and the prison authorities were not negligent in not having more prison officers in the yard. He was also satisfied that the only way the incident could have been prevented was by searching every prisoner every time he moved from one area to another. As a matter of balance, he was of the view that more and more frequent searches than were actually carried out would undoubtedly be regarded as excessive and could be argued to amount to harassment of the prisoners.

Small children and supervision

In *Mulvey (a minor) v. McDonagh*[16] the infant plaintiff claimed damages in respect of personal injuries allegedly suffered as a consequence of an assault by another pupil on the last day of her first year at school. The central allegation was that the school authorities had been negligent in their failure to prevent the plaintiff being assaulted and bullied over a long period: it was alleged that they had failed to monitor the conduct of the pupils in circumstances where the plaintiff maintained she had been bullied on a number of occasions since the previous October and complaint had been made about it.

However, having heard the evidence in relation to the complaints made and the level of monitoring of the school yard by the school authorities (which had, in fact, been increased as a result of the plaintiff's complaints), Johnson J. accepted that some incidents had taken place during the school year but where there was a dispute between the plaintiff's and school's evidence, he preferred the latter. In addition, not being satisfied that the plaintiff had suffered the injuries alleged, he dismissed the claim.

[1997] I.R.L.R. 589 (CA) (Evans, Waite, Swinton-Thomas LJ.J.) where the defendant's duty of care not to cause foreseeable injury, including mental injury, to the plaintiff, who was one of his officers (and who alleged that she had been the victim of sexual discrimination) was characterised by the English Court of Appeal as "equivalent to an employer's duty to provide his employees with a safe system of work, or *with the duty of the headmaster or governing body of a school to safeguard its pupils from the ill effects of bullying by fellow pupils, for whose acts there is not, strictly, a vicarious responsibility*" (*Emphasis* added, references omitted).
[16] [2004] 1 I.R. 497.

Insofar as the standard of care was concerned, he was satisfied that it was "... that of a prudent parent exercising reasonable care ...". He also accepted that this must be taken in the context of a "prudent parent behaving reasonably with a class of twenty-eight four year olds having their first experience of mingling socially with other children."[17] Johnson J. was also satisfied that this care had been taken and he did not consider that:

"... the suggestion that there should be a further and higher degree of liability, namely that of professional negligence, is a situation which has ... yet been achieved in Irish law".[18]

Balancing supervision and humaneness

However, there may be circumstances when supervision and intervention could be oppressive such as to interfere with the essence of what school should be about. Excessive supervision and control might be inconsistent with the learning experience. These twin concepts of supervision and balance between that supervision and humaneness in the regime are recurring themes in the related cases and are equally applicable in the school setting too.

In *Kavanagh v. Governor of Arbour Hill Prison, Ireland and Attorney General*[19] another prisoner plaintiff failed in his action against the prison authorities in respect of an assault on him by another prisoner. The essence of the claim was that there had been negligence in failing to supervise properly the prisoners as they moved through the prison, thus providing an opportunity for the attack, in circumstances where there was tension in the aftermath of the foiling of a planned prison break. However, there was no evidence that the authorities knew, or ought to have known, that any resentment or hostility existed towards the plaintiff, who was one of four prospective escapees and the allegation of failure to supervise the prisoners was robustly rejected by

---

[17] *Ibid.*, p.504.
[18] See *Scott v. Lothian Regional Council*, unreported, Outer House, Scotland, September 29, 1998 where the test applied was as to whether it had been proved that the teacher was "guilty of such a failure as no guidance teacher of ordinary skill would be guilty if acting with ordinary care." See, also, McMahon and Binchy, *op. cit.*, n.10, *supra*, para.16.17. "The problems of care and control in a school bear some resemblance to those confronting a parent in the home but they are far from identical. It is possible that in a future decision Irish courts will drop the reference to careful parent and stress the fact that it is the standard of the reasonable school teacher or manager which should prevail." In *Bradford-Smith v. West Sussex County Council*, The Times Law Reports, January 29, 2002, Judge L.J. also clearly favoured the professional negligence test.
[19] Unreported, High Court, Morris J., April 22, 1993.

the court. Insofar as a prisoner had a sharp blade, it was further alleged that this demonstrated a clear and obvious failure to take all reasonable steps to protect the plaintiff while he was in the prison.

Morris J. (as he then was) was satisfied that as a matter of probability, the blade had found its way into the prison during a visit to one of the prisoners. Given the type of prison in question, the trial judge accepted that "the requirements and procedures of such a prison must be appropriate to the type of prison that it is" and he also accepted the evidence that a rigid regime as might be appropriate for a high security institution would generate feelings of frustration and ill-will among prisoners in this prison. Morris J. dismissed the plaintiff's claim; however, as to the balance that requires to be struck, what he stated is worth setting out. He noted:

> "The system of searching has been in existence for approximately fifteen years and ... from time to time at regular intervals, the system is reviewed and reconsidered by the prison authorities. It has (been) found to be and remains ... the correct and proper method for this type of prison. The authorities accept that, from time to time, small objects such as drugs (or indeed the blade in this case) will find its way into the prison. To ensure that this does not happen would involve comprehensive strip searching procedures and would involve restricting the nature of the visits available to the prisoners. This would ... seriously disrupt the smooth operation of the prison and would cause serious resentment among the inmates. In my view, a balance is required to be struck as to what is reasonable ... there is a clear necessity to maintain a humane regime within the prison and that the steps now taken by the authorities are all that can reasonably be taken for the protection of the plaintiff consistent with that objective."

These principles were also applied in *Boyd & Boyd v. Ireland and the Attorney General*.[20] They were similarly applied in *Bolger v. Governor of Mountjoy Prison, Ireland & Attorney General*[21] where a remand prisoner, a few hours after his arrival, was subjected to a sudden and unprovoked assault in which boiling water was poured over him by another prisoner and which resulted in burns to 10% of his body surface. Insofar as a balance required to be struck between the duty to take reasonable care to prevent such injuries and the maintaining of a humane regime, O'Donovan J. noted:

---

[20] Unreported, High Court, Budd J., May 13, 1993. The plaintiffs' claims were also dismissed.
[21] Unreported, High Court, O'Donovan J., November 12, 1997.

"... when considering the extent of the duty of care owed by a prison authority to a prisoner, a balance must be struck between precautions which are acceptable and those which are excessive. The question therefore arises as to whether or not, in the light of what they knew or ought to have known about [the assailant's] previous behaviour while a prisoner of the State, the duty of care for the safety of other prisoners in their custody which was owed by the prison authorities in Mountjoy Prison, required that they should segregate [him] from other prisoners or deny him access to buckets of hot water."[22]

In this quotation, substituting "disruptive pupil" for "assailant" or "prisoner" and "school" for "prison authority" provides an appropriate touchstone for analysing the central liability issue that also arises in schools. In this case, on the evidence, the court was not satisfied that the assailant's history suggested that he was so dangerous that, in the interests of the safety of others, the prison authorities should have recognised a need to segregate him. As segregation, in this context, was tantamount to solitary confinement and given that, at the material time, he was serving a ten-year sentence, O'Donovan J. was of the view that:

"... it would have been an entirely excessive precaution were he to be segregated from other prisoners on account of his past history. Neither do I think that [in light of his past history] it was incumbent on the prison authorities to deny him access to hot water which ... he would require for the purpose of washing himself and ... for making himself a cup of tea ... a facility which is available to all prisoners. To punish an adult prisoner in that way for an offence which he had committed when only a boy would, in my view, be grossly excessive."

Exclusion may be necessary

There may be circumstances, however, where discharging the duty which is owed will require a person's exclusion. In *Hall v. Kennedy*,[23] Morris J. (as

---

[22] This should be compared with the approach of Glass and Samuels JJ.A. in *Haines v. Warren* NSW Court of Appeal (CA 85 of 1986, CL 348 of 1984), discussed further at p.161 *infra*.
[23] Unreported, High Court, Morris J., December 20, 1993. This was another case involving assault on a licensed premises, where the plaintiff failed. On the facts, the assailant had shown none of the signs or manifestations of drunkenness as would have alerted a reasonable publican or his staff to the prospect that he might assault another customer. It was held that the assailant's response to what he had regarded as

he then was) stated:

> "The obligations of the [publican] at law is to take all reasonable care for the safety of the [customer] while on the premises. This would include in this case ensuring that [another] customer in the premises did not assault him. The necessary steps would include, in an appropriate case, removing such a customer from the premises, refusing to serve him drink [and] staffing the bar with sufficient barmen or security staff so as to ensure the safety of the [customer]."

With appropriate modification, this dictum captures the essence of what is required. These principles, modified in respect of an assault in a café/snooker hall, were applied in *Wallace v. Flynn*.[24] There, Kelly J. was of the view that the obligations owed to the injured plaintiff were those set out in *Hall* in respect of a publican's duty to his customer. They were, he stated "applicable here subject to whatever modifications are necessary having regard to the different character of [the] premises." In this regard, there is no good reason to consider that those obligations would not, in addition, be imposed on schools, with further modification as necessary. Indeed, this approach is broadly consonant with cases from the United States and Australia, which usefully illustrate the application of these principles in the school setting.

Discipline may also be necessary

In *Hamilton v. Independent School District No. 114*,[25] the defendant school authority was responsible for the operation of public schools and sponsored various spectator events during the school year, including athletic competitions, to which admission was charged. After a basketball game organised by a school, one 13-year old student, who had attended the game, hid in the shadows in order to push another student into a snowbank. He pushed his fellow student into the plaintiff who fell and suffered serious injury to her hip. She sued for negligence.

The school principal, who was present at the game, was responsible for student discipline and gave evidence that he considered uninvited physical

---

an insult by the plaintiff was "hot-tempered and spontaneous" and could not have been foreseen by the defendant publican.

[24] Unreported, High Court, Kelly J., May 1, 2002. Liability was not imposed, however: the security arrangements which had been made were reasonable, in all of the circumstances of the case.

[25] 355 NW 2d 182 (1984) Minn. App., September 25, 1984 (C9–84–1012), Popovich C.J., Sedgwick, and Lansing JJ., *per* Popovich C.J.

contact between students contrary to school policy. He indicated that students were expected to adhere to the same standard of conduct at school events as was expected during the school day, whether inside or outside the building. He was the only person exercising any supervisory function at the time.

During the school year, the assailant and his friends had frequently "picked on" the other pupil by calling him names or hitting him in the arm or head. Approximately two weeks earlier, the same two pupils had been involved in another incident at a school basketball game when the (victim) pupil had been pushed and tripped. Although he became upset, he was not physically injured. The incident was reported by his mother to the principal, who verbally reprimanded the assailant and instructed him to go into the gym or leave the school grounds. He took no further action because he regarded the incident as petty.

In summarily dismissing the plaintiff's claim, the trial court found that, as a matter of law, any negligence on the part of the school authorities did not, in this case, cause the plaintiff's injuries. The trial judge stated:

> "I cannot think of a fact situation which so clearly falls into the category of cases denying liability, simply because no amount of monitoring or supervision by school employees could have prevented Mrs. Hamilton's injury. Conceding that there is a basis for a finding of negligence based upon inadequate supervision and crowd monitoring, and also that there was direct notice of [the] past bullying tactics toward [the other pupil], I can think of nothing the school district could have done to restrain [the bully], except (1) to have barred him from all basketball games, or (2) to have hired a teacher to remain within a couple of feet of [the bully] from the time that he entered until he left school property. Neither of these alternatives was feasible, realistic or required. ..."

These conclusions, in the context of *Muldoon*, in particular, and the other cases already referred to, seem unexceptional. However, the trial judge was not satisfied to base his decision thus. He continued:

> "I prefer to base my decision upon my conclusion that if the presence of [the pupil's mother] and plaintiff immediately to his right and left did not deter [the bully's] sudden attack upon [him], no number of school employees would have prevented it, especially outside the school building on a sidewalk filled with adults leaving the basketball game."

As in the other cases, the duty and causation issues were clear. It was held that school authorities are required to exercise ordinary care to prevent foreseeable misconduct of students. In order to recover damages, a plaintiff must prove that a general danger was foreseeable and that supervision would have prevented the accident. The onus on the plaintiff was to prove that it was likely that the misconduct would have been prevented had the duty been discharged.

Having said that, the Minnesota Court of Appeal considered that there was an issue of fact to be determined on causation, as there was an issue in relation to whether or not reasonable supervision might prevent sudden injuries by interrupting misconduct or deterring it altogether considering the evidence of the earlier attack by the bully and lack of supervision by the school authorities. Accordingly, the matter was remitted to the trial court for determination.

In the Australian case of *Haines v. Warren*[26] the plaintiff sued the defendant as nominee of the New South Wales Department of Education in respect of an incident, during the course of which she was injured,[27] that took place in the grounds of her school in March 1982. At the time, she was a 15-year-old pupil in the coeducational school, which was attended by several hundred boys and girls. She was in good health, weighing about 7 to 7½ stone.

During the midmorning recess on the day in question she was standing with some friends in the off quadrangle area, a comparatively small space adjacent to the main quadrangle, that included a grassed area shaded by trees to one side of a pathway leading to a flight of steps. She was standing on the grass area facing the steps when a boy named Alfonso of approximately the same age came from behind and picked her up by grasping her legs below the knees. While she struggled to free herself he carried her a few paces and dropped her. When she fell she landed on a corner of a concrete slab embedded in the grass striking her tailbone. There was no supervisor in the off quadrangle area at the time. The practice was to have a teacher there at lunchtime but not during the morning recess.

Although the court was of the view that the evidence tendered to show negligence on the part of the school authority was "comparatively meagre", there was no evidence at all from the school. The plaintiff's evidence was to

---

[26] NSW Court of Appeal (CA 85 of 1986, CL 348 of 1984) Glass, Samuels and Priestly JJ.A., December 23, 1986.
[27] The plaintiff suffered a prolapsed intervertebral disc at the L4–5 level, with a major neurological deficit in her lower limbs, subsequently necessitating a partial excision of the disc. Because of her injuries, and the loss of motivation that ensued, she left school early and did not fulfil her ambition to become a nurse, the court concluding that her earning capacity had been reduced by sixty per cent. She was awarded A$250,000, and the defendant appealed.

the effect that Alfonso was "always cheeking people and calling people names" and that he had been in a fight with a few boys. However, a witness recounted an experience she had had with Alfonso the previous year when he had called her "a slut", upon which she pushed him and he retaliated by punching her in the neck. She also described his general behaviour during the period of eleven months between that incident and the incident involving the plaintiff, as she was keen to keep out of his way. She often saw him spitting at people, pushing, causing trouble and fighting with boys and misbehaving towards both boys and girls.

During the morning recess, the evidence indicated that there was a supervisor on duty in the canteen area adjacent to the quadrangle, from where he or she could see into the quadrangle which was the main playground, but could not see into the off quadrangle area. The evidence also indicated that the schoolboys tended to fight fairly regularly and that the presence of a master did not always prevent it.

The trial court had found that there had been a breach of duty in two respects: the failure to discipline Alfonso and the failure to provide adequate supervision. The court also found that each of these failures was causally related to the injury suffered by the plaintiff. Thus, the trial judge noted:

> "Prior to the assault Alfonso's conduct was [n]ever reported to any of the teachers at the school but as the aggressive conduct ... regularly took place in the quadrangle, the teachers knew or should have known of his aggressive disposition and his readiness to give full vent to it. ... However the evidence discloses that a course of aggressive behaviour on the part of Alfonso had been followed regularly for a period of at least a year. The condonation of this behaviour by the school authorities must have left Alfonso with the impression that he was free to act as he chose. However those in authority at the school had ample time had they been so minded to follow a course of firm disciplinary action against Alfonso which would have made clear to him that violent conduct would attract serious consequences. If there had also been an adequate system of supervision Alfonso would have been aware that any aggressive conduct on his part in the quadrangle or off-quadrangle area would not have gone unnoticed. In the light of the evidence and the inferences therefrom I am satisfied that the taking of the steps to which I have referred would have prevented or minimised the injury which was in fact received by the plaintiff and the plaintiff has established liability on the part of the school authority."

This must be considered to be relatively unexceptional, in terms of conclusion. However, on appeal, the defendant school authority submitted that the evidence only established four kinds of misconduct, *viz.* spitting, pushing, causing trouble and fighting, that the first three were not fraught with the risk of injury to other pupils, that conduct of one of the four kinds happened twice a week and that there was no basis for inferring that any one kind predominated.

Accordingly, it was argued, it was not behaviour which "signalled the future occurrence of conduct fraught with the risk of injury". Even if Alfonso's conduct was of such a kind, it was also argued, he had been disciplined from time to time and warned of the consequences. In relation to the failure to supervise the playground adequately, it was submitted that the area was so small that it was not a breach of duty not to have it under view at all times. Furthermore, it was argued that the conduct of Alfonso on the day in question in picking the plaintiff up by the legs, carrying her a few paces while she struggled and then dropping her tail first was not intrinsically dangerous. In effect, it was innocent play that was a sudden occurrence allowing no opportunity for a supervisor to intercept or deter it.

The Court of Appeal was satisfied that Alfonso's "manoeuvre was not inherently dangerous. But for the plaintiff's struggles, Alfonso may well have performed no more than a balletic lift. But for the slab, it would have been harmless. Its duration could not have exceeded ten seconds."[28] However, Glass J.A. was also satisfied that to leave the area, which was supervised at lunchtime, unsupervised during the mid-morning recess, demonstrated a want of reasonable care.[29]

But, this did not determine the matter. The question to be addressed was, whether or not, if the area had been properly supervised, the plaintiff's injury would have been prevented. The Court of Appeal was not satisfied that it would have been.

> "Owing to its nature and the conduct of Alfonso in the main quadrangle where supervision was provided, it does not seem probable that the presence of a supervisor would have deterred its execution. Owing to

---

[28] Samuels J.A., who was in the minority, essentially agreed that it was no more "than a piece of horse play, unremarkable, I would have thought, between young persons, lacking any overtly aggressive elements or, so far as can be seen, any desire to inflict pain or humiliation. It was thoughtless perhaps and a little rough, but its serious consequences do not appear to have been intended."

[29] However, Samuels J.A. disagreed, arguing that no inference adverse to the defendant could be drawn by assuming that the area was supervised during the lunch hour but not during the mid morning recess – especially as the positioning of a teacher in the area appeared to have more to do with supervising children entering and leaving the school through a gate in the area than with actually supervising the area.

its duration it does not seem probable that a supervisor in the area would have been able by admonitory words to discourage or by physical intervention to frustrate the carriage of the plaintiff before she was dropped on the slab."[30]

Thus, the plaintiff failed on the allegation that there was a failure of adequate supervision. However, in relation to the allegation that there had been a failure to discipline Alfonso, the Court of Appeal noted the absence of an explanation from the school authority in relation to the plaintiff's evidence and that of the other witnesses. It concluded:

"[Alfonso's] antisocial conduct directed at boys and girls alike occurred in the quadrangle and should have come under the notice of the supervisor stationed there. It was of such a character as to present, if not checked, a foreseeable risk of injury to other students. To assign a teacher who would act as a permanent restraining influence on him would doubtless exceed the requirements of due care. But the precaution of detaining him in the classroom during recess unless or until his behaviour improved was practicable. If this precaution had been adopted at some stage during the eleven months of unchecked aggression, it seems probable . . . that by March 1982 he would either have improved or still be detained during recess and the plaintiff would not have been subjected to the rough treatment which she suffered at his hands on that day."[31]

In *Bradford-Smart v. West Sussex County Council*[32] the plaintiff appealed to the Court of Appeal against the High Court's dismissal of her claim[33] for damages against West Sussex County Council for psychiatric injury caused

---

[30] Priestly J.A., who agreed with Glass J.A. in dismissing the appeal, however, was of the view that the evidence did, in fact, support the argument that but for the failure to supervise, Alfonso would not have acted as he did and, thus cause the plaintiff's injuries.
[31] Samuels J.A. disagreed, holding that the finding was purely speculative. He did not consider "that any disciplinary regime of a kind which ordinary humanity and current pedagogic standards would have permitted, would probably have deterred Alfonso from doing what he did on this occasion." And, therein lies the essential problem of balance, also seen in other cases. Priestly J.A., who agreed with Glass J.A., expressed no view on the arguments that there had been a failure to discipline Alfonso.
[32] *Times Law Reports*, January 29, 2002 (Court of Appeal, Judge and Hale L.JJ. & Sir Denis Henry)
[33] *The Times*, December 5, 2000 (Garland J.).

by bullying when she was a pupil at Ifield Middle School, and for which the defendant council was responsible.

Judge L.J. (for the court) accepted that the plaintiff was a victim of bullying, albeit outside the school, on the bus to and from school and on the estate where she lived. In the High Court, the scope of the school's duty of care towards its pupils was determined as going no further than to prevent the bullying actually happening inside the school.[34] It was argued that it was wrong in principle to adopt a line of demarcation at the school gate: the essence of the argument focussed not on what the school did in relation to the plaintiff but what it did not do in relation to the bullies who were pupils at the same school. In general, a day school is not directly in control of the activities of its pupils once they left its charge:[35] that is the responsibility of parents.

Judge L.J. accepted that a school might on occasions be in breach of duty for failing to take such steps as were within its power to combat harmful behaviour of one pupil towards another even when they were outside school;[36] those occasions would, however, in his view, be few and far between.[37]

Reprise

The moral of the cases is clear. Reasonable care must be exercised. What is reasonable depends on the circumstances of the case. Issues relating to the adequacy of supervision, as is evident from the cases, reduce to consideration of the evidence in any particular instance. The proportionality of the response – in terms of social control – and the efficacy of that response, are important factors to be taken into account in any assessment of reasonableness. In short, therefore, if injury is reasonably foreseeable as a result of a school's acts or omission, liability may be imposed. This may apply even where the injury is caused by the criminal or intentional acts of a third party. Indeed, it might be noted that, arising from this general principle, the injury that is

---

[34] See, *Phelps v. Hillingdon London Borough Council* [2001] 2 A.C. 619, *The Times*, July 28, 2000.

[35] However, see *R v. Newham London Borough Council, Ex parte X* [1995] E.L.R. 303, *The Times,* November 15, 1994 where Brooke J. had rejected the argument that a head teacher could not use his disciplinary powers against a pupil who attacked a boy outside the school.

[36] See, also, the approach of Finlay P., as he then was, in *State (Smullen & Smullen) v. Duffy & Ors* [1980] I.L.R.M. 46 (HC) discussed further at p.167 *infra.*

[37] This was not such a case and the plaintiff's appeal was dismissed.

foreseeable need not necessarily be to another pupil or person actually on the school premises.

Disciplinary Procedures[38]

General

The focus of this chapter, thus far, has been on liability in negligence for harm occurring where it is alleged that there should have been preventative intervention. That is not to say, however, that that is the only legal recourse that an aggrieved person might have. It may be that, in certain circumstances, judicial review of the failure to intervene may be sought. Such was the English case of *R v. Head Teacher of Fairfield Primary School and others ex parte W*.[39] Here, the father of a ten-year old boy sought judicial review of the action that a head teacher, and the board of governors and the local education authority, had taken after a particularly serious playground injury was inflicted on his son by another pupil.

On November 26, 1996, the 10-year-old applicant's arm was broken by another boy, "C", while the two were waiting in the lunch queue at their school, and as a result of which he had to go to hospital. Essentially, the parents sought an order of certiorari to quash the head teacher's decision to take no disciplinary action against "C" beyond a verbal admonition and, secondly, a declaration that neither the head teacher nor the governors had complied with their statutory obligations in respect of discipline arising out of the incident. The applicant's father was extremely upset and annoyed about what had happened, particularly because he was of the view that, for some time, bullying had been endemic in the school, his son had been bullied by "C" for many years in and out of the school and the school's attitude to bullying was inadequate to meet the perceived problem.

After the child had recovered from his injuries, he returned to school and there was disagreement about whether, and if so, what conditions should be applied to his return to ensure his safety in the future. On a trip by pupils of the school to France, in which both the applicant and "C" participated, it was hoped that there no longer remained any bad feeling between the two children. However, by the time the matter came on for trial, which was at the end of the school year, both the applicant and "C" were due to leave the school in question, following which they were to go to separate secondary schools.

---

[38] See, also, Department of Education and Science Circular M33/91.
[39] Q.B.D. CO/541/97, July 18, 1997, Scott Baker J.

The school argued that what had occurred was a "playground incident and something over which the court would not be likely to interfere with the head master's discretion as to how to deal with it."[40] Because both the applicant and the person who caused his injuries had, by this time, left the school and had gone to different schools, the judge hearing the application concluded that the dispute had ceased to be of practical significance: in the circumstances, the court declined to proceed further given that any relief that might be granted would have no practical effect.

Although relief was refused on the particular facts of this case, the tenor of the judgment clearly indicates that decisions by school authorities in respect of what appears to be a failure to take disciplinary action against children who injure others may, in certain circumstances,[41] be reviewed by the courts.

Acting immediately – fairness of procedures

A question may arise as to how the actions of a school may be judged in circumstances where, in order to prevent a situation from escalating, immediate action has to be, and is, taken. This question arose in *State (Smullen & Smullen) v. Duffy & ors.*[42] There, the High Court was satisfied that the arrangements for dealing with expulsions and suspensions of boys who had been involved in a violent incident outside the school were proper, just and equitable. Furthermore, the court was satisfied that, if those arrangements were properly complied with and implemented in a *bona fide* manner, proceedings or consequences resulting from them could not be said, under any circumstances, to be contrary to natural justice. The draft articles of management, in accordance with which the school in question was being run provided that, subject to the directions of the board, the principal should

---

[40] The local education authority commissioned an inspection that, in the view of the judge, went a considerable way to vindicating the concerns of the applicant's father about the management of this school. Although the trial judge was satisfied that he had a clear picture of the wider public considerations that the applicant's father was anxious to have explored in the judicial review proceedings, the court was of the view that these were issues of fact that were not proper matters for such proceedings.

[41] At first instance in *Murtagh & anor v. Board of Governors of St Emer's National School*, Barron J., in the High Court, while refusing the relief sought on the grounds that he was satisfied that the board of management had not acted in breach of fair procedures, as had been alleged, held that judicial review could properly lie in relation to disciplinary decisions in national schools, since such matters lay in the public domain. The Supreme Court reversed on the facts, see, [1991] 1 I.R. 482, [1991] I.L.R.M. 549 (SC), which is discussed further below at p.169.

[42] [1980] I.L.R.M. 46 (HC).

inter alia control the internal organisation, management and discipline of the school and should have power for any cause which he or she judged adequate to dismiss, subject to the approval of the board, or to suspend pupils from attendance. On the dismissal or suspension of any pupil the parent was required to be notified of a right to appeal to the board. Finlay P. (as he then was) noted:

> "It would seem an essential power to give to the principal of a school with disciplinary responsibility and powers over a number of pupils that he or she should be entitled, after a *bona fide* investigation carried out in the informal way which one would expect from a schoolmaster with pupils under his care rather than from a court on the trial of a criminal charge, to make an immediate suspension of one or more pupils in order to maintain peace and discipline within the school."

For the principal to have immediately suspended, as he did, based on the evidence available to him, members of both of the rival gangs who were involved in the violent incident outside school, was "a minimum responsible decision for a schoolteacher with obligations to maintain discipline and safety within his school." The failure to interview one particular boy, in the court's view, did not affect the validity of the decision reached or the fairness or *bona fides* of the method by which it had been reached.

On the important question of legal representation of the applicants, who were suspended, at any meeting or hearing of the school board in connection with their suspension, Finlay P. was of the view that it was:

> "... inherent in the general provision for the discipline of a school and indeed in the interests of pupils of a school and the relationships which should exist between them and the school authorities and between their parents and the school authorities that communication should, in the first instance at least, be direct and should not preferably, and certainly not as a right, be through legal representatives."

For schools, the conclusion of Finlay P. is apposite. On his assessment of where the truth lay on the facts, he considered that the board was:

> "not only entitled to, in effect, expel the two boys from the school but that they would be failing in their duty to the school and to the other pupils attending it had they not taken that step. Largely different considerations might well apply if the board of management and, or alternatively, the principal had decided between two contending or

warring parties in the fight and had retained some of them and expelled the others."

The implication is clear. Failure to act decisively may open a school and its board of management to actions in negligence and breach of duty, where steps are not taken to prevent a foreseeable risk of injury or harm.[43] Finlay P. finished by noting:

> "What the school did seems ... to be the proper and reasonable thing having regard to their magisterial responsibility and their obligation to enforce and maintain discipline, namely, to suspend from the school and thus separate the two rival gangs who had met in a fight of violence."

Acting fairly – scope of judicial review

Not all disciplinary decisions of a school or its board of management, however, are amenable to judicial review. In *W*, it will be recalled, any decision on judicial review would have been moot, as the applicant, in that case, had already left the school in question and gone on to secondary school. In *Smullen*, the decision under review involved the suspension of two boys which *de facto* amounted to their expulsion. It was, accordingly, a decision with serious consequences.

That was not the case, however, in *Murtagh & anor v. Board of Governors of St Emer's National School*.[44] Here, the Supreme Court refused to interfere with the decision by a national school board of management to suspend the applicants' eleven-year-old son for three days for having insulted a teacher and refusing to apologise. In the Supreme Court, Hederman J. dealt with the matter in summary fashion. He held that a three-day suspension of a pupil from a national school either by the principal or the board of management of that school is not a matter for judicial review:

> "It is not an adjudication on, or determining of, any rights, or the imposing of any liability. It is simply the application of ordinary disciplinary procedures inherent in the school authorities and granted to them by the parents who have entrusted the pupil to the school.
>
> A three day suspension for an admitted breach of discipline would be no more reviewable by the High Court, than for example, the

---

[43] See pp.20–21 *supra*.
[44] [1991] 1 I.R. 482; [1991] I.L.R.M. 549 (SC). See *supra*, p.167.

ordering of a pupil as a sanction to stay in school for an extra half hour to write out lines, or to write out lines while he is at home."

McCarthy J. doubted that such a decision was amenable to review by the courts. He held that:

"The enforcement of discipline in a national school is a matter for the teachers, the principal teacher, the chairperson of the board of management and the board itself. It is not a matter for the courts, whose function, at most, is to ensure that the disciplinary complaint was dealt with fairly."

O'Flaherty J., for his part, stated that the proceedings were:

"... a ridiculous waste of public time and should never have been initiated; having been initiated they should not have been entertained but should have been dismissed as quite inappropriate for judicial review."

Wrongdoing off school premises

The school disciplinary process may be invoked not only in relation to incidents that occur on the school premises, but also in relation to incidents off premises, and even out of school hours.

The issues that arise for consideration in such circumstances came under judicial scrutiny in *Student A & Student B v. Dublin Secondary School*,[45] a case involving alleged drug use outside of school hours and off premises. Here, two teenagers in a Leaving Certificate class challenged the decision of their private school to expel them for smoking cannabis at a private party outside of school hours. The boys had admitted to having cannabis for their own use at a private party in a pub outside Dublin, at which it was also alleged that there was widespread underage drinking. A teacher at the school was in the pub and, having become aware of their having cannabis, he informed the headmaster. The boys were expelled the following day.

The parents maintained that they were unaware of a school rule to the effect that pupils found using illegal drugs in whatever circumstances would be expelled. While not condoning the use of cannabis, they would not support such a rule. They had met the headmaster and written to the board of governors in an effort to have the decision reversed. The governors upheld

---

[45] [1999] I.E.II.C. 47 (November 25, 1999).

the decision and the parents sought an interlocutory injunction restraining the expulsions.

It was indicated to the court that the school operated a policy of "zero tolerance" towards drugs and it stood over its decision. In reply, the parents relied on Department of Education guidelines regarding a code of discipline and behaviour for schools; these stated that sanctions to reflect disapproval of students' behaviour should contain a degree of flexibility and that expulsion should be resorted to only in the most extreme circumstances – after other sanctions and efforts at rehabilitation were exhausted. It was maintained that the penalty imposed was "savage" and that the boys had been expelled even before they had a chance to confirm that they did have the cannabis or were even spoken to.

The court was only concerned with whether there was a reasonable basis for the school to regard cannabis use as constituting a serious offence, as it was also a criminal offence. The trial judge was of the view there could be no doubt the school was entitled to take an extremely severe line on drug use because any slippage of discipline could have the most deleterious implications for student users, other students and the school generally. Kearns J. noted that a "zero tolerance" policy was not unreasonable but the boys and their parents were entitled to make submissions to the board before the ultimate penalty was imposed. He stated:

"... expulsion is the most draconian punishment a school can impose, and such are the implications of expulsion ... that such decisions can be properly regarded as quasi-judicial in nature."

But, he continued:

"I have the greatest difficulty in accepting the proposition that it is necessary to have any specific rules or Code of Conduct in a school which would emphasise to the parents or pupil that drug abuse is considered a serious transgression by a school authority. It cannot be seriously argued in my view that where a serious transgression occurs which is not addressed by school rules, either because they do not exist or make specific reference to the transgression in question, that the school as a result can take no steps to discipline the offender. There may be grey areas where particular concerns of a school authority should be spelled out in the school rules to ensure that parents and students are fully aware both of a rule and the disciplinary policy. However, the kind of offence in the instant case must be regarded as falling into the category where both parents and pupil alike must reasonably expect a school authority to take serious action in the event of transgression."

Significantly, then, Kearns J. stated:

"Once a court decides that a school has in general terms been fair I would take the view that it should not lightly interfere with the autonomy of the school or do anything which might have the effect of damaging its capacity to discipline its students, given that the school, with its vast experience and knowledge of its pupils usually knows best.

[I]t does not seem to me appropriate for a court to state whether a punishment should be suspension or expulsion in an individual case unless there appears to be a want of any reasonable basis for the decision of the school authority. In the same way as the courts extend deference to expert tribunals, it seems to me much the same sort of consideration demands that the court should be extremely slow to intervene in cases of this nature."

He also considered that an opportunity of making representations prior to the imposition of the most severe penalty to be imposed by a school was "an essential requirement of natural justice".[46] Where the Department of Education guidelines on discipline did not apply, e.g. to unrecognised private schools, as was the school in this case, the judge pointed to the approach that should be adopted, as follows:

- if a long-term suspension or expulsion was to take place, rules of natural justice required that students or parents should be permitted to make representations on penalties;

- in the context of any meeting or hearing for this purpose, it is not desirable that lawyers be involved at this stage of the process and in matters of this sort legal intervention ideally should be kept to a minimum;

- exceptional circumstances of the type occurring in *Smullen*, may justify immediate or even long-term suspension without notice or invocation of other procedures, e.g. where there is danger to life and property;

- where Department of Education and Science Guidelines or the provisions of the Education Act 1998 do not apply to a particular school, it is important

---

[46] Kearns J. was of the view that the headmaster had wrongly concluded that he had no option but to expel the boys automatically before any submissions were heard.

for such schools to have clear rules of conduct and to ensure that parents and pupils are made fully aware of them and the school's disciplinary policy. In addition, it would be prudent for schools to adopt a practice of requiring parents to read and sign such rules, particularly where any rule relates to behaviour of students off the school premises and outside school hours.

Although conceding that legal representation may become necessary, but "only ... as a last resort in matters of this nature", in relation to the second of these points, insofar as the involvement of lawyers was concerned, Kearns J., in an implicit endorsement of what was stated in *Smullen* noted:

> "There is something inherently offensive in the concept of school authorities being obliged to thrash out difficult problems of discipline with parents, particularly at the initial stages, if either side goes to such a meeting with legal representation."

This approach was followed in the next case which is described, which also considers another aspect of fairness of procedures – the right to know what is alleged before action is taken.

Injunctive relief

In the High Court, in *Wright v. Board of Management of Gorey Community School*[47] the central allegation against two brothers again involved alleged drug use which occurred, this time, during an all night charity hockey marathon at the defendant school. Here, one brother had previously been suspended for admittedly bringing cannabis to the school and apparently sharing it with his brother (which was contested) and with a number of other pupils. On that occasion, both this student and his parents had signed an acknowledgement, in the context of the lifting of an indefinite suspension, that any recurrence or similar activity would result in his immediate and permanent expulsion from the school. The brothers were suspended pending the investigation of the allegations made in relation to the hockey marathon.

Having carried out an inquiry, the principal concluded that the brother previously suspended had bought cannabis and arranged to have his brother deliver it to the school. All of this was denied by the brothers as were certain factual allegations. The parents, having initially signalled their intention of withdrawing their sons from the school voluntarily, later changed their mind

---

[47] [2000] I.E.H.C. 37 (March 28, 2000).

on the basis that to do so in the context of allegations which were denied would mean that they were leaving under a cloud.

At a meeting of the board of management, the principal outlined the results of his investigation indicating, among other things, that the brothers had denied the allegations and also indicating his view that the incident in question alone would not be sufficient to warrant his recommending the expulsion of one brother. However, other allegations were also made. The parents also made a submission and questioned the principal on his account to a certain extent.

The board then deliberated in the absence of the principal and parents and later advised the parents that one brother was to be expelled and the other suspended for some three months. On an application for an injunction seeking their immediate re-instatement in the school, pending the trial of the action, in which they claimed, among other things, a declaration that unfair procedures were adopted against them O'Sullivan J., echoing the approach of *Smullen* and *Student A*, stated:

> "... in the case of a school, the requirement of maintaining discipline and authority means that the requirement of fair procedures does not demand something approaching the formality of a courtroom situation even where expulsion, which is the ultimate sanction with very serious consequences for the person expelled, is open for consideration. I am far from persuaded, for example, that it is necessary (or desirable) to arrange for the cross-examination by lawyers of student witnesses in a case such as the present."

He considered that, even though the parents had legal advice, there was a fair question to be tried, as it was arguable that the charges and details of the evidence upon which they were based became known to the parents only in the course of the proceedings before the board itself. O'Sullivan J. accepted:

> "... that the accused should be given a reasonable opportunity to hear the case (*i.e.* charges and an account of the evidence) against him, to respond to it with evidence of his own if he wishes and to address the deciding body. I also consider that such a reasonable opportunity includes being given advance notice of the charges and the gist of the evidence upon which they are based, so as to enable a considered response to be given, if necessary after taking legal advice."

But, that was not the end of the matter; he also had to consider where the balance of convenience lay and concluded that it lay in refusing the pupils' re-instatement. He noted:

> "If I were to re-instate the plaintiffs and they were to lose their action, enormous damage would have been done to the authority and policy of the defendant school, faced with the grave responsibility of dealing with any threat from drug abuse.
> On the other hand, if I were now to refuse the injunction and the plaintiffs eventually win their case, they will in all probability in the meantime have had access to appropriate schooling, neither of them is facing a watershed examination. ... Equally, if they win their case their reputations can be vindicated ...".

On balance, the court was, accordingly, satisfied that the injunction should be refused.

Reprise

In essence, in a school disciplinary process fair procedures must be followed which requires: (i) informing the pupil (and the parents) of the allegations and the gist of the evidence supporting them and (ii) allowing the making of representations before the deciding authority, *i.e.* the board of management, before sanction is imposed. Lawyers, it will have been seen, are not particularly welcome, at least not in the first instance. Finally, the general reluctance of the courts to interfere in a process that is fair is obvious for the reasons set out in the various dicta already referred to. Once a court has decided that a school has, in general terms, been fair it will not lightly interfere with the school's autonomy. In the enforcement of discipline, as a result of a breach of a school policy – whether in relation to bullying or otherwise – the courts will allow schools and their management a wide latitude and discretion, subject to fair procedures.

THE STATUTORY MECHANISMS

General

Statutory provisions, in relation to decisions concerning the expulsion and suspension of pupils from school, merit consideration in the context of what has already been described, in terms of judicial review proceedings. Having said that, it also merits noting that decisions of appeal committees and of the Secretary-General of the Department of Education and Science are also amenable to judicial review, in an appropriate case.

Education Act 1998

Section 28 of the Education Act 1998 provides as follows:

(1) The Minister, following consultation with patrons of recognised schools, national associations of parents, recognised school management organisations and recognised trade unions and staff associations representing teachers, may from time to time prescribe procedures in accordance with which-

(2) (a) the parent of a student or, in the case of a student who has reached the age of 18 years, the student, may appeal to the board against a decision of a teacher or other member of staff of a school,
 (b) grievances of students, or their parents, relating to the students' school (other than those which may be dealt with under paragraph (a) or section 29), shall be heard, and
 (c) appropriate remedial action shall, where necessary, be taken as a consequence of an appeal or in response to a grievance.

In prescribing such procedures, however, the Minister is required to have regard to the desirability of determining appeals and resolving grievances in the school concerned. But, in any event, section 29 of the Act, provides that where a school's governing board: (a) permanently excludes a student from a school, or (b) suspends him or her from attendance for a prescribed period the parent (or in the case of a student who has reached the age of 18 years, the student), may following the conclusion of any appeal procedures provided by the school or the patron (in accordance with section 28) appeal that decision to the Secretary-General of the Department of Education and Science. That appeal will then be heard by a committee which must include in its membership an Inspector (and other persons the Minister considers appropriate).

The procedures require that: (a) the parties to the appeal are assisted to reach agreement on the matters the subject of the appeal where the appeals committee is of the opinion that reaching such agreement is practicable in the circumstances, (b) hearings are conducted with the minimum of formality consistent with giving all parties a fair hearing, and (c) appeals are dealt with within a period of 30 days from the date of the receipt of the appeal by the Secretary-General (except in certain prescribed circumstances).

Following determination of the appeal, the appeals committee notifies the Secretary-General in writing of its determination and the reasons for that determination. Where a complaint is upheld in whole or in part, and it appears to the appeals committee that any matter which was the subject of the complaint (so far as upheld) should be remedied, the committee must make recommendations to the Secretary-General as to the action to be taken. Thereupon, the Secretary-General must notify the complainant and the board of the determination of the appeals committee and the reasons and (s)he may give such directions to the board as appear to the Secretary-General (having regard to any recommendations made by the appeals committee) to be expedient for the purpose of remedying the matter which was the subject of the appeal: the board must then act in accordance with those directions.[48]

Apart from the appellate procedures, the statutory provisions, on one reading, might reasonably be considered simply to reflect the ordinary public law requirements which have already been described.

Education (Welfare) Act 2000

Codes of behaviour

Section 23 of the Education (Welfare) Act 2000 requires the board of management of a recognised school, after consultation with the principal, teachers and parents of students at the school, and the educational welfare officer assigned, to prepare a code of behaviour in respect of the pupils. That code of behaviour must specify:

(a) the standards of behaviour to be observed by each student attending the school;

(b) the measures that may be taken when a student fails or refuses to observe those standards;

(c) the procedures to be followed before a student may be suspended or expelled from the school concerned;

(d) the grounds for removing a suspension imposed in relation to a student, and

(e) the procedures to be followed relating to notification of a child's absence from school.

The code of behaviour must be prepared in accordance with guidelines issued by the National Education Welfare Board,[49] following consultation with parents', school management and teachers' organisations. In addition, the principal before enrolling a child, is obliged to provide the parents with a

---

[48] These provisions are amplified in Department of Education and Science Circular Letter M48/01 and the annexes thereto.

[49] As of the date of publication, such guidelines have not been issued.

copy of the code of behaviour for that school and is empowered, as a condition of registration, to require the parents to confirm in writing that the code of behaviour is acceptable to them and that they will make all reasonable efforts to ensure compliance by the child. This accords significantly with what Kearns J. set out in *Student A*, which, pending the introduction of guidelines, provides a useful touchstone.

Expulsion

Insofar as expulsion from school is concerned, section 24 of the Education (Welfare) Act 2000 provides that where a board of management considers that a student should be expelled from school it must, before doing so, notify in writing the relevant educational welfare officer of its opinion and the underlying reasons. The educational welfare officer then must make all reasonable efforts to ensure that provision is made for the continued education of the student in question and:

(a) make all reasonable efforts to consult with the principal of the school, the student and parents, and "such other persons as the educational welfare officer considers appropriate", and

(b) convene a meeting attended by those persons as agree to attend.

A student may not be expelled from a school before the passing of 20 school days following the receipt of a notification by the educational welfare officer. But, this is without prejudice to the right of a board of management "to take such other reasonable measures as it considers appropriate to ensure that good order and discipline are maintained in the school concerned and that the safety of students is secured." In this regard, it must be considered that the principles enunciated in, in particular, *Smullen*, are relevant and that this statutory provision is an additional and not a substituting requirement.

Appeals by National Education Welfare Board of decision of boards of management

Pursuant to the provisions of section 26 of the Education (Welfare) Act 2000 the National Education Welfare Board may appeal *inter alia* a decision to expel a student to the Secretary-General of the Department. In addition, the National Educational Welfare Board may, at the hearing of an appeal brought by a parent or student against a decision to expel him or her, make such submissions (whether in writing or orally) to the appeals committee, as it considers appropriate.

Where a decision to expel a pupil is upheld by an appeals committee or where no appeal is brought against that decision, section 27 of the Act provides that the Board must make all reasonable efforts to have the child enrolled in another recognised school. Where it fails to do so, despite such efforts, it is empowered, with the consent of the parents of the child and the Minister, to "make such other arrangements as it considers appropriate to ensure that the child receives a certain minimum education". It is then required to monitor the progress of that education. This, too, must be considered to be an additional and not a substituting requirement.

SCHOOL DISCIPLINE: BALANCING INDIVIDUAL STUDENT RIGHTS AND THE COMMON GOOD

Dympna Glendenning[*]

Introduction

One of the global problems facing agencies and institutions that are responsible for the care and education of children to-day is the disruptive or aggressive behaviour occurring in a minority of children. There is growing concern among some teachers that their efforts to educate students, who are willing to learn, are being eroded by the persistent interference of a minority of students.[1] School discipline is one of the newly regulated spheres of life in this jurisdiction. Recent legislation, teachers fear, has left Principals and school management uncertain as to the scope of their disciplinary powers to sanction disruptive students and fearful of legal consequences if they impose serious sanctions. Moreover, when long term suspension or permanent exclusion (expulsion) is imposed on the more seriously disruptive students, following a successful appeal under the Education Act 1998 (section 29), they frequently return to disrupt the classroom and the cycle begins anew. Teachers point to the fact that they also have rights, as employees, to a safe place of work and a safe system of work[2] and that, as part of their conditions of employment, they are entitled to work without fear of attack or verbal abuse and without excessive stress.[3]

---

[*] B.A., M.Ed., Ph.D., Barrister.
[1] This was a major concern at teacher conferences held at Easter 2004 and in December '04 at a TUI conference. See Oliver Mahon B.L., *Irish Vocational Education Association (IVEA) Journal* and O. Mahon, *The Principal's Legal Handbook*, IVEA, 2002, Chap.2.
[2] Safety, Health and Welfare at Work Act 2005 commenced on September 1, 2005: S.I. No.328 of 2005 and S.I. No.548 of 2005.
[3] *Ibid.*, s.22 for health surveillance.

In response to teacher concerns the Minister for Education and Science has established a commission on school discipline to examine and report on the issues involved. This chapter discusses some of the legal issues involved in striking an appropriate balance, in school discipline between the interests of the school community and the interests of individual students in recognised schools.[4] At the outset, it is important to determine whether the schools are in State ownership or whether they are State-aided denominational schools as this factor is significant when considering the school disciplinary context.

PRELIMINARY POINT

By comparison with the European norm, in which a State system of education runs parallel to a denominational system, most schools in Ireland are owned by the dioceses or religious orders or by trustees under Deeds of Trust the main exception being the vocational sector in which the State owns the schools which are administered by the vocational education committees (VECs)[5] and the teachers are employed by the VECs. The fact that the majority of schools in Ireland are not State schools, but regulated[6] denominational schools, adds complexity to the disciplinary context as consultation with the parties in education[7] may be required to takes place in advance of prescription by the Minister for Education and Science (the Minister). For example, section 28 of the Education Act 1998 (the 1998 Act), requires such consultation prior to the prescription of Grievance and other procedures which would enable students and their parents to appeal their grievances against the decisions of teachers and staff members and their grievances against the school.[8] To date, however, no such procedures have been prescribed. It appears that any consultation which has taken place between the parties in education has not resulted in a consensus which would enable the Minister to prescribe these procedures to date.[9]

---

[4] Schools recognised by the Minister under s.10 of the 1998 Act.
[5] The State also owns and manages the dwindling system of Model schools and Educate Together schools are owned by limited companies.
[6] See the Education Act 1998; the Education (Welfare) Act 2000: the Equal Status Acts 2000–2004, the Ombudsman for Children Act 2002, the Education for Persons with Special Educational Needs Act 2004.
[7] Patrons of recognised schools, national associations of parents, recognised school management organisations, recognised trade unions and staff associations representing teachers.
[8] See Appendix 1 to this chapter for s.28 of the 1998 Act.
[9] As of January 2006, the date of going to press.

School Policies on Discipline

Section 23 of the Education (Welfare) Act 2000 (the 2000 Act) requires the board of management (the board), following consultation with the principal, teachers, parents of students and the educational welfare officer (EWO), to prepare a code of behaviour (the Code) in respect of students registered at the school. The Code must specify:

"(a) the standards of behaviour that shall be observed by each student attending the school;
(b) the measures that may be taken when a student fails or refuses to observe those standards;
(c) the procedures to be followed before a student may be suspended or expelled from the school concerned;
(d) the grounds for removing a suspension imposed in relation to a student; and
(e) the procedures to be followed relating to notification of a child's absence from school."

The Code must be drafted in accordance with guidelines to be issued by the National Educational Welfare Board (the NEWB) following consultation with the parties in education.[10] Prior to registering a student at the school, the Principal is required to provide the parents of the student with a copy of the Code and may, as a condition of registration, require the parents to confirm in writing that the Code is acceptable to them and that they will make "all reasonable efforts to ensure compliance with such code by the child."[11] However, this provision appears of limited value, as the school/teachers have no real sanction against parents who fail to respect their written undertaking. On request by a student, or a parent, the Principal must furnish him/her with a copy of the Code.[12]

Expulsion from a Recognised School

Where the board, or a person acting on its behalf, is of the opinion that a student should be expelled from the school, written notification must be

---

[10] The 2000 Act, s.23(3).
[11] Ibid., s.23(4).
[12] Ibid., s.23(5).

given to the EWO of its opinion and the reasons for the expulsion.[13] The EWO is then required to make all reasonable efforts to ensure that continuing provision is made for the student concerned.[14] This provision may not relieve the school of responsibility for the further placement of the student, however, and we must await judicial interpretation of this important point in this jurisdiction.[15] A student shall not be expelled from a school before the passage of 20 days following the receipt of a notification by an EWO under section 24(4). However, section 24(4)] is stated to be:

> "without prejudice to the right of a board of management to take such other reasonable measures as it considers appropriate to ensure that good order and discipline are maintained in the school concerned and that the safety of students is secured."[16]

Clearly the 20 day rule in section 24(4) does not fetter the discretion of the employer (the board of management) to take other measures, so long as they are reasonable, to maintain good order and discipline. So, if a student becomes violent or aggressive, the board retains the authority to suspend him or her for the full 20 day period having considered the circumstances. Alternatively, in-house suspension could be imposed on the student with care, education, homework and supervision elements in place. In the case of a 20 day suspension from school, the courts in this regard have not yet been called upon to determine whether obligations fall on the school to set and correct the suspended student's homework.

If the student it is proposed to expel has a disability, then there are important provisions in the Equal Status Acts 2000–2004 which must be taken into consideration[17] prior to any expulsion and these are discussed more fully in page 118. Where a student has a disability that, in the circumstances, could cause harm to the person or to others, treating that student differently, to the extent reasonably necessary to prevent such harm,

---

[13] *Ibid.*, s.24(1).
[14] *Ibid.*, s.24(2).
[15] See the case of *Ali v. Board of Governors of Lord Grey School, Times Law Reports*, April 9, 2004 which held that the Head teacher and governing body bore the primary duty in law to educate a child who had been accepted into their school. Sedley L.J. stated that the bare existence of the LEA's fallback duty [somewhat similar to the fallback duty on the Educational Welfare Officers in s.24(2) of the 2000 Act], did not relieve the school of its duties.
[16] The 2000 Act, s.24(5).
[17] Note s.4 of the Equal Status Act 2000 as amended is without prejudice to ss.7(2)(a), 9(a) and 15(2)(g) of the 1998 Act.

does not constitute discrimination on the disability ground.[18] With reference to "educational establishments", section 7(4)(b) contains an exemption which aims to extend to certain situations where a student, because of his or her disability, would prove disruptive to a degree that would disrupt or negate the education of other students in the school.[19] So, if a student's disability was making impossible, or having a seriously detrimental effect on, the provision by an educational establishment of its services to other students, this would not constitute discrimination under the Act[20] a point that was established in *Clare v. Minister for Education and Science*.[21]

When seeking to permanently exclude or expel a student the onus would fall on the board to establish that the student was making it impossible or having a seriously detrimental effect on the educational services being provided to other students in the school or that the presence of the student in the school could cause harm to the student or to others in the school.[22] This brings to the fore the importance of good communication with parents, appropriate and adequate record keeping and monitoring of a student's disruptive behaviour in accordance with a well drafted and carefully implemented Code of Behaviour[23] grounded in fair procedures and natural justice.

If a recognised school[24] is seeking to permanently exclude (expel) a student who has special educational needs, the provisions of the Education for Persons with Special Educational Needs Act 2004 (the 2004 Act) apply as most of its provisions have now been commenced.[25] The 2004 Act makes

---

[18] Section 4(4) and s.4 generally. S.4 of the Equal Status Act 2000 as amended is without prejudice to ss.7(2)(a), 9(a) and 15(2)(g) of the 1998 Act.
[19] In the Dáil Debates (Cols. 958–964, 513)the Minister made it clear that the exclusion of a student in such circumstances would require a stringent test *i.e.* that the student's disability "must make impossible or have a seriously detrimental effect on the school's provision of its services to other students. ... It is not intended to cover cases where it would inconvenience the school to have a pupil with a disability nor are the perception or attitudes of other pupils or their parents relevant.[W]here an educational establishment seeks to avail of such an exemption, it will be a matter for that establishment, not the complainant, to show that the exemption applies."
[20] *Ibid.*, s.7(4)(b) and s.7 generally.
[21] Unreported, High Court, July 30, 2004.
[22] *Ibid.*, s.4(4).
[23] Drafted in accordance with s.23 of the Education (Welfare) Act 2000.
[24] A school recognised pursuant to the Education Act 1998.
[25] The following Statutory Instruments have been brought into force by the Minister: On July 14, 2005, S.I. No.507 of 2005 was signed by the Minister thereby commencing ss.1, 2, 14(1)(a), 14(1)(c), 14(2)–14(4), 19–37, 40–44 and 50–53: on July 14, 2005, S.I. No.508 of 2005 which appointed October 1, 2005 as Establishment Day for the National Council for Special Education (NCSE) under s.19 of the 2004 Act: on July

further provision for the education of people with special educational needs, wherever possible, in an inclusive environment with those students who do not have such needs.[26] In determining whether a student with special educational needs was lawfully excluded or expelled, a court would be likely to interpret the provisions of the 2004 Act harmoniously with the relevant provisions of the Equal Status Act 2000–2004, the Education Act 1998, the Education (Welfare) Act 2000, the Safety Health and Welfare at Work Act 2005 and any other germane legislative and constitutional provisions.

The 2004 Act seeks to ensure that children with special educational needs will have the same right to avail of and benefit from appropriate education as their peers who do not have such needs wherever possible. The National Council for Special Education (the Council) established under the Act will designate the schools which children with special educational needs will attend either of its own volition or at the request of parents of a child who has had an education plan prepared under section 8(1)[27] and boards of management may appeal that designation[28] to the Appeals Board. The Act seeks to balance the right of students with special needs to an integrated education, wherever possible, with the effective education of other children in the class or school. Provision is made for assessments, the making of education plans and for the delivery of services to children with special educational needs. Section 2, which has been commenced, provides:

> "A child with special educational needs shall be educated in an inclusive environment with children who do not have such needs unless the nature or degree of those needs of the child is such that to do so would be inconsistent with—
> (a) the best interests of the child as determined in accordance with any assessment carried out under this Act, or
> (b) the effective provision of education for children with whom the child is to be educated."

It is one of the duties of a school to ensure that it complies, *inter alia*, with section 2.[29]

14, 2005, S.I. No.509 of 2005 was signed by the Minister setting up the Appeals Board under s.36 of the 2004 Act: on September 30, 2005, S.I. No.636 of 2005 was signed by the Minister which commenced ss.45–49.

[26] In addition to that which already exists pursuant to the Education Act 1998 (the 1998 Act), the Education (Welfare) Act 2000 and the Equal Status Act 2000–2004 all of which carry the presumption of constitutionality.

[27] S.10(1).
[28] *Ibid.*, s.10(3).
[29] See s.14 for the school's duties.

If a school is seeking to permanently exclude a child with special educational needs, the best interests of the child must first be determined in accordance with an assessment, for which provision is made in the 2004 Act.[30] In the event of a dispute arising as to the balance to be achieved between the child's best interests and the effective provision of education to other children to be educated, it will be for the Appeals Board or following mediation, the courts,[31] if called upon, to determine where the appropriate balance lies having considered all the circumstances of each case. Once again the significance of on-going monitoring and good record keeping and parental consultation on the part of the school is self-evident here. Questions may be raised in regard to the constitutionality of the mediator's function under the 2004 Act in the light of Article 34 [32] of the Constitution in view of the fact that the mediator will be adjudicating, *inter alia*, on fundamental rights. However, the 2004 Act carries the presumption of constitutionality and the mediator's function in the Act is arguably in the interest of the common good so it is unlikely that the courts would find this provision to be unconstitutional.

FAIR PROCEDURES AND NATURAL JUSTICE CONSIDERATIONS

A school's disciplinary decisions may be challenged on the grounds that the decision-maker failed to implement fair procedures or natural justice principles, concepts which are distinctive although closely related. It is well settled that a person who may be adversely affected by a decision relating to his/her rights or liabilities must not be condemned without a hearing but must be given an opportunity to state his/her case.[33] In this jurisdiction, natural justice is buttressed and extended by constitutional justice and in particular the well established guarantee of fair procedures implicit in Article 40.3 of the Constitution.[34] These principles apply in the school context where the rights and liabilities of students are being seriously affected by a decision

---

[30] In ss.3 and 4 of the Act.
[31] Note the provision in s.38(7) which permits a court hearing proceedings under ss.38(1)(b) when making any decision as to costs to have regard to the fact that the plaintiff/applicant refused to participate in the mediation provided or that they did not participate in good faith and the court may have regard to the mediation report.
[32] Article 34 provides: "Justice shall be administered in courts established by law by judges appointed in the manner provided by this Constitution. ...".
[33] *Maunsell v. Minister for Education* [1940] I.R. 213; *State (Gleeson) v. Minister for Defence* [1976] I.R. 280.
[34] *In re Haughey* [1970] I.R. 217; *Garvey v. Ireland and Others* [1981] I.R. 750.

although case law indicates that the courts tend to apply them less stringently in the school setting.

In *Student A and Student B v. A Secondary School*, [35] Kearns J., as he was then, stated that, once a school has been in general terms fair, that the courts should not lightly interfere with the autonomy of the school or do anything which might have the effect of damaging its capacity to discipline its students, given that the school unusually knows best. The judge also held that in the context of any meeting or hearing concerning long-term suspension or expulsion from the school, it was not desirable that lawyers be involved at this stage of the process and, in matters of this kind, legal intervention should ideally be kept to a minimum.

In *Wright (a Minor) v. The Board of Management of Gorey Community College*,[36] O'Sullivan J. stated that he considered that:

> "... in the case of a school, the requirement of maintaining discipline and authority means that the requirement of fair procedures does not demand something approaching the formality of a Courtroom situation even where expulsion, ... is open for consideration. I do accept, however, that the accused should be given a reasonable opportunity to hear the case (i.e. charges and an account of the evidence) against him, to respond to it with evidence of his own if he wishes and to address the deciding body. I also consider that such a reasonable opportunity includes being given advance notice of the charges and the gist of the evidence upon which they are based, so as to enable a considered response to be given, if necessary after taking legal advice.

O'Sullivan J. cited with approval the earlier decision of Finlay J., as he was then, in *State (Smullen) v. Duffy*[37] which concerned a gang fight among students of a community school, outside the school gates, during which one student was stabbed and was later hospitalised. O'Sullivan J. considered that Finlay J. had set the correct standard applicable to a school investigation and determination of this kind. In the *Smullen* case Finlay J. ruled that in exceptional circumstances, for example, where there was a threat to life and property posed by the presence of the student, a school could lawfully impose immediate long-term suspension without notice or procedures. He held that the general school disciplinary scheme was essentially fair and wise and that the immediate suspension was justified in the light of the inherent powers vested in the Principal with disciplinary responsibilities. On the issue of

---

[35] Law Reports, *Irish Times*, January 31, 2000.
[36] Unreported, High Court, March 28, 2000.

whether the parents of the student were entitled to be legally represented at the board meeting which made the decision to expel, the judge stated:

> "... I am satisfied that there is no obligation either on the principal or upon the Board of Management in this case to permit any legal representation ... of the prosecutors or of their mother at any meeting or hearing in connection with this suspension. It seems to me inherent in the general provision for discipline of a school and indeed in the interests of pupils of a school and the relationships that should exist between them and the school authorities and between their parents and the school authorities that communication should, in the first instance at least, be direct and should not preferably, and certainly not as a right, be through legal representatives.".

As the law relating to fair procedures/natural justice is evolving, these principles may have wider application in schools in the future. The school should also bring to the attention of the student's parents their right to appeal the decision of the board of management pursuant to the Education Act 1998 and the timeframe imposed by the Act.

SECTION 29 APPEALS

Section 29 of the 1998 Act provides for an appeal procedure when students are, *inter alia*,[38] permanently excluded (expelled) from school or are suspended for a prescribed period[39] or when a school refuses to enrol a student. Parents of the student or the student, if they have reached their 18th birthday, may appeal that decision. Appeals may also be taken by the National Educational Welfare Board (NEWB) against the decision of the board relating to (a) the permanent exclusion of a student from a school and (b) refusal to enrol a student in a school under section 29.

The Minister has appointed appeal committees under section 29(2) to hear and determine these appeals. Each committee must include in its membership an Inspector of the Department of Education and Science (DES)

---

[37] [1980] 2 I.L.R.M. 46 at 50–52.
[38] Or when the Minister makes a decision pursuant to s.29(1)(d) of the 1998 Act following consultation with the parties in education.
[39] See s.24 of the Education (Welfare) Act 2000 and in particular s.4(4) which provides: "A student shall not be expelled from a school before the passage of 20 school days following the receipt of a notification under this section by an educational welfare officer."

and "such other persons as the Minister considers appropriate."[40] Where a committee is appointed, the Minister also appoints the chairperson from their number who, in the case of an equal division of votes, has a second or casting vote.[41] As may be seen, the committees are entirely comprised of ministerial nominees. Perhaps the composition of the appeals committees needs to be representative of the parties in education so as to reflect a more balanced decision-making procedure. In January 2005, it was estimated that of the 47 students who appealed against their "permanent exclusion" since 2001, only 5 were actually expelled.[42] If these figures are correct, in means parents succeeded in overturning the expulsion on appeal, or schools were required to withdraw the expulsion, in 42 cases out of 47[43] during this period but the balance may have altered since that date.[44] To the best of my knowledge, no legal challenge to a determination of a section 29 Appeals committee[45] or to a direction of the Secretary General to the board of management,[46] either by a school or a student, has been heard in our courts to date.

In England, changes have been made to the local authority independent appeal panels, which regulate school exclusion decisions, so as to achieve a better balance between the interests of the excluded students and the interests of others in the school. These panels were previously required, when making their decisions, to consider only the impact of the exclusion on the pupil concerned. Now they must also consider the impact of their decisions on other pupils and on persons teaching at the school thus balancing the rights of the common good of the school community and individual pupil rights. These panels must also include a head teacher in their composition. If the panels in this jurisdiction are adjusted to reflect more representative decision-making and a better balance between the rights of the parties, permanent exclusions will most likely increase and appropriate provision for excluded children then becomes a priority. These measures affect children's statutory and constitutional rights to education and they will require careful, coordinated, long-term planning and provision.

---

[40] The 1998 Act, s.29(2).
[41] *Ibid.*, s.29(3).
[42] Sean Flynn, Education Editor, "Hanafin to set up commission on school discipline", *Irish Times*, January 5, 2005: Rebecca Smithers, *The Guardian*, "Exclusion Panel wields power over Schools, October 12, 2002.
[43] *Ibid.*
[44] I have been unable to obtain figures for the remainder of 2005.
[45] The 1998 Act, s.29(5).
[46] *Ibid.*, s.29(7)(b).

DETENTION OF CHILDREN

The courts are not unaware of the problems being experienced by schools in regard to disruptive students. In *T.D. and Others v. Minister for Education*[47] which dealt with the accommodation and treatment of a number of disadvantaged children, Hardiman J. stated in the Supreme Court:

> "Where a young person becomes uncooperative and unwilling to assist in his own education, difficult to accommodate in schools or institutions because he is felt to be a threat to other students and staff, and prone to taking drugs, a very difficult situation arises. This situation is acute whether the young person is being cared for by the State or by his parents." [48]

Hardiman J. referred to the young person's right, on approaching his or her majority, not to be unlawfully detained in circumstances where they have not been convicted of any crime. While an element of containment may be feasible and consistent with some form of education, he stated, it may be increasingly difficult as the young person approaches his majority. As a place offering an element of containment or detention moves towards a totally secure environment, the more closely it resembles a prison or place of detention for persons convicted of criminal offences.[49] The efficacy of very secure detention for educational and social purposes of a person approaching his 18th birthday, Hardiman J. continued, must at least be variable and the legality of secure detention may not be entirely guaranteed merely by the fact that it takes place in an institution other than a penal one. From any perspective, a real likelihood of progress and co-operation are certainly necessary, he concluded, to mandate the forcible detention of a person coming close to his majority who is not being prosecuted for, or convicted of, any criminal offence.[50]

HEALTH AND SAFETY

As well as their common law duties, boards of management have duties under the Safety, Health and Welfare at Work Act 2005 and regulations made thereunder, to ensure, so far as is reasonably practicable, the safety, health and welfare of their employees. This means that the board is required

---

[47] [2001] 4 I.R. 259.
[48] *Ibid.*, p.344.
[49] *Ibid.*, pp.344–345.
[50] *Ibid.*, p.345.

to provide a working environment for employees that is, safe and without risks to their health, safety and welfare, but this clearly that is not an absolute duty. In the context of school discipline, this would probably mean that the board, when making a decision, is required to balance the degree of risk involved to students and staff by retaining a violent student in school, and the damage which would most likely accrue to the education of other students, against the individual student's loss of education and the educational alternatives available to the student. What if the school makes alternative provision for the student on his or her reinstatement? Some of the principles in recent House of Lords cases are of interest to the school disciplinary setting and although they are not binding on Irish courts, they may be of persuasive influence.

RECENT HOUSE OF LORDS CASES

The Case of "L" and In-School Detention

In the case of pupil L (*Re L (a minor)*), the stated refusal of teachers to work with him forced the school to establish an alternative regime for him in which he was taught by supply teachers apart from his classmates.[51] L was expelled from a secondary school as a result of his involvement (to some extent) in a violent and injurious assault on a fellow pupil in the school toilets. The following day, the headmaster permanently excluded L and his decision was later upheld by the school's governing body. On appeal, the appeal panel directed that L should be reinstated immediately. L did not rejoin mainstream classes but spent the school day in a 10-foot square room, where he was joined later by another pupil. L was not permitted to speak or associate with any other pupil until the second pupil arrived. He was prohibited from speaking with staff members save for his supervisor and any other willing staff member and he sat his GCSE in a different room to his classmates. L was not permitted to join in communal acts of worship. A mathematics teacher, who had previously taught at the school prior to retiring, but was not a union member, taught mathematics to L but he received no other face to face tuition although teachers in other subjects set him work and marked it. L sought judicial review of the school's decision. L complained that the regime put in place for him in school did not amount to "reinstatement" under the Schools Standards and Framework Act 1998 and so this arrangement did not give effect to the panel's decision that he be reinstated in school.

---

[51] [2003] U.K.H.L. 9.

This case brought to the fore the balance which a school must strike between the interests of an individual pupil and those of the total school community. In a 3-day hearing, Ms Cheri Booth QC argued that L had been denied "a proper education" and the school was in breach of its obligations to reinstate him under the School Standards and Framework Act 1998. Lord Scott stated that "His [the excluded pupil's] loss of social contact with other pupils at the school for a relatively short period had to be measured against the possible disruption to the teaching of the other pupils at the school." The possible effect on the victim of the assault, if one of the assailants had been allowed to resume social contact with others, also had to be taken into account, he stated. Lord Walker and Lord Hobhouse agreed. However, Lord Hoffman and Lord Bingham disagreed stating "The pupil must be substantially reintegrated in the social and educational life of the school and nothing short of that will do." Finally, the House of Lords upheld the right of the school to make alternative educational provision for L, provided it was reasonable and proportionate. One needs to be mindful, however, that this was a 3:2 decision.

The L case would probably not have reached the courts if changes in the appeal panel regulations had been in place prior to the original exclusions. From January 2003 onwards, local authority appeal panels must include serving teachers and pupils will not be reinstated simply because of a school's procedural mistake. Furthermore, the independent local authority panels are now required to balance the interests of excluded pupils against the interests of others. The government had previously issued guidelines to such panels that they should not normally recommend reinstatement of pupils in cases which involved threats and violence. What if the teachers refuse to teach the violent student on his or her return to the school?

The Case of "P" and the Legality of Strike Action

In a recent case, *Re P (a Minor)*,[52] the House of Lords[53] considered whether the strike action taken by a group of teachers, who refused to teach a reinstated pupil, was lawful under the English legislation.[54] This was essentially a dispute over terms and conditions of employment[55] and whether there was a contractual obligation on teachers to teach P in the particular circumstances

---

[52] [2003] U.K.H.L. 8 on appeal from [2001] E.W.C.A. Civ. 652.
[53] While such cases are not binding on an Irish court, they are frequently persuasive but one needs to be mindful of the different legislation applying in this jurisdiction.
[54] The Trade Union and Labour Relations (Consolidation) Act 1992, s.219 and ss.226–234.
[55] *In re P (a Minor)*, at n.30, *per* Lord Bingham, para.24.

Balancing Individual Rights and the Common Good

of the case. The appellant was a student at a voluntary aided school in central London. His teachers found him to be disruptive in class and abusive in the playground. On the June 6, 2000, the headmaster directed that P be permanently "excluded" or expelled from the school. P appealed to the board of governors and on the June 30, 2000, it directed that he be reinstated. Accordingly, the headmaster instructed the teachers to take P back into their classes. The union contended that the headmaster's direction to teach was unreasonable. Nonetheless, P returned to school. Following further disruptive incidents involving P the following year, some teachers lodged complaints to their union, the National Association of School Masters/Union of Women Teachers (NASUWT) stating that they should not be required to continue to teach P. The union gave notice to the governors that they intended to ballot their members on whether they should strike, or take industrial action short of strike, in furtherance of their objections to having to teach P.

Following the ballot, which was unanimous in favour of industrial action, the teachers refused to teach P in their classes. The headteacher arranged for P to occupy a separate room, supervised by a supply teacher, and do work which was set by other teachers. P then took an action against the union.[56] When the case came before the House of Lords, on appeal, the main issues to be determined were (i) the measure or scope of immunity enjoyed by the unions from actions against them by employers based on the tort of inducing breaches of contract by employees and (ii) the validity of the ballot taken in the particular circumstances. The crux of the matter in relation to the ballot was, whether it was invalidated and the union's entitlement to immunity lost, because it failed to treat two members at the school, as persons entitled to vote.[57] Lord Bingham stated with regard to the first issue:

> "But the immunity has never been, and is not now, unqualified. Under the law as it now stands, immunity is enjoyed only if the inducement is an act done in contemplation or furtherance of a trade dispute (Trade Union and Labour Relations (Consolidation) Act 1992, section 219) and only if the breach induced has the support of a properly conducted ballot (1992 Act, sections 226–234)."[58]

---

[56] Under s.235A of the Trade Union and Labour Relations (Consolidation) Act 1992) which gives a statutory cause of action to an individual against a trade union in certain circumstances.
[57] However, this omission did not effect the outcome of the ballot.
[58] At para.2 of his judgment.

The Court held this was a genuine trade dispute which related to the terms and conditions of the teachers' employment and that the dispute had been the subject of a proper ballot and it dismissed P's appeal against the union.

One must be mindful, however, that the right to education is constitutionally protected in Ireland. However, the right of teachers in Ireland to withdraw their services was recognised by Kenny J. in the High Court in *Crowley v. Ireland*[59] when he stated:

> "The State cannot by laws compel teachers to teach when they do not wish to do so, though it may and should protect their right to teach when they wish to do so and others want to prevent them."

Even if teachers had a right to refrain from teaching, however, he continued, it was not a right which could be exercised for the purpose of frustrating, infringing or destroying the constitutional rights of others.[60] It was established in the *Crowley* case that the children's constitutional right to free primary education was infringed by the teachers' union[61] and substantial damages were awarded to a number of those children in subsequent cases.[62] One needs to be mindful, therefore, that the right to education is a Constitutional right in this jurisdiction.

STUDENTS WITH SCHOOL ATTENDANCE PROBLEMS

If a disruptive student has school attendance related problems, as is frequently the case, then the NEWB should be contacted as it may, with parental consent, arrange for an assessment[63] of the child.[64] Where a parent refuses such consent, the NEWB may apply to a judge of the Circuit Court (for the Circuit in which the child resides) for an Order that an assessment of the child be carried out. If satisfied at the hearing of an application, that such an assessment is warranted, the Court may order that the assessment be made and specify the manner, the place it is to be made and the person who will make the assessment.

---

[59] [1980] I.R. 102.
[60] *Ibid.*
[61] The INTO.
[62] *Conway v. INTO* [1991] 2 I.R. 305; *Hurley v. INTO* [1991] 2 I.R. 328; *Sheehan v. INTO* [1997] 2 I.R. 327: many of these cases were settled out of court, see further Glendenning, *Education and the Law* (Butterworths, 1999), p.376 *et seq.*
[63] Intellectual, emotional and physical only.
[64] S.10(6).

Apart from the statutory obligations falling on schools and principals, further obligations could fall on the Principal and teachers under the common law. Accordingly the importance of referral onwards of a student for professional assistance cannot be overstressed, as the board the Principal and the teachers could be held liable in negligence for failing to do so. In the *Dorset* case, Lord Browne-Wilkinson, applying the professional standard, ruled that the headmaster has a duty of care to exercise the reasonable skills of a headmaster in relation to the child's educational needs:

> "If it comes to the attention of the headmaster that a pupil is underperforming, he does owe a duty to take such steps as a reasonable teacher would consider appropriate to try to deal with such underperformance ...".[65]

It should be noted, however, that the courts in this jurisdiction have not applied the professional standard of care to teachers to date but rather that of reasonable care in all the circumstances of the case or the *in loco parentis* standard.[66]

Nonetheless, teachers and principals would be well advised to refer all pupils who are underperforming or who, in their opinion, have special educational needs or disability or behavioural problems for an assessment and the letters of referral should be appropriately retained.

When section 3 of the Education for Persons with Special Educational Need Act 2004 is commenced, principals will have further statutory obligations in relation to assessments and the preparation of education plans for those students who have special educational needs. The performance of any function conferred on the principal under the 2004 Act may be delegated by him/her to a teacher in the school as the principal considers appropriate.[67]

THE LEGALITY OF EXCLUSION

In England, the legislation permits head teachers to exclude a pupil for a total of 45 days in a school year and in all cases, of more than a day's exclusion, work is required to be set and marked for the pupil.[68] In the

---

[65] *X Minors v. Bedfordshire C.C. and other cases* [1995] 2 A.C. 633: see also *Phelps v. London Borough of Hillingdon*, HSE, July 27, 2000.
[66] *Maher v. Board of Management of Presentation Junior School* [2004] I.R. 337.
[67] S.18. The function then becomes performable by the delegatee.
[68] School Standards and Framework Act 1998, ss.64–68.

House of Lords case, *Ali v. The Head Teacher and Governors of Lord Grey School*, the liability of a school for the unlawful exclusion of a pupil came before the Court. Lord Justice Sedley stated as follows:

> "School exclusions are a serious matter. A disturbingly high proportion of the prison population has begun by being excluded from school. But a refractory pupil can disrupt the education of others and make teachers' work impossible. Legislation, guidance and case-law have sought in recent years to balance between justice to pupils in trouble and justice to the school as a functioning unit. That is one aspect of the present case."[69]

A, who admitted being present, was one of three students suspected of starting a fire in his school at lunch time. A was excluded from school, indefinitely at first and later for a fixed term, on suspicion of being involved in the arson incident. All three students were charged with arson (on March 8, 2001) but the proceedings were discontinued for want of sufficient evidence (on March 29, 2001). By the time A was admitted into a new school, he had been without schooling for almost 11 months. It was not until the March 21, 2001 that the head teacher wrote to A's parents to notify them that she was excluding A until April 5, 2001. On April 25, the deputy head wrote to A's parents further excluding A until May 15, 2001 (the day following his SATS examination). The letters did not convey the legally necessary information about the right of access to the governing body. During all this time, self-assessed revision work in English, Mathematics and Science was provided for A to do at home and he was allowed to return to the school to sit his examinations (which he passed) but not otherwise. A contended that his exclusion and removal from school were unlawful and a breach of his right to education under Article 2 Protocol 1 of the European Convention on Human Rights (ECHR)[70] and he sued the head teacher and the governors for damages.

The trial judge found that neither the exclusion nor the subsequent removal from the school roll had complied with the procedural requirements of the School Standards and Framework Act 1998 but that this did not entitle A to damages for breach of his Convention rights. When the matter came before the Court of Appeal, it held that the early part of the exclusion (during which the student was afforded appropriate education through the provision of homework), did not breach the Convention. When the temporary exclusion

---

[69] [2004] E.W.C.A. Civ. 382 at para.2 of the judgment.
[70] See below.

ended, the Court stated, his continued exclusion was unlawful and the school had a clear obligation to admit him once it became clear that there were no grounds to exclude him on a permanent basis. The Court ruled that A's Convention rights were denied even though the school offered to continue providing him with homework. Moreover, the Court refused to accept the contention that section 19 of the Education Act 1996 (the 1996 Act) meant that neither the Head nor the governors were liable for the students' education because, from the moment of exclusion, the Act placed the responsibility for a child's education on the local education authority (LEA). The Court found that the Head teacher and governing body bore the primary duty in law to educate a child who had been accepted into their school.

On appeal to the House of Lords, Sedley L.J. stated that, although the first phase of the exclusion had been unlawful (because it was indefinite), there was no breach of A's Convention rights because he was given self assessing work in preparation for his SATS examination. In the second phase of the exclusion, once the permitted period of 45 days temporary exclusion had expired, the school had a duty either to re-admit A or to exclude him permanently. Having done neither, the exclusion then became a nullity and breached A's Convention rights although the school still offered to provide him with substitute work. Furthermore, the unlawful removal of A's name from the school roll did not end the breach which lived on until A was admitted into a new school. The bare existence of the LEA's fallback duty in section 19 of the 1996 Act, the court stated, did not relieve the school of its duties because in law it was the headteacher and the governing body who carried the primary duty to educate a child who has been accepted by their school and they were not entitled to exclude that child except as authorised by law.[71] Sedley L.J. stressed that in phase 1 of the exclusion, the legal vice was not the act of exclusion but the failure to set a term to it. In phase 2, the legal vice was the failure of the governing body to become involved and of the headteacher to inform the parents of their right to involve the governors. From the completion of the SATS examination, the school offered to provide A with work but the offer was not accepted. In the absence of an acceptable explanation, phase 3 of the exclusion had to stand on the same footing as the second. Once the period of 45 days temporary exclusion had expired, A's continued exclusion was incontestably unlawful and it was done in

---

[71] Under s.24 of the Education (Welfare) Act 2000, when the EWO receives the written notification of the board etc. (s.24(1)), the EWO must make "all reasonable efforts to ensure that provision is made for the continued education of the student ...". Does that relieve the principal/board/or other delegatee from responsibility for the further education of the excluded student?

defiance of a clear statutory prohibition and was a legal nullity. Readmission then became the only option. The House of Lords held that the school was not liable to pay damages to A under section 8 of the Human Rights Act 1988 from March 8, 2001 to June 6, 2001. However, the Court allowed the appeal, from June 7, 2001 to January 20, 2002. Accordingly, A was entitled to damages for breach of his Convention rights since his right to education thereunder had been breached during the latter period only and the action proceeded to the assessment of damages unless it was settled by the parties prior to that date.[72]

Since the European Convention on Human Rights is now part of Irish law, subject to the Constitution, under the European Human Rights Act 2002, it is relevant to the school disciplinary context. Article 2 of Protocol 1 provides:

> "No person shall be denied the right to education. In the exercise of any functions which it assumes in relation to education and to teaching, the State shall respect the right of parents to ensure such education and teaching in accordance in conformity with their own religious and philosophical convictions."

Clearly the first part of the above article is the person's right to education while the second part is a parental right. Now that the Convention is part of Irish law, albeit subject to certain limitations, interaction between the ECHR and educational rights in Ireland is awaited with much interest.

THE CONCEPT OF REASONABLE FORCE

In coping with the levels of disruptive behaviour in some contemporary classrooms, it may be necessary for teachers to have an understanding of the legal concept of "reasonable force" in the context of maintaining student discipline. To illustrate the concept in another common law jurisdiction, I will take the example of an Illinois high school teacher who intervened in a classroom fight in which two 16 year-old girls challenged each other shouting obscenities. When they ignored the teacher's plea for order and continued to fight, he stepped between them and grabbed the most belligerent student by the elbow to hasten her exit from the classroom. Later the student alleged that the teacher had caused injury to her elbow and she sued the School

---

[72] Sedley L.J. advised that careful attention be paid to the decision in *Anufrijeva v. Southwark LBC* [2004] 1 All E.R. 833.

District and the teacher for breach of her rights under the Fourth and Fourteenth amendments. The Seventh Circuit Court of Appeals affirmed a lower court's ruling and applied a test of reasonableness in which an immediate, effective action by the teacher was compelled in the circumstances. Given the particular context of the school environment, in which students do not enjoy the same liberty as would a private citizen, and because classroom order and effective discipline are crucial to education, the Court ruled that the teacher's action in applying physical force to restrain and control students was reasonable when there is a threat of injury or damage to property.[73]

In Ireland the legal provisions relating to "reasonable force" are to be found in the Non-Fatal Offences against the Person Act 1997 (the 1997 Act) which abolished the common law rule of law under which teachers were immune from criminal liability in respect of physical chastisement of pupils.[74] Thus, the current position is that any physical chastisement of a pupil by a teacher would leave the teacher open to both civil and criminal proceedings. On the other hand, the 1997 Act permits a person to use "reasonable force" in the following circumstances:

"(a) to protect himself or herself or a member of the family of that person or another, from injury, assault or detention caused by a criminal act; or
(b) to protect himself or herself or (with the authority of that other) another from trespass to the person; or
(c) to protect his or her property from appropriation, destruction or damage caused by a criminal act or from trespass or infringement; or
(d) to protect property belonging to another from appropriation, destruction or damage caused by a criminal act or (with the authority of that other) from trespass or infringement; or
(e) to prevent a crime or breach of the peace.[75]
(2) "use of force in subsection (1) is defined and extended by section 20.

---

[73] *Wallace v. Batavia School District*, 68 F. 3 d 1010: see 104 Ed. Law Rep. 132: also D. Frisby and J. Beckham, "Developing School Policies on the Application of Reasonable Force", 122 Ed. Law Rep. 27 (January 8, 1998).
[74] Corporal punishment was prohibited by Circular in 1982 but it was not abolished by law until 1997: smacking was banned in UK state schools in 1986 and the ban was extended to include fee-paying schools in 1996.
[75] S.18(1) of the 1997 Act.

Thus, a teacher may use "reasonable force" in self-defense or to prevent a pupil from committing a crime or from injuring themselves or others or to protect another's property or in any of the circumstances outlined above. However, a teacher's conduct would have to be reasonable and proportionate in the light of all the circumstances and the use of excessive force could result in criminal charges or a civil action for damages in certain circumstances. England has made some legislative amendments in that regard: the Education Act 1997 added a section to the Education Act 1996 Act to clarify, to some degree, when teachers may use physical force to restrain a pupil. It is notable that the provisions of the 1996 Act are not restricted to the school premises, but apply when the school has "lawful control or charge of the pupil". The Act permits teachers to use "reasonable force" to prevent a pupil:

- from committing a criminal offence (or what would constitute a criminal offence if they were old enough);
- from injuring themselves or others;
- from damaging property; and
- from acting in a manner that it contrary to good order and discipline at the school.

Moreover, the English Department of Education and Skills (DESC) has provided guidance through Circular 10/98[76] to schools and teachers. Such Circulars represent best practice and the courts may take them into account when cases come before them. Circular 10/98 suggests that reasonable physical intervention by a teacher might be:

- physically interposing between pupils;
- blocking a pupil's path;
- holding;
- pushing or pulling;
- leading a pupil by the hand or arm;
- shepherding a pupil away by placing a hand in the centre of a back or, in extreme circumstances, using more restrictive holds.

---

[76] Para 21.

One can see, however, how such interventions could get out of hand and lead, either directly or indirectly to litigation. Parental assaults on teachers in England have increased recently[77] and the courts have taken a firm line against such assaults. In 2002, the English courts jailed a parent for three months who pleaded guilty to common assault on her daughter's teacher.[78] Neither are assaults on teachers in this jurisdiction unknown. There has been an expansion of police patrols in and around schools in England and, as an extreme measure, full time uniformed police officers have been based in some schools in England's worst affected criminal areas as part of the government's new policy on truancy and bad behaviour[79] Hopefully, these latter measures will not be needed in this jurisdiction if the matter is adequately and appropriately addressed in time.

---

[77] Bev. Marshall, Yorkshire regional officer for the National Union of Teachers (NUT), cites a survey on assaults on teachers in England which shows that they had risen from 34 in 1988 to 130 in 2001.
[78] Will Woodward, "Parent Jailed for Hitting Teacher", *The Guardian*, July 31, 2002.
[79] See DESC, Circular 10/98. para.10.

MAKING PARENTS PAY: THE LEGAL ENFORCEMENT OF SCHOOL ATTENDANCE IN ENGLAND

NEVILLE HARRIS[*]

INTRODUCTION

In October 2005 the Labour Government in the United Kingdom published what it has described as pivotal proposals to carry forward its extensive programme of education reforms into a new phase. The proposals are contained in a White Paper of over 100 pages, which, if the Government holds sway in the face of opposition from within its own party, will in due course be followed by Labour's ninth Act of Parliament on education since coming to power in 1997.[1]

The White Paper, *Higher Standards, Better Schools for All*,[2] proposes increased independence for individual state schools and a schools system that is more responsive to the wishes and demands of parents, who are to be 'empowered'. School governors, head teachers and other teachers who already feel somewhat battered by the constant winds of legislative change and policy implementation that successive governments have imposed upon them will doubtless view these latest proposals with some world-weariness, notwithstanding any positive benefits that they may perceive in the Government's vision.

---

[*]LL.B, LL.M. Ph.D, Barrister, Professor of Law, The University of Manchester, UK.

[1] Education (Schools) Act 1997; School Standards and Framework Act 1998; Teaching and Higher Education Act 1998; Learning and Skills Act 2000; Special Educational Needs and Disability Act 2001; Education Act 2002; Higher Education Act 2004; Education Act 2005.

[2] HM Government, *Higher Standards, Better Schools for All. More choice for parents and pupils*, Cm 6677 (The Stationery Office, 2005).

One of the underlying aims of these proposals is to model state schools on independent (private) schools, particularly emulating their ethos, which is associated with a strong sense of individual school identity and mission, an emphasis on academic achievement, and good standards of discipline. The increased autonomy for state schools, through the acquisition of 'self-governing Trust' status,[3] will partly be at the expense of local education authority control. These authorities underwent a mini-renaissance under Labour, following the diminution of their powers under the Conservative governments from 1979-1997, but that will end. Their role will become residual, but one area of responsibility that they will retain is the enforcement of school attendance, including the service of a notice on parents of truanting children requiring them to satisfy the authority that the child is receiving a suitable education and, in default, serving a school attendance order and prosecuting if it is disobeyed.[4]

The enforcement of school attendance is an area which, in itself, has been subject to many reforms in recent years. Indeed, truancy was identified by the Government when coming to office as one of the major contributory factors to both educational under-achievement and wider social exclusion. It was the subject of the first report by the Social Exclusion Unit[5] which the Government established to look into not only truancy and exclusion from school but also a range of other social and economic problems such as teenage pregnancy and the skills gap. Over the years the powers and mechanisms for enforcing school attendance in England, including the sanctions that can be imposed on parents in cases of non-attendance (truancy), have been increased significantly. Developments have included the restoration of the courts' power to imprison the parents for their child's persistent truancy and the introduction of a power for police officers and designated officers of local education authorities to hand out penalty notices to parents.

Furthermore, governing bodies have been required to set targets for reductions in pupil absences in their schools.[6] Yet as the White Paper

---

[3] The process of acquiring this status would be initiated by the school's governing body, following consultation with parents. These trust schools would be able to control their own admissions, assets and personnel arrangements: *ibid.*, Chap.2.
[4] Education Act 1996, s.437. The school attendance order cannot be served until at least 15 days from the date of service of the notice.
[5] Social Exclusion Unit, *Truancy and School Exclusion* (London: The Stationery Office, 1998).
[6] See the School Standards and Framework Act 1998, s.63, as amended by the Education Act 2002, s.53; the Education (School Attendance Targets) Regulations 2005 (S.I. 2005/58, as amended). This duty applies only to state schools, who educate approximately 93% of school pupils in England. The targets do not need to distinguish between authorised and unauthorised absences.

acknowledges, these changes have not stemmed the increases in unauthorised absence from school. Indeed, the overall level of truancy has increased since 1996–97;[7] and on average 50,000 children in England are absent from school without authority on each school day.[8] This is despite government expenditure of £885 million on school attendance initiatives between 1997-98 and 2003-04, with a further £500 million committed by the end of 2005-06.[9] Although it appears that the Government does not intend to carry through the idea, floated by the Prime Minister, of withholding part of the social security benefits (such as child benefit) of parents of persistent truants,[10] it has nevertheless renewed its promise to "clamp down on truancy."[11] In fact, the White Paper proposals are somewhat thin on new ideas for ameliorating the problem; and for the most part the idea seems to be to apply more pressure on schools and local education authorities to utilise their existing powers and procedures more effectively and on parents to meet their responsibilities.

This chapter examines what is now quite a complex legal regime for the enforcement of school attendance, highlights the major initiatives to tackle truancy, and discusses the developing case law. It begins by examining the nature of the parental duty to ensure their child receives education and its relationship to the child's right to education.

THE RIGHT TO EDUCATION AND SCHOOL ATTENDANCE

It is widely accepted that the right protected in the first sentence of the European Convention on Human Rights (ECHR), Article 2 of Protocol 1, which provides that "No person shall be denied the right to education", is a right of the child, whereas the obligation in the second sentence of the Article, to ensure that such education and teaching as the state assumes responsibility for is in conformity with parents' "own religious and philosophical convictions," refers to a right of the parents.[12] The child's right to education is also, of course, protected under Article 28 of the UN Convention on the Rights of the Child (UNCRC), which in addition places States Parties under a specific positive obligation to "[t]ake measures to encourage regular attendance at schools and the reduction of drop-out rates." This duty seems

---

[7] See below, p.213 *et seq.*
[8] National Audit Office, *Improving School Attendance in England*, HC 212 (London: The Stationery Office, 2005), p.4.
[9] *Ibid.*, p.5.
[10] *Hansard*, House of Commons Debates, May 1, 2002, col. 940.
[11] N.2 *supra*, para.7.33.
[12] See *Eriksson v. Sweden*, Series A no 156 (1989) 12 E.H.R.R. 183 §93.

to imply less tolerance of home education than under the ECHR.[13] Indeed, home education does appear capable of bringing children's rights into conflict with those of parents, but is sanctioned under English law as a means by which the parent may fulfil his or her statutory duty to ensure that their child who is of compulsory school age[14] receives an "efficient full-time suitable ... to his age, ability and aptitude, and ... to any special educational needs he may have, either by regular attendance at school or otherwise."[15]

Parents can therefore educate their child at home, irrespective of the child's wishes, as long as the education provided meets these requirements. If a local education authority considers that the child is not receiving a suitable education it must serve a school attendance order requiring the parent to cause the child to become a registered pupil at the school named in the order, otherwise an offence is committed.[16]

Home education seems to be a growing trend: in 2004 some 21,000 5-16 year olds were being educated at home compared to 12,000 in 1999.[17] It is not clear what proportion of these home educated pupils are being taught by parents or by a visiting teacher employed by the local education authority. Either way, the concern is that these children may miss out on social interaction that is crucial to proper social development. Yet as Stanley Burnton J. commented in one recent case, "[e]ducation at home is different from education at school, but it is not necessarily less favourable to the pupil."[18] Some, however, argue that there are insufficient safeguards to the child's right to education, notwithstanding the local education authority's role in assessing the suitability of home educational provision by parents.[19]

In addition to the statutory duty on the parent to ensure the child's efficient full-time education, which is enforceable in the courts on the action of local education authorities (see below), the child's right to education is also supported by the statutory duties on local education authorities to ensure that efficient primary, secondary and further education is available to meet

---

[13] See *Kjeldesen, Busk Masden and Pedersen v. Denmark* (1979-89) 1 E.H.R.R. 711 and *Family H v. U.K.*, Application No. 10233/83 (1984) D.R. 105.
[14] Broadly speaking, ages 5 to 16: Education Act 1996, s.8.
[15] Education Act 1996, s.7.
[16] *Ibid.*, ss.437 and 443.
[17] Figures cited in L. Rogers, "Number of children taught at home soars", *The Sunday Times*, June 26, 2005.
[18] *VK v. Norfolk County Council and the Special Educational Needs and Disability Tribunal* [2005] E.L.R. 342, Q.B.D., *per* Stanley Burnton J. para.47.
[19] See O. Hyams, *The Law of Education* (2nd ed., Bristol: Jordans, 2004), paras 5.16 and 5.17.

the needs of the population in their area and that there are sufficient schools to ensure all pupils have the opportunity of appropriate education.[20]

While the latter would seem to imply that all children are guaranteed a place at school, the courts have held that it is only a "target duty" on local education authorities, so that when particular circumstances arise that are beyond an authority's control, such as teacher shortages due to limited financial resources, the authority may not be in breach of its duty.[21] In a case where children were unable to attend school because it had been closed for one day in a week in order to forestall industrial action by ancillary staff, the court found no breach of duty.[22]

While the exceptional nature of these situations suggests that interference with the child's right to attend school will in practical terms almost always be illegitimate, it must also be noted that when schools exercise their right to exclude a pupil on disciplinary grounds (or, more rarely, on health grounds), the local education authority's duty to make alternative educational provision for the pupil[23] does not require it to place him or her in a mainstream school (a placement in a "pupil referral unit" is common). Under government guidance, which local education authorities are required by law to take into account,[24] such alternative provision must be made within 16 days of the child's exclusion;[25] but the White Paper proposes a reduction to 6 days.[26]

It is also proposed that during those first five days when the child is unlikely to be receiving formal schooling of any kind the parent should be expected to take responsibility for their child by, for example, ensuring that he or she is "supervised doing schoolwork at home or, for example, at a relative's house."[27] A new offence is to be created, with the punishment of fines, for parents whose excluded children are found in a public place during school hours.[28]

---

[20] Education Act 1996, ss.13 and 14.
[21] *R .v Inner London Education Authority ex parte Ali and Murshid* [1990] 2 Admin. L.R. 822.
[22] *Meade v. Haringey London Borough Council* [1979] 2 All E.R. 1016.
[23] Education Act 1996, s.19.
[24] The Education (Pupil Exclusions and Appeals) (Maintained Schools) (England) Regulations 2002 (S.I. No.2002/3178), reg.7(2).
[25] Department for Education and Skills, *Advice and Guidance to Schools and Local Authorities on Managing Behaviour and Attendance: Responsibility for educating pupils out of school and re-integrating them into school* (London: Department for Education and Skills, 2005) (accessible via www.dfes.gov.uk/behaviourandattendance/guidance/IBAGuidance).
[26] *Op. cit.*, para.7.15.
[27] *Ibid.*, para.7.13.
[28] *Ibid.*

Once a young person aged under 16 is placed at a pupil referral unit or other arrangements have been made for his or her education not at school by the local education authority his or her attendance there is required in exactly the same way as if he was a school pupil;[29] but the parent would be acquitted of an offence if he or she could show that the child is receiving suitable education elsewhere.[30]

There have been a number of human rights challenges to the arrangements made by local education authorities for the education of children who are not attending school. One question is whether the ECHR right to education has been infringed by the provision of fewer hours of education (as few as eight per week) compared to that available to full-time pupils,[31] while it has also been argued that the right to privacy and family life in Article 8 of the Convention includes a right to be educated in a way that is conducive to the development of one's personality through interaction with other pupils.[32] Generally, however, the courts have acknowledged the wide discretion that enables authorities to tailor provision in the light of the various financial and other considerations that bear upon them and therefore condition the human rights in question.[33]

The acid test is one of legality. The courts' view is that if the authority is acting legitimately for the purposes of the Education Acts then it is highly likely to be meeting its human rights obligations.[34] Only when it fails to address compliance with its human rights obligations when going through the process of deciding how to exercise its discretion is it likely to be held in breach of the Human Rights Act 1998 in not paying proper regard to a relevant provision of the Convention. This happened when a Muslim girl who had been refused permission to attend school while wearing the jilbab (full-length cloak with head covering) successfully invoked Article 9 of the Convention, protecting her right to manifest her religious beliefs.[35] The

---

[29] Education Act 1996, s.444ZA, inserted by the Education Act 2005, s.116.
[30] *Ibid.*, s 444ZA(6).
[31] *The Queen on the application of B v. Head Teacher of Alperton Community School and Others; The Queen v. Head Teacher of Wembley High School and Others ex p. T; The Queen v. Governing Body of Cardinal Newman High School and Others ex p. C* [2001] E.L.R. 359.
[32] *Ibid.*
[33] See N. Harris, "Education: Hard of Soft Lessons in Human Rights?" in C. Harvey (ed.), *Human Rights in the Community. Rights as Agents for Change* (Oxford: Hart, 2005), 81–112.
[34] E.g. *A v. Head Teacher and Governors of Lord Grey School* [2004] E.L.R. 169, CA.
[35] *R (SB) v. Head Teacher and Governors of Denbigh High School* [2005] E.L.R. 198, CA.

school's fault lay in drawing up its school uniform policy without asking itself if it was acting in compliance with the Article.

A child's basic right to attend school is also supported via the parents' duty to ensure that a child, once a registered pupil at a school, "attends regularly;" failure in that duty makes the parents guilty of an offence[36] that has been held to be one of strict liability.[37] However, in one case in 1999, where the child was nearly 16 and had run away from home, the court considered that an absolute discharge was probably the maximum sentence that should be imposed on the mother in respect of the child's truancy and wondered whether prosecution had been appropriate in the circumstances.[38]

In another case, in 2003, the appellant, who had been convicted of this non-attendance offence and was fined £75 plus costs, argued that as the offence is one of strict liability it is contrary to Article 6(2) of the ECHR, which establishes the presumption of innocence until proven guilty according to law.[39] The court held that while the offence was one of strict liability that did not mean that the presumption of innocence did not apply to it: the authorities still had to establish proof of certain facts, for example that the child was a registered pupil, was of compulsory school age, had failed to attend regularly and, if the issue was raised, did not have a recognised excuse for absence. That meant that the court did not consider that Article 6(2) was engaged at all.

The two judges disagreed, however, on whether, had the Article been engaged, the justification for imposing criminal liability without fault would have stood up to the test as to its being proportional to the objective sought to be achieved, namely that convictions are facilitated and parents may face up to their responsibility. Maurice Kay J., who considered that it was proportionate, argued that "the wholly ignorant and blameless parent in respect of a child who does not attend school regularly ought to be an extreme rarity."[40] Elias J., however, considered that there was a lack of proportionality. For example, instead of imposing strict liability the law could apply a reverse burden of proof by requiring the parent to demonstrate the steps he or she had taken to secure the child's attendance.[41] Moreover, while the penalty for a conviction would generally be a small fine, there was

---

[36] Education Act 1996, s.444(1).
[37] *Crump v. Gilmore* (1970) 68 L.G.R. 56.
[38] *Bath and North-East Somerset District Council v. Warman* [1999] E.L.R. 81.
[39] *Barnfather v. London Borough of Islington Education Authority and the Secretary of State for Education and Skills* [2003] E.L.R. 263, Q.B.D.
[40] *Ibid.*, para.30.
[41] *Ibid.*, para.52.

"a real stigma attached to being found guilty of a criminal offence of this nature. It suggests either an indifference to one's children, or incompetence at parenting, which in the case of the blameless parent will be unwarranted."[42]

The question of parental awareness of the child's absence is however relevant as a potentially exacerbating factor. Under an amendment introduced under the Criminal Justice and Court Services Act 2000, if the parent "knows that his child is failing to attend regularly at the school and fails without reasonable justification to cause him to do so" he is guilty of a separate offence under the same section.[43]

Whilst the other offences relating to truancy carry a maximum penalty, on conviction, of a fine of £1,000, the offence introduced by the 2000 Act in March 2001 carries a maximum penalty of a £2,500 fine and/or imprisonment for a term not exceeding three months.[44] If the parent is prosecuted under this provision but the court acquits him or her, then, if the court considers that the strict liability offence has been committed it may proceed to convict the parent of that offence.[45] Note that fines imposed following prosecutions for truancy offences tend to be less than £100 and can be as low as £1;[46] and while a fine would appear to be the most common sentence it is not clear how many parents receive a conditional or absolute discharge.

The statute prescribes, in section 444, defences to a charge of failing to ensure a child's regular attendance (which means attendance at the times stipulated by the school or local education authority[47]) and these are considered to be exhaustive.[48] The first is absence "with leave".[49] Separate regulations provide that save in exceptional circumstances, leave can only be granted for a maximum of 10 school days per school year.[50] This provision enables parents to request permission for the child to attend a family holiday during term time, although the Government has encouraged schools not to

---

[42] *Ibid.*, para.57.
[43] i.e., the Education Act 1996, s.444. The new offence is in s.444(1A).
[44] *Ibid.*, s 444(8A).
[45] *Ibid.*, s 444(8B).
[46] *Hansard*, House of Commons Debates, November 14, 2000, col.909, *per* Mr Boateng, Under Secretary of State; *Hansard*, House of Lords, October 21, 2000, col.929, *per* Baroness Blatch.
[47] *Hinchley v. Rankin* [1961] 1 All E.R. 692.
[48] *Spiers v. Warrington Corporation* [1954] 1 Q.B. 61.
[49] Education Act 1996, s.443(3)(a).
[50] Education (Pupil Registration) Regulations 1995 (S.I. No.1995/2089), regs.(3) and (4).

grant it because it disrupts the child's education and sends out the wrong message to parents and other pupils about the importance of attendance. According to the current White Paper[51] permission is often refused these days.

The second of the defences actually combines two separate grounds: that the child was "prevented from attending by reason of sickness or unavoidable cause."[52] The courts have confirmed that the sickness must relate to the child and not to the parent.[53] They have also considered the meaning of "unavoidable cause."

In *Jarman v. Mid-Glamorgan Education Authority*,[54] the court considered that the unavoidable cause defence did not avail the mother of two pupils at a school where corporal punishment was administered who had kept them away from school because of her opposition to corporal punishment and its potential effect on her children, one of whom had been caned on the hand for missing detention. May L.J. said that "the words 'unavoidable cause' ... should in no way be equated with 'reasonable grounds'."

A similar approach was taken in *Bath and North-East Somerset District Council v. Warman*,[55] where a 15 year old girl left home to live with her long term boyfriend. She did not attend school and her mother was prosecuted. The girl did not tell her mother her whereabouts. Rose L.J. said that "[h]owever hard it may appear to be," the construction placed upon the provision by the relevant case authorities "makes the conclusion inescapable that the circumstances of this case did not give rise to unavoidable cause for the child's absence from school."[56] As noted above, the court nonetheless questioned the value of a prosecution in such a case.

These issues were re-visited in June 2005 in *The Queen (R) v. Leeds Magistrates Court and Others*,[57] which is an important decision because it confirms that sickness" may relate to mental as well as physical factors; and it hints that unavoidable cause may in some cases arise out of circumstances not directly concerned with the child. As in the *Bath* case the child in question was aged 15. She was absent from school for 117 days and her mother was prosecuted. The mother claimed that her daughter's absence from school was due to bullying by other pupils, which had caused the girl to become "stressed." She also said that the girl had talked about suicide, leading to the

---

[51] N.2 *supra*, para.7.30.
[52] Education Act 1996, s.444(3)(b).
[53] *Jenkins v. Howells* [1949] 2 K.B. 218.
[54] *The Times*, February 11, 1985.
[55] [1999] E.L.R. 81.
[56] *Ibid.*, p.84H.
[57] [2005] E.W.H.C. 1479 (Admin.).

mother withdrawing her from school and that her daughter had been put on anti-depressants by her GP. Both the girl herself and her sister also gave evidence regarding bullying.

The magistrates concluded that the girl was not away from school due to unavoidable cause, although they acknowledged the effect of name-calling upon her. They also held that there had been no violation of Article 8 of the ECHR, right to respect for private and family life, because the interference with private or family life was "necessary and justified and is a proportionate and legitimate aim" (for the purposes of Article 8(2)), namely to secure school attendance.

On appeal, Davis J. acknowledged that section 444 could result in what some people might regard as "hard results."[58] However, he said that the underlying policy was "reasonably clear: that is to say to seek to ensure the attendance at school of children and to underline the responsibilities of parents in that regard."[59] He found that the magistrates had concluded that there was not a significant risk of suicide and therefore on the evidence they were entitled to conclude that the child was not absent due to "unavoidable cause."

Counsel for the local education authority had conceded in argument that if there *were* evidence of a significant risk of suicide, that would amount to a defence, although it was more likely to be on the basis of sickness than unavoidable cause. With regard to Article 8, the court rejected the idea that the magistrates had focused on the wider issue of policy as to whether in these kinds of case interference with that right would be necessary and justified. The court held that they had rightly focused on the individual circumstances of the case.[60]

Finally, Davis J. considered whether unavoidable cause always had to be assessed with reference to the child, as the previous case law indicated. He concluded that the individual circumstances of the parent would not always be irrelevant, because it might be "that there are some cases where the circumstances of the parent may impact upon [those] of the child".[61] It has long been the case that truancy is more prevalent among those children whose family circumstances are difficult. The law has not permitted those factors to limit the parental obligation although it might have mitigated the sentence in particular cases.

Whether Davis J.'s acknowledgment that the parents' circumstances

---

[58] *Ibid.*, para.23.
[59] *Ibid.*
[60] *Ibid.*, para.25.
[61] *Ibid.*, para.30.

might impact upon the child for the purposes of the above defence alters the position remains to be seen. Unfortunately he did not develop the point and his comment might be taken to reflect a mere theoretical position. On the other hand, one can think of cases where, for example, a mother is a victim of domestic violence and goes into hiding with the child, which might be the kind of situation envisaged by the judge.

The other statutory defences to the non-attendance offences under section 444 are where the child is absent for a day of religious observance[62] or where the school "is not within walking distance ... and ... no suitable arrangements have been made by the local education authority for [the child's] transport ... or for boarding accommodation."[63] The local education authority is under a duty to provide transport for those not living within walking distance.[64] In considering whether it is necessary to provide transport to facilitate attendance at a school not within walking distance, the local education authority would need to consider whether, for example, the child was at risk of being bullied at a nearer school.[65]

There are no national statistics on prosecutions in truancy cases or their

---

[62] Education Act 1996, s.444(3)(c).
[63] *Ibid*, s 444(4)); "walking distance" is 2 miles, or 3 miles if the child is 8 or over, measured by the "nearest available route" (s 444(5)). There is considerable case law on what amounts to "suitable arrangements" for this purpose: see *R v. Rochdale MBC ex p Schemet* [1994] E.L.R. 89; *Re C* [1994] E.L.R. 273; *R v. Dyfed CC ex p S* [1994] E.L.R. 320; *Re S* [1995] E.L.R. 98; *R v. Bedfordshire County Council ex parte DE*, July 1, 1996, Q.B.D. (unreported); *R v. Kent County Council ex p C* [1998] E.L.R. 108, Q.B.D.; *R (Jones) v. Ceredigon County Council* [2004] E.L.R. 506. In considering whether it is necessary to provide transport to a school not within walking distance, the local education authority would need to consider whether, for example, the child was at risk of being bullied at a nearer school.
[64] Education Act 1996 s.509(4)(a), as amended following *Rogers v. Essex County Council* [1986] 3 All E.R. 321, where it was held that the age of the child and the nature of the route to school would be a relevant consideration as to whether transport to school should be provided. See also *R v. Devon County Council ex parte Paul George* [1988] 3 All E.R. 1002, where the House of Lords held that the parent has do that which is reasonably practicable to get the child to school, including accompanying him or her in situations where it would be unsafe for the child to go to school unaccompanied. In *R v. Essex County Council ex p EB* [1997] E.L.R. 327 the court confirmed that safety of the route was not a matter for the court to determine. McCullough J. said that the Secretary of State (i.e. officials) could do that and thus judge the reasonableness of the local education authority's conclusion. In a move to facilitate parental choice, the law is to be amended so that socially disadvantaged children who wish to attend a school up to six miles away will also qualify for free transport: n.2 *supra*, para.3.15.
[65] *R v. Carmarthenshire County Council ex p White* [2001] E.L.R. 172, Q.B.D.; *The Queen on the application of J v. Vale of Glamorgan County Council* [2001] E.L.R. 758, C.A.

outcomes. However, it was estimated in 2004 that each year approximately 7,500 parents are prosecuted and that 80% of prosecutions result in a conviction.[66] However, there is now a fast-track management procedure that local education authorities can use in truancy cases; it enables cases to be brought swiftly before the courts if the parent of a persistent truant fails to ensure that the child attends school regularly.

Under fast-track the parent is contacted and a review date is set for six weeks later; at the same time, the local education authority serves a summons and asks for a court date (set at 12 weeks later). If, by the time of the six weeks review, the attendance has not improved the case will proceed to court, unless compelling mitigating factors have emerged.[67] Figures published by the Department for Education and Skills (DfES) show that in the period April-July 2005 a total of 9,239 cases entered the fast-track process. Of these, 3,319 did not result in prosecution, in most cases (2,724) because attendance had improved. Therefore only 20.5% of cases (1,902) resulted in prosecution.

Is Prosecution the Answer?

As we saw above, the child's right to education is protected by a range of criminal sanctions linked directly to a failure to attend school. This fact demonstrates the importance attached to school attendance, or at least to receipt of an effective education, and thus to the parental obligation. The Government's policy was in part informed by the report on truancy and exclusion by its Social Exclusion Unit, which concluded that:

> "[p]arents bear the primary responsibility for ensuring that their children attend school regularly and home circumstances exert an important influence over pupils' attendance and punctuality. Poor parental supervision and lack of commitment to education are crucial factors behind truancy ... Some families condone unauthorised absence, for example, for family shopping trips. Others expect school-age children to look after younger brothers or sisters during the day, or to take on excessive responsibilities for helping out at home."[68]

---

[66] National Audit Office, *Improving School Attendance in England*, H.C. 212 (London: The Stationery Office, 2005), para.3.24.
[67] DfES, *Fast Track to Prosecution Framework – Towards Better Case Management*, www.dfes.gov.uk/schoolattendance (November 3, 2005).
[68] Social Exclusion Unit, *Truancy and School Exclusion* (London: The Stationery Office, 1998), para.1.8.

Yet there are important questions of principle and utility concerning prosecution of parents. Do the underlying objectives of maximizing the pressure on parents to ensure their children receive a full-time education justify the punishment of parents who may be innocent (parents are aware of their child's absence from school in only 50% of cases[69]) or ineffectual, for something that is outside their control? And, more pragmatically, does prosecution work?

The fact that truancy levels have increased rather than fallen since the new offence with stiffer penalties was introduced in 2001, leading to several highly publicized cases of imprisonment of parents that one would assume would have acted as a deterrent,[70] might suggest not. Moreover, fining parents who may already be under financial strain will not be conducive to family stability. Neither will imprisonment, although rarely imposed.

Research in the UK has shown that the overall effectiveness of prosecution in non-attendance cases is somewhat uncertain. In some cases, especially where the child is of primary school age (under 11), it can improve attendance; but it is ineffective where the causes of truancy lie outside the direct control of the parent.[71] The fast-track procedure, noted above, does seem to be effective in preventing recidivism. Probably because the service of the summons makes the threat of prosecution real, the procedure does seem to be effective in encouraging parents to improve their child's attendance. On the other hand, it appears that it might not be sufficient in cases of more entrenched truancy.[72]

The fact remains that truancy is a complex problem with a variety of causes some of which, such as bullying or victimization in school, may have nothing to do with the behaviour of the parent. Moreover, some parents lack the capacity to alter their child's behaviour, particularly once the child has reached adolescence, when the risk of truancy is at its greatest. In one survey the parents "cited a multitude of social disabilities – the overburdening anxieties connected with unemployment, poverty, illness and other family

---

[69] Hansard, House of Commons Debates, July 1, 2004, col. 423, *per* Mr I. Lewis, Under Secretary of State.

[70] In particular, the widely reported case of Patricia Amos, who was sentenced initially to a 60 day term: see A. Gillan, "Judge refuses bail for mother of truants", *The Guardian*, May 16, 2002. See also the case of a Suffolk woman reported in "Pregnant mother of truant spends Christmas in jail", *The Guardian*, December 27, 2002.

[71] National Audit Office, *Improving School Attendance in England*, H.C. 212 (London: The Stationery Office, 2005); S. Kendall and others: *School Attendance and the Prosecution of Parents: Effects and Effectiveness* (Slough: NFER/LGA, 2004).

[72] K. Halsey et al, *Evaluation of Fast-track to Prosecution for School Non Attendance* (Slough: NFER, 2004).

responsibilities – to explain inability to persuade their child to attend school regularly".[73] Yet the Labour Government has been desperate to enforce parental responsibility right across the education system while also acknowledging a need both for tackling some of the underlying problems such as bullying and boredom/alienation among those nearing the end of their period of compulsory schooling (as reflected in their plans for "personalised learning", including the choice of studying for specialized diplomas[74]), but also tougher action to ensure parents play their part. This may be seen as part of Labour's "Third Way" course between state support and the encouragement of personal/private initiative, of balancing citizenship rights and responsibilities.[75]

ALTERNATIVES TO PROSECUTION

A long-standing alternative to prosecution is an application for an education supervision order (ESO) under the Children Act 1989.[76] Before instituting a prosecution the local education authority must consider the appropriateness of applying for an ESO, and even if a parent has been or is being prosecuted the court can generally require the authority to apply for such an order.[77]

An ESO requires the local education authority, generally through its education welfare service,[78] to provide support and guidance to the family. The official guidance says that an ESO is not likely to be effective where the parents are "actively hostile to intervention" and that if that is the case alternative strategies such as prosecution might be called for.[79] The effect of

---

[73] P. Carlen et al., *Truancy: The Politics of Compulsory Schooling* (Buckingham: Open University Press, 1992), p.137.
[74] See n.2, Chap.4.
[75] See generally, HM Government, *New ambitions for our country. A New Contract for Welfare* Cm 3805 (London: TSO, 1998); H. Dean, *Welfare Rights and Social Policy* (Prentice Hall, 2002); C. Howarth, P. Kenway and G. Palmer, *Responsibility for All. A National Strategy for Social Inclusion* (London: NPI/Fabian Society, 2001).
[76] Children Act 1989, s.36. The local authority can subsequently prosecute under s.444 of the Education Act 1996: see *Graves v. London Borough of Islington* [2004] E.L.R. 1.
[77] Education Act 1996, s.447.
[78] On the recruitment and training of education welfare officers, see generally Department for Education and Skills, *Advice and Guidance to Schools and Local Authorities on Managing Pupil Attendance* (London: DFES, 2005) (www.dfes.gov.uk/behaviourandattendance/).
[79] Department for Education and Employment, *DfEE Guidance on Education Supervision Orders (Children Act 1989)*, p.2 (www.dfes.gov.uk/behaviourandattendance/).

the order is that the supervisor must "advise, assist and befriend and give directions" to secure that the child is "properly educated".[80] Directions might, for example, require the parents to attendance a meeting with teachers or require an assessment by an educational psychologist.[81] The advantage of this process is that it is likely to focus on the underlying causes of truancy, but the drawback is the cost in terms of public expenditure. If the parent fails to co-operate with their supervisor a separate offence arises under the Children Act 1989, but prosecutions are rare. Care proceedings arising out of truancy are only likely to occur where failure to attend school is one of a range of problems affecting a child's upbringing.[82] In any event, the local authority will investigate where a child persistently fails to comply.[83] This will fall under the remit of children's services authorities, which combine education and social functions for children, under the Children Act 2004.

One of the measures in operation for a number of years, having started around 20 years ago in Bradford and a few other areas, has been the use of truancy sweeps or patrols. Truancy patrols generally comprise a trained officer of the local education authority's education welfare service and a police officer. They search shopping malls and other areas where children are likely to be found. According to Government figures 12,000 children were stopped by 900 truancy patrols in England from April 29 to May 30, 2002. Around 50% were found to be with a parent and 68% were from secondary schools. Of those accompanied by a parent, around half did not have a good reason for being absent from school. Children who are unaccompanied by an adult are normally asked to accompany the truancy team back to school or to an agreed central location.

Indeed under the Crime and Disorder Act 1998, where the local education authority has designated premises for this purpose (and police have been notified of them), a police officer above the rank of Superintendent may authorise constables to exercise the following power in a designated area and at a designated time or times:

> "If a constable has reasonable cause to believe that a child or young person found by him in a public place in a specified area during a specified period—
>
> (a) is of compulsory school age; and

---

[80] Children Act 1989, Sch.3, para.12.
[81] Department for Education and Employment, *DfEE Guidance on Education Supervision Orders (Children Act 1989), op. cit.*, p.6.
[82] See, e.g., *O, Re (A Minor) (Care Proceedings: Education)* [1992] 4 All E.R. 905.
[83] Children Act 1989, Sch.3, para.19.

(b) is absent from a school without lawful authority ...
the constable may remove the child or young person to designated premises, or to the school from which he is so absent."[84]

Neither the child's nor the parent's consent is required. Clearly this process will not displace other procedures for imposing responsibility on the parents of truants, but it could deter truancy as well as helping to protect at least some of the children from dangers that may arise when they are away from the generally more protective environment of home or school. This power has been complemented since 2002 in 10 identified crime areas by the deployment of police officers in or around schools, as part of a policy known as Safer Schools Partnerships.

Penalty notices have also recently been introduced, under the Anti-Social Behaviour Act 2003, as an early deterrent aimed at preventing the establishment of a pattern of persistent truancy. An authorized officer, such as a police officer or a designated officer of the local education authority, may issue a notice where he or she has reason to believe that a child's parent has committed a school attendance offence.[85]

If the parent meets their responsibility regarding the education of their child within 42 days from receipt of the notice a prosecution may not be brought against them.[86] And if they pay the fixed penalty notice (£50, if paid within 28 days, or £100 if paid within 42 days) in accordance with the notice they will not be taken to court. The official guidance indicates that notices will be used where the truancy is parentally-condoned, where the parent is capable of remedying the problem but is unwilling to do so, and prosecution might be a 'heavy-handed' approach.[87]

Penalty notices have yet to become commonplace. Indeed, much less use is made of them than the fast-track prosecution procedure. Only 2,339 penalty notices were issued in England in the four months from April-July 2005, less than a third of the number of fast-track prosecution cases in this period.[88] However, the fact that in 1,176 (50%) of the cases the penalty was

---

[84] Crime and Disorder Act 1998, s.16.
[85] Education Act 1996, ss 444A and 444B, inserted by the Anti-social Behaviour Act 2003, s.23.
[86] The Education (Penalty Notices) (England) Regulations 2004 (S.I. No.2004/181).
[87] DfES, *Guidance on Education-Related Parenting Contracts, Parenting Orders and Penalty Notices* (London: DfES, 2004), para.64.
[88] DfES, *Data: Penalty Notices and Fast-track (for truancy) and Parenting Orders and Parenting Contracts (For truancy and exclusions)* (2005) www.dfes.gov.uk (November 3, 2005).

still unpaid after 42 days[89] raises doubts about the effectiveness of this measure and perhaps has influenced the course taken by local education authorities.

Parental responsibility is also enforced through the use of parenting contracts and parenting orders.[90] The latter were originally introduced under the Crime and Disorder Act 1998 with a view to controlling lawless behaviour by young people. They were extended by the Anti-Social Behaviour Act 2003 to cases where young people are excluded from school on disciplinary grounds or fail to attend regularly at a school at which they are a registered pupil (see below). As is implicit in the nature of contracts, parents cannot be compelled to enter into a parenting contract with their school's governing body or the local education authority; it is a voluntary arrangement.

Figures covering the period April-July 2005 show that 3,682 parenting contracts were proposed in England, of which 3,465 (94%) were accepted by parents.[91] The 2003 Act prescribes the purpose of requirements that may be included in the contract, which may include attendance at a guidance or counselling programme, as being to "ensure" the child's regular attendance at his or her school.[92] It therefore eschews the more modest aim of securing a mere improvement in the child's attendance. The official guidance indicates that a parenting contract will be appropriate where the parent is "willing to address their child's truanting behaviour, but needs support to do so effectively".[93] The parenting contract is not binding: the Act states that it gives rise to no obligations in contract or tort.[94]

If the parent is convicted of a school attendance offence[95] the court can make a parenting order.[96] The order, which can be imposed for up to twelve months, can require particular action on the part of the parent, including attendance at guidance or counselling classes up to once a week for a period not exceeding three months. These classes are intended to impart good

---

[89] *Ibid.*
[90] Anti-Social Behaviour Act 2003, s.19. There is guidance, which authorities and schools are required to take into account: DfES, *Guidance on Education-Related Parenting Contracts, Parenting Orders and Penalty Notices* (London: DfES, 2004).
[91] DfES, *Data: Penalty Notices and Fast-track (for truancy) and Parenting Orders and Parenting Contracts (for truancy and exclusions)* (2005) www.dfes.gov.uk (November 3, 2005).
[92] Anti-Social Behaviour Act 2003, s.19(5) and (6)(b).
[93] DfES, *Guidance on Education-Related Parenting Contracts, Parenting Orders and Penalty Notices* (London: DfES, 2004), para.46.
[94] Anti-Social Behaviour Act 2003, s.19(8).
[95] That is, an offence under the Education Act 1996, ss.443 or 444: *supra*.
[96] Crime and Disorder Act 1998, s.8.

parenting skills. Breach of the order without reasonable excuse carries a penalty of a fine of up to £1,000.[97]

Parenting orders have become fairly common in the criminal justice system and the evidence is that they can improve parents' confidence in exerting some control over their misbehaving children, although they appear not to have affected the children's behaviour overall.[98] Their impact in the context of school attendance is as yet unknown, but relatively few orders have been made. In the period April-July 2005, only 201 parenting orders were made in England following a truancy prosecution.[99]

Clearly it would be better if the use of such measures were avoided and the problem nipped in the bud. Schools have been advised by the DfES and the Office for Standards in Education to respond early to truancy by contacting parents and attempting to find out its cause(s), but also to remind parents of their responsibilities while in addition ensuring that rigorous procedures are in place for registration of attendance and referral to the local education authority for action when non-attendance persists.[100] As noted earlier, targets for reductions in non-attendance rates have also been used with a view to encouraging schools to be proactive in ensuring that pupils attend.

CONCLUSION

While the Government can point to an improvement in the overall rate of school attendance over the period 1996/97–2004/05, this is due entirely to a reduction in *authorized* absences.[101] The Government has strongly discouraged the removal of children from school during term-time for family holidays and this might be one reason for the fall. Yet the rate of *unauthorized* absence in 2004-05 was at its highest level across this nine year period:

---

[97] *Ibid.*, s.9(7).
[98] D. Ghate and M. Ramella, *Positive Parenting – the National Evaluation of the Youth Justice Board's Parenting Programme* (London: Youth Justice Board, 2002).
[99] DfES, *Data: Penalty Notices and Fast-track (for truancy) and Parenting Orders and Parenting Contracts (For truancy and exclusions)* (2005) www.dfes.gov.uk (November 3, 2005).
[100] See DfES, *Guidance on Education-Related Parenting Contracts, Parenting Orders and Penalty Notices* (London: DfES, 2004); Office for Standards in Education (Ofsted), *Improving Attendance and Behaviour in Secondary Schools* (London: Ofsted, 2001).
[101] DfES, *Pupil Absence in Schools in England 2004/05 (Provisional)*, SFR 40/2005 (London: DfES, 2005), Table 1.

across all schools an average of 0.79% of school sessions (half-days) were missed due to truancy, with a higher rate in secondary schools and special schools. Among pupils whose absence was authorized, the average number of half-days missed was 14 per secondary school pupil and 8 per primary school pupil.[102] It is clear that truancy is an entrenched problem that is resistant to legal remedies. That having been said, it is also clear that legal intervention in truancy cases, at least in the form of actual or threatened court action, is still relatively uncommon.

The figures quoted above, which are the first produced since local education authorities were required to supply data on the use of these measures to the DfES, suggest that authorities and schools are not invoking the various and expanding legal processes in a way that the Government might have envisaged. Indeed, the White Paper now promises "greater use of fines and further truancy sweeps in urban areas" (where rates of truancy are the highest).[103]

Over the years a number of teachers have told the author that the absence, for whatever reason, of pupils who are known to be disruptive and difficult to manage can sometimes come as a relief to staff, thereby acting as a disincentive to positive intervention to restore attendance. Yet schools have come under increasing pressure to improve pupil attendance rates; and now, under proposals in the White Paper, they will be expected to form or join partnerships with other schools to reduce persistent truancy. All secondary schools are to be expected to be a member of such a partnership by 2007.[104]

Truancy is a problem whose scale and detrimental effects for the individual and society fully justify every effort to quell it. In the light of all the new measures that have been taken, no-one could accuse the Government of complacency. However, the effectiveness of the legal machinery for enforcement of school attendance that has been put in place, with broader options for local education authorities, can only really be assessed when proper use is made of it. Perhaps, though, the apparent reticence shown by the authorities reflects doubts about its potential efficacy.

It is likely that it also reflects social justice concerns: that those parents who are most likely to be subjected to the force of the law, including the sanctions of the criminal law – such as fines and possibly imprisonment – tend to be among the most disadvantaged members of society.

While the punitive character of fines and penalty notices sits uneasily with the idea of supporting the disadvantaged that social agencies such as

---

[102] *Ibid.*, Table 6.
[103] N.2 *supra*, para.7.33.
[104] *Ibid.*, paras 7.5 and 7.20.

schools and local education authorities are culturally attuned to (notwithstanding Foucault's idea of schools as part of the apparatus of disciplinary power over individuals),[105] over the past decade the notion of effective parental responsibility has entered the zeitgeist. Government has been keen to promote it at every opportunity, particularly in the context of education, such as through home-school agreements and the participation of parents in their children's learning. As a continuing problem, truancy is likely to be met with firmer rather than reduced intervention. One way or another, the parents will take the rap and be made to pay for their children's truancy.

---

[105] M. Foucault, *Discipline and Punish* (Harmondsworth: Penguin, 1977).

THE OFFICE OF OMBUDSMAN FOR CHILDREN IN IRELAND

DYMPNA GLENDENNING[*1]

INTRODUCTION

The Office of Ombudsman, when appointed by government,[2] derives its authority from its independence, impartiality and competence to achieve fair play for persons who have suffered a wrong in a specific area of public life. Provision for such an Office may be made in Constitutions, or by way of statute law or by non-statutory methods. Whatever measure is chosen for the delivery of the Office of Ombudsman at governmental level, the hallmark of the Office is its independence,[3] a matter which is discussed later. We can trace the origin of the Office of Ombudsman to the practice and policy of the Nordic islands and, in particular to Sweden, where in 1809 a Parliamentary Ombudsman, independent of the Executive, was established by the Constitution to safeguard citizen's rights. Norway appears to have been the first country to establish a statutory Commissioner, or Ombudsman with express powers to protect children's rights.[4]

---

* B.A., M.Ed, Ph.D., Barrister.
[1] This article deals only with the said Office in the Republic of Ireland: for Northern Ireland see The Commissioner for Children and Young People (Northern Ireland) Order 2003: see also Annual Report 2003–2004; Consultation Response by the NI Commissioner for Children and Young People (NICCY) to the Five Library Boards Draft Financial Plans for the Period April 2005–March 2006; also NICCY's response to the Proposal to adopt a framework Decision on the Recognition and Enforcement in the EU of Prohibitions Arising from Convictions for Sexual Offences Committed Against Children.
[2] An Ombudsman does not have to be appointed by government but may be employed in a specific business etc. Such an Ombudsman does not have any governmental powers.
[3] As Kevin Murphy, the second Public Services Ombudsman, stated: "I am required by law to be independent in the exercise of my functions and this independence is the foundation stone of the Office. I must be able to operate without being influenced by Government Action. Not alone must my office be independent in fact, it must also be seen as such by those who use the service I provide."
[4] Since 1981, the Ombudsman for Children in Norway has striven continuously to

Northern Ireland, Scotland and Wales have established somewhat different enabling structures. The Care Standards Act 2000 in Wales provided for the establishment of the Office of a Children's Commissioner and the Children's Commissioner's Act 2001 extended the Commissioner's powers and added new functions. In England the Care Standards Act 2000 set up a National Care Standards Commission and a Children's Rights Director. Northern Ireland's Commissioner for Children and Young People was appointed pursuant to the Commissioner for Children and Young People (Northern Ireland) Order 2003.[5] Scotland's Commissioner for Children and Young People was appointed under the Commissioner for Children and Young People (Scotland) Act 2003. In the Republic of Ireland (Ireland hereafter) an Ombudsman for Children, Ms. Emily Logan, was appointed pursuant to the Ombudsman for Children Act 2002[6] (the 2002 Act hereafter). Ms. Logan has recently published her First Annual Report (2005) having completed her first year in Office.[7] This chapter considers the Office of Ombudsman for Children as established in Ireland[8] and in particular the Ombudsman's function in examining and investigating complaints against public bodies,[9] recognised schools[10] and voluntary hospitals.[11]

---

improve national and international legislation relating to children's welfare. Mr Trond Waage has been Ombudsman for Children since 1996.
[5] See S.I. No.439 of 2003 (N.I. 11).
[6] Ms Logan took up office on March 26, 2004 having been appointed Ombudsman for Children by President McAleese in December 2003.
[7] Ombudsman for Children, Annual Report 2005, Government Publications, Dublin 2.
[8] D. Glendenning, "The Ombudsman for Children: an analysis of the Irish model as it relates to recognized schools", Geoffrey Bennett and David Palfreyman (eds.), *Education and the Law* (Carfax Pubs, Taylor and Francis Group), vol.13, nos. 2 and 3, June-September, 2004, 133–143; Frank Martin, "The Ombudsman for Children: An Analysis of the Strengths and Weaknesses of the Irish Model" in *Administration*, Summer Issue, 2004; G. Shannon, *Children and the Law* (Round Hall, Sweet and Maxwell, 2001), pp.15–17.
[9] Under s.8 of the 2002 Act.
[10] Those schools recognised by the Minister for Education and Science pursuant to s.10 of the Education Act 1998.
[11] *Ibid.*, s.9. The term "voluntary hospital" in the 2002 Act means "a voluntary hospital within the meaning of the Health (Eastern Regional Authority) Health Act 1999 or a voluntary hospital specified in *Schedule* 2." Those hospitals listed in *Schedule* 2 are Mercy Hospital, Grenville Place, Cork; South Infirmary-Victoria Hospital Limited, Cork; and St. John's Hospital, St. John's Square, Limerick.

ORIGINS OF THE OFFICE OF OMBUDSMAN FOR CHILDREN

The Office of Ombudsman for Children is one of a number of international initiatives with a common objective: to promote and safeguard the rights of children and young persons. While that Office was initially perceived as being an independent Office for dealing with complaints concerning children, since the adoption of the United Nations Convention on the Rights of the Child 1989 (UNCRC), European legislation reflects a dual function for that Office firstly, in dealing with complaints concerning children, and secondly, as an advocate for children's rights. The UNCRC has codified and identified international norms on children's rights and has facilitated a broad consensus on family, society and international obligations to children, some of which were already embodied in earlier UN instruments.[12] Possibly the most progressive concept in the UNCRC was that of moving from the notion of protection of children to the assertion of children's rights,[13] a move which many commentators feel should now be incorporated into the Irish Constitution (1937) which guarantees fundamental rights including equality.[14] It is against the human rights background, constitutional framework and wider legislative programme of reforms relating to children's rights, that the Office of Ombudsman for Children in Ireland needs to be appraised.

Human Rights in the UNCRC

Article 2 of Part 1 of the UNCRC provides:

"1. "State parties shall respect and ensure the rights set forth in the present Convention to each child within their jurisdiction without discrimination of any kind, irrespective of the child's or his or her

---

[12] The Geneva Declaration of the Rights of the Child (1924); The Declaration of the Rights of the Child (1959) and recognised in the Universal Declaration of Human Rights; The International Covenant of Civil and Political Rights (in particular Arts. 23 and 24); The International Covenant on Economic, Social and Cultural Rights (in particular Art. 10) and in the statutes and relevant instruments of specialised agencies and international organisations concerned with the welfare of children.

[13] See further S. Karp, U.N. Committee on the Rights of the Child to the Irish delegation, Geneva, January 1998. William Duncan, The Constitutional Protection of Parental Rights in *Report of the Constitutional Review Group*, May 1996, p.612 at 625; generally at 330.

[14] Frank Martin, *op. cit.*, n.8; William Duncan, The Constitutional Protection of Parental Rights in Report of the Constitutional Review Group, Government Publications, May 1996, p.612 at 625; generally at 330; G. Shannon, *op. cit.*, n.8.

parent's or legal guardian's race, colour, sex, language, religion, political or other opinion, national, ethnic or social origin, property, disability or other status."
2. States Parties shall take all appropriate measures to ensure that the child is protected against all forms of discrimination or punishment on the basis of the status, activities, expressed opinions, or beliefs of the child's parents, legal guardians or family members."

The UN Committee on the Rights of the Child has made it clear that Article 2 imposes an obligation upon State Parties to ensure that all Convention rights apply to all children in the State including refugees, visitors, children of migrant workers and those who are in the State illegally.[15]

Recent Reforms in Ireland : Children's Rights and Welfare

In November 2000 the Irish Government launched its "National Children's Strategy: Our Children–Their Lives"[16] (the Strategy hereafter) which is a co-ordinated and comprehensive action plan for the next decade for all children. The Strategy is the single largest initiative to progress the implementation of the UNCRC and it covers a wide range of policy areas such as a National Children's Advisory Council, a National Children's Office, Dáil na nÓg (Youth Parliament) and an Ombudsman for Children. This progressive policy for children builds on earlier legislative measures, laid down over the previous decade, and it is against this inclusive background that the Children's Ombudsman is considered in this chapter.

The Sexual Offences (Jurisdiction) Act 1996 targets the child sex tourist by providing that Irish citizens, or those persons ordinarily resident in Ireland, who participate in sex with children while abroad, may be prosecuted in the Irish courts. Section 24 of the Non-Fatal Offences Against the Person Act 1997 prohibited corporal punishment of children in school and abolished the rule of law by which teachers were immune from criminal liability in respect of physical chastisement of children bringing Ireland into line with the rest of Europe in that regard. Further statutory safeguards for children were introduced by the Child Trafficking and Pornography Act 1998 which made the production, distribution and possession of child pornography a crime. Another significant statutory measure is the Protection of Persons

---

[15] See further Implementation Handbook for the Convention on the Rights of the Child, UNICEF, p.26
[16] Government Publications, Molesworth St., Dublin 2.

Reporting Child Abuse Act 1998 as it provides safeguards for any person acting "reasonably and in good faith" when reporting suspicion of abuse of a child provided such abuse is reported to "an appropriate person"[17] *i.e.* a designated officer of a Health Board (now the Health Service Executive Area)[18] or a member of An Garda Síochána. The Illegal Immigrants (Trafficking) Act 2000 targets professional trafficking of human beings some of whom may include children. In addition, there are specific procedures under the Refugee Act 1996, to deal with situations where an unaccompanied minor arrives in the State. When fully implemented the Children Act 2001 will reform the law relating to juvenile justice and children requiring care, protection and control.[19]

ROLE AND FUNCTIONS: OMBUDSMAN FOR CHILDREN

The *Seanad Debates* are instructive as to the intention of the Oireachtas regarding the function of the Office of the Children's Ombudsman. These debates indicate that the Ombudsman was not intended to be a counsellor, a teacher,[20] or an inspector, or to have an educational function other than where these are necessarily incidental to the other functions of the Office.[21] Neither did the Oireachtas intend that the Ombudsman should replace existing appeal procedures or interfere with the judicial process or investigate employer-employee relationships.[22] Instead, it was the intention of the Oireachtas that the Ombudsman would an advocate for children's rights and welfare but that s/he would not protect children's rights and welfare directly, as that onus must necessarily fall primarily on parents, the health boards, the courts and society.[23]

Pursuant to the 2002 Act, the Ombudsman is independent in the performance of the functions assigned to her/him[24] and is required, in the

---

[17] Protections for Persons Reporting Child Abuse Act 1998, s.1.
[18] See Health Act 2004. The health boards have been abolished and replaced by a number of Health Service Executive Areas (HSEAS). On January 1, 2005 the Health Service Executive became responsible for the delivery of all health and social services nationally. All services previously delivered by the health boards are now delivered by the HSEAS.
[19] See S.I. No.151 of 2002; S.I. No.527 of 2003; S.I. No.468 of 2004.
[20] *Ibid.*, Col.501.
[21] *Ibid.*, Cols 527–530.
[22] 169 Seanad Debates, Cols 466–467.
[23] *Ibid.*, Cols 527–530, Minister of State for Children, M. Hanafin TD.
[24] The 2002 Act, Chapter 2, s.6(1).

performance of her/his functions, to have regard to the best interests of the child concerned and, in so far as practicable, to have regard to the age and the understanding of the child and to his or her wishes.[25] The Ombudsman has a broad remit and a dual function in promoting children's rights and welfare[26] and in examining and investigating complaints against public bodies,[27] voluntary hospitals and recognised schools.

Promotional Function of Ombudsman

Section 7 provides for the function of the Ombudsman for Children in promoting the rights of children as follows:

"(1) The Ombudsman for Children shall promote the rights and welfare of children and without prejudice to the generality of the foregoing, he or she shall—
 (a) advise the Minister or any other Minister of the Government, as may be appropriate, on the development and co-ordination of policy relating to children,
 (b) encourage public bodies, schools and voluntary hospitals to develop policies, practices and procedures designed to promote the rights and welfare of children,
 (c) collect and disseminate information on matters relating to the rights and welfare of children,
 (d) promote awareness among the members of the public (including children of such age or ages as he or she considers appropriate of matters, (including the principles and provisions of the Convention) relating to the rights and welfare of children and how those rights can be enforced,
 (e) highlight issues relating to the rights and welfare of children that are of concern to children,
 (f) exchange information and co-operate with the Ombudsman for Children (by whatever name called), of other states,
 (g) monitor and review generally the operation of legislation concerning matters that relate to the rights and welfare of children, and
 (h) monitor and review the operation of this Act, and whenever

---

[25] *Ibid.*, s.6(2).
[26] *Ibid.*, s.7.
[27] Construed in accordance with Sch.1 in Pt 1 of the Act which list includes, *inter alia*, the Department of Education and Science.

he or she thinks it necessary, make recommendations to the Minister, or in a report under section 13(7) or both for amending this Act.

2(a) The Ombudsman for Children shall establish structures to consult regularly with groups of children that he or she considers to be representative of children for the purposes of his or her functions under this section,

(b) In consultations under this subsection, the views of a child shall be given due weight in accordance with the age and understanding of the child.

(3) The Ombudsman for Children may undertake, promote or publish research into any matter relating to the rights and welfare of children.

(4) The Ombudsman for Children may, on his or her own initiative, and shall, at the request of the Minister or any other Minister of the Government, give advice to the Minister or the Government concerned on any matter (including the probable effect on children of the implementation of any proposals for legislation) relating to the rights and welfare of children.

(5) For the purposes of this section, persons under the age of 18 years who are enlisted members of the Defence Forces shall not be regarded as children in any case where they are subject to military law under the Defence Forces Acts 1954 to1998.

(6) In this section "the Convention" means the Convention on the Rights of the Child done at New York on 20th November 1989 as amended by any protocol thereto that is for the time being in force in the State."

Investigatory function of ombudsman

Sections 14 and 15 of the 2002 Act confer on the Ombudsman similar investigatory powers as were conferred on the Public Services Ombudsman under the Ombudsman Act 1980, section 7. These powers include the power to compel the production of documents and information and the attendance of witnesses. Key considerations for the Ombudsman's Office are firstly, whether the complaint lies within its remit and secondly, whether the complainant has taken reasonable steps to resolve the matter at local level.[28] Furthermore, when discharging her/his investigatory function concerning complaints against public bodies, voluntary hospitals and recognised schools,

---

[28] Annual Report of the Ombudsman (2005), p.11.

the action complained of must be one which is taken in the performance of an inherently flawed administrative function.[29] The Ombudsman may undertake an investigation either on her/his own initiative or arising out of a complaint made by a child, a family member or a person having a professional relationship or other appropriate relationship with the child.

If a parent is not the complainant, then one of the parents must be informed that a complaint has been initiated so as to ensure that parental constitutional rights, or the rights on the Family under Article 41, are not breached (*Dáil Debates*, 169 Col.467). There are some circumstances in which this requirement could adversely impact on the child's rights, e.g. where the complaint is against the parent(s) or where the child is approaching adulthood and does not wish to have parental involvement. The constitutional protections of the married Family in Article 41 may insulate the married Family from the investigations of the Ombudsman for Children, even where such intervention would clearly benefit or safeguard the child. Unless the Constitution is amended to take further account of children's rights, the Ombudsman's function may be restricted in these sensitive spheres.

Complaints taken against Schools and Voluntary Hospitals

The Ombudsman may investigate complaints taken against recognised schools in connection with the performance of administrative functions under section 9 of the Education Act 1998 and against voluntary hospitals within the meaning of the Health Act 1999 and against those hospitals listed in Schedule 2 of the 2002 Act, where, having carried out a preliminary examination, it appears to the Ombudsman that—

(i) the action has or may have adversely affected a child, and

(ii) the action was or may have been—
   (I) taken without proper authority,
   (II) taken on irrelevant grounds,
   (III) the result of negligence or carelessness,
   (IV) based on erroneous or incomplete information,
   (V) improperly discriminatory
   (VI) based on an undesirable administrative practice, or
   (VII) otherwise contrary to fair or sound administration.

The Ombudsman's powers, under section 9 of the Act of 1998, are discretionary and she may decide not to take up these complaints. If she

---

[29] The 2002 Act, Chap.4, s.8.

decides to exercise this discretion to take up a complaint in schools, then she must comply with section 9 of the 2002 Act. Section 9(2) provides:

> "The Ombudsman for Children may investigate an action under subsection(1)(a) only where the procedures prescribed pursuant to section 28 of the Act of 1998 have been resorted to and exhausted in relation to the action".[30]

Since no procedures have been prescribed by any Minister for Education and Science under section 28 of the 1998 Act to date, it appears, the Ombudsman may investigate any administrative action of a recognised school under section 9 of the Education Act 1998 provided it falls within the scope of her investigative functions under section 9 of the 2002 Act.

Functions of a School: Section 9 of the Education Act 1998

Section 9 of the 1998 Act provides:

> "A recognised school shall provide education to students which is appropriate to their abilities and needs and, without prejudice to the generality of the foregoing, it shall use its available resources to—
> (a) ensure that the educational needs of all students, including those with a disability or other special educational needs, are identified and provided for
> (b) ensure that the education provided by it meets the requirements of education policy as determined from time to time by the

---

[30] Section 28 of the 1998 Act provides:
   (1)   The Minister, following consultation with patrons of recognised schools, national association of parents, recognised school management organisations and recognised trade unions and staff associations representing teachers, may from time to time prescribe procedures with which—
      (a) the parent of a student or, in the case of a student who has reached the age of 18 years, the student, may appeal to the board against a decision of a teacher or other member of staff of a school,
      (b) grievances of students, or their parents, relating to the student's school (other than those which may be dealt with under paragraph (a) or section 29 shall be heard and
      (c) appropriate remedial action shall, where necessary, be taken as a consequence of an appeal or in response to a grievance.
   (2)   In prescribing procedures for the purposes of this section the Minister shall have regard to the desirability of determining appeals and resolving grievances in the school concerned.

Minister including requirements as to the provision of a curriculum as prescribed by the Minister in accordance with section 30,
(c) ensure that students have access to appropriate guidance to assist them in their educational and career choices,
(d) promote the moral, spiritual, social and personal development of students and provide health education for them, in consultation with their parents, having regard to the characteristic spirit of the school,
(e) promote equality of opportunity for both male and female students and staff of the school,
(f) promote the development of the Irish language and traditions, Irish literature, the arts and other cultural matters,
(g) ensure that the parents of a student, or in the case of a student who has reached the age of 18 years, the student, have access in the prescribed manner to records kept by that school relating to the progress of that student in his or her education,
(h) in the case of schools located in a Gaeltacht area, contribute to the maintenance of Irish as the primary community language,
(i) conduct its activities in compliance with any regulations made from time to time by the Minister under section 33,
(j) ensure that all the needs of personnel involved in management functions and staff development needs generally in the school are identified and provided for,
(k) establish and maintain systems whereby the efficiency and effectiveness of its operations can be assessed, including the quality and effectiveness of teaching in the school and the attainment levels and academic standards of students,
(l) establish or maintain contacts with other schools and at other appropriate levels throughout the community served by the school, and
(m) subject to this Act and in particular section 15(2)(d), establish and maintain an admissions policy which provides for maximum accessibility to the school."

Although the above functions of a school are to be discharged by the board of management or manager or board of governors,[31] in practice, they fall to be implemented by the teachers and other staff, under the direction of the

---

[31] The Education Act 1998, s.15(2).

Principal,[32] and the board/manager/governors.[33] Where following an investigation under the 2002 Act into an action, it appears to the Ombudsman that the action adversely affected a child *and* fell within section 8(b) or section 9(1)(ii) of the 2002 Act, then s/he may recommend to the public body, school or voluntary hospital concerned:

(a) that the matter in relation to which the action was taken be further considered,

(b) that measures or specified measures be taken to remedy, mitigate or alter the adverse effect of the action, or

(c) that the reasons for taking the action be given to the Ombudsman.[34]

If the Ombudsman thinks fit, she may request the public body, school or voluntary hospital to notify her within a specified time of its response to the recommendation. Where it appears to the Ombudsman that the measures taken or the proposed measures to be taken in response to a recommendation are not satisfactory, she may cause a special report on the case to be included in her Annual Report which is laid before the Dáil and Seanad[35] or it may also be included in a special report made by her under section 13(7).

EXCLUSIONS AND LIMITATIONS

Exclusions under the 2002 Act

Section 11(1)(a) of the 2002 Act provides for a number of exclusions in which the Ombudsman is precluded from investigating any action by or on behalf of a public body, school or voluntary hospital. If the action is one, *inter alia*, in relation to which:

(iii) the child affected by the action has a right of appeal, reference or review to or before a person other than a public body or, if appropriate, the school or voluntary hospital concerned,

the Ombudsman may not investigate that action.

---

[32] See s.22(1) of the Education Act 1998. Note that the vocational schools have their own distinctive structures under the VEC Acts 1930–2001.

[33] See further *Legal Statutes Annotated*, 2003, The Ombudsman for Children Act 2002, annotated by Kevin C. Boyle, p.22-12.

[34] S.13(3) of the 2002 Act.

[35] *Ibid.*, in accordance with s.13(7).

There is no appeal from section 29 of the Education Act 1998 which establishes a mechanism for an appeal to the Secretary General of the Department of Education and Science (DES) in certain circumstances.[36]

Part VIII of the Education Act 1998 makes provision for examinations. Section 51(1)(f) of the 1998 Act, sets down the terms under which candidates may appeal against the results of examinations and the procedure for such appeals. The Children's Ombudsman is precluded by section 11(1)(f) of the 2002 Act from investigating any action taken by or on behalf of a public body, school or voluntary hospital, if the action is one which relates to the results of an examination within the meaning of section 49 of the Act of 1998.[37] There is no appeal to the Children's Ombudsman from section 51 of the Education Act 1998, which provides for the appointment by the Minister of a person or body of persons to advise him or her on any matter relating to the examinations,[38] or to supervise or review any part of the conduct of the examinations including appeals by candidates against the results of the examinations. However, the Public Services Ombudsman, Ms Emily O'Reilly, is empowered pursuant to the Ombudsman Act 1980 (sections 7, 8, and 9) to investigate certain matters in respect of examinations and these powers are detailed in Appendix B of the Ombudsman for Children's Annual Report (2005).

Further Limitations on the Ombudsman's powers

The following spheres are expressly omitted from the Ombudsman's remit: the courts, security matters, and military activities. Where the State fails to vindicate the fundamental rights of children, the Ombudsman may not investigate as such matters must come before the High Court in the normal manner. The Ombudsman is precluded from acting where legal proceedings have been initiated or where a statutory right of appeal to a court exists or where there is a right of appeal existing to an independent tribunal or referees drawn from outside the Civil Service. Decisions relating to asylum, immigration, citizenship or naturalisation are excluded from the Ombudsman's

---

[36] See also Pt 2 of the Act of 2002 which provides, *inter alia*: "The reference in the said Pt 1 to the Department of Education and Science does not include a reference to an appeals committee within the meaning of s.29 of the Act of 1998; a person or body of persons appointed under s.51(2) of the Act of 1998."

[37] Under the 1998 Act the term "examination" means an examination relating to post-primary, adult and vocational training as may from time to time be conducted in accordance with procedures determined by the Minister or by a body of persons established by the Minister and to which this part applies in accordance with s.50.

[38] For example the State Examinations Board.

remit under the 2002 Act. Neither may the Ombudsman investigate any action taken in the administration of the prisons or other places for the custody and detention of children other than certified reformatory or industrial schools under the Department of Education and Science (DES). Effectively, all institutions providing for the custody or detention of children which fall under the jurisdiction of the DES and the Department of Health and Children lie within the Ombudsman's remit. All relevant institutions under the jurisdiction of the Department of Justice, Equality and Law Reform are excluded from the scope of the Ombudsman's powers under the 2002 Act.

In effect, this means that children detained in prisons, Garda stations and other places of detention fall outside the Ombudsman's investigatory powers.

A recent study of 50 children coming before the Dublin Children's Court conducted by the *Irish Association for the Study of Delinquency* (2005) found, *inter alia*, that detention was used for half of the children convicted,[39] a sanction which is clearly in breach of Article 37 of the UNCRC which provides that the arrest, detention or imprisonment of a child be used only as a measure of last resort and for the shortest appropriate period of time.[40] Not surprisingly, the exclusion of this group of children from the 2002 Act is of great concern to the Ombudsman's Office. In her Annual Report 2005 the Ombudsman notes that 166 children (15 to 17 years) were detained in prisons in Ireland in 2004 and 147 were detained this year (up to May 2005). The Report states:

> "The Ombudsman for Children's Office is concerned that, at present, significant numbers of children are detained in St. Patrick's Institution and adult prisons throughout the State and that the Ombudsman for Children is currently precluded from acting on complaints received from such children insofar as they relate to matters pertaining to their detention."[41]

The exclusions in the 2002 Act contrast sharply with the provision made in the relevant legislation in the neighbouring jurisdictions of Scotland and Northern Ireland. In the Commissioner for Children and Young People (Scotland) Act 2003, there are no express exclusions in regard to asylum,

---

[39] Carol Coulter, Legal Affairs Correspondent, "Report urges setting up youth justice system", *Irish Times*, August 1, 2005, p.4.
[40] Art.37(6).
[41] At p.24 of the Annual Report (2005).

immigration, naturalisation or citizenship or in regard to the administration of prisons or other places of detention. Neither does the Commissioner for Children and Young People (Northern Ireland) Order 2003 contain any such express exclusions. Clearly the 2002 Act affords a lesser level of protection for certain groups of children in this jurisdiction than that which applies in Northern Ireland which breaches the spirit of the Good Friday Agreement as it fails to deliver parity of protection and equality of treatment to children in this jurisdiction.[42]

During the passage of the Ombudsman for Children Bill through the Oireachtas, considerable concerns were expressed in regard to the detention of children in inappropriate places[43] and an amendment was inserted in section 11(2)(a) which provides for the removal of the exclusion at the discretion of the Minister for Health and Children with the consent of the Minister for Justice, Equality and Law Reform. This anomaly in the legislation Act needs to be removed in the opinion of the author.

INDEPENDENCE OF OFFICE OF OMBUDSMAN: MINISTERIAL VETO

Although the President must appoint the nominee of the Dáil and Seanad, the Office of Ombudsman for Children is stated to be an independent Office in section 6(1) of the 2002 Act which provides:

"The Ombudsman for Children shall be independent in the performance of his or her functions under the Act."

It was intended that the Office of Children's Ombudsman would be protected from political pressure and influence at local, national and European level and from pressures arising out of paid employment. Such independence, however, is seriously compromised by section 11(4) of the 2002 Act which provides:

"Where a Minister of the Government so requests in writing (and attaches to the request a statement in writing setting out in full the reasons for the request), the Ombudsman for Children shall not investigate, or shall cease to investigate, an action specified in the request, being an action of—

---

[42] The Good Friday Agreement (1998) recognises the failure of partition and commits us to building a society based on equality and justice for all people on this island.
[43] Seanad Éireann, Vol.169, February 27, 2002, Committee Stage.

(a) a Department of State whose functions are assigned to that Minister of the Government, or
(b) a public body (other than a Department of State) whose business and functions are comprised in such a Department of State or in relation to which functions are performed by such a Department of State.
(whether or not all or any of the functions of that Minister of the Government stand delegated to a Minister of State at that Department of State)."

In effect subsection (4) above confers on any Government Minister the power to prevent or terminate any investigation by the Ombudsman into Departments of State, to which functions have been assigned by that Government Minister, or a public body, whose business or functions are comprised in such State Department, or in relation to which functions are performed by such State Department.

According to the Seanad Debates on the issue, one of the reasons for inserting this provision was "to prevent an errant Minister or an errant Ombudsman having unfettered influence in particular matters."[44] Such Ministerial "requests," if they are made must be detailed in the Ombudsman's annual report[45] thereby bringing them to public attention. The Office of the Ombudsman for Children is a national human rights institution established under statute law to which "the Paris Principles"[46] apply. Given this context, any ministerial veto on the investigative powers of the Office seems highly inappropriate as it compromises that very independence expressly conferred on the Office in section 6(1) of the Act and traditionally accorded the Office internationally.

A further limitation is placed on the Ombudsman's powers when she is appearing before the Public Accounts Committee, under section 18(2), the Ombudsman is precluded from questioning or expressing an opinion on the merits or objectives of any policy of the Government or a Minister. However, this constraint relates only to an appearance before the Public Accounts Committee and the Ombudsman may voice such opinions and questions as part of her/his promotional role under section 7 of the Act. The Report of the Constitution Review Group recommended that, if the independence of the Office of Ombudsman is to be secured, a new Article needs to be inserted

---

[44] 169 Seanad Debates, Col.545.
[45] S.13(7) of the Act of 2002.
[46] United Nations Principles relating to the Status and Functioning of National Human Rights Institutions for the Protection and promotion of Human Rights.

The Office of Ombudsman for Children in Ireland

in the Constitution confirming the establishment of that Office as may be determined by law. Effectively, this would insulate the Office from vested interests and undue deference to the Oireachtas and it would facilitate independent and impartial decisions.[47]

FIRST ANNUAL REPORT OF OMBUDSMAN

The Ombudsman's First Annual Report (the Report hereafter) was published in 2005. During its first year, the office dealt with 1777 complaints of which approximately 14% were made by children. As one would expect, the immediate family was the main complainant on behalf of the child. Of the total number of complaints, more than 51% of these were concerned with education and more than a quarter of that number dealt with special education. Of the remaining 49% of complaints, 34% of these were concerned with child protection; approximately 28% related to social welfare entitlements while the remainder related to civil proceedings, custody, asylum and administration cases.[48] The Report is critical of the fact that Codes of Behaviour/Discipline in schools have been developed pursuant to section 23 of the Education (Welfare) Act 2000, without consulting children. It considers this practice to be in breach of the spirit of Article 12 of the UNCRC[49] and has made a submission to that effect to the DES Taskforce on Student Behaviour. Article 28(2) of the UNHCR is also relevant in this context as it requires State Parties to "take all reasonable measures to ensure that school discipline is administered in a manner consistent with the child's human dignity and in conformity with the present Convention." These two Articles appear to copper-fasten the child's right, particularly as they grow towards maturity, to consultation in regard to the drafting of Codes of Behaviour in schools.

Section 5 of the Report is headed "Limitations and exclusions in the Ombudsman for Children Act 2002". The Report states that the Ombudsman for Children's Office is concerned that certain of the limitations and exclusions in the Act the Ombudsman's investigatory powers, may preclude

---

[47] Government Publications 1996, pp.426–427 referring to the Office as established under the Ombudsman Act of 1980.
[48] *Ibid.*, p.12.
[49] Art.12(1) states: "States Parties shall assure to the child who is capable of forming his or her own views the right to express those views freely in all matters affecting the child, the views of the child being given due weight in accordance with the age and maturity of the child."

the Office from executing effectively its role and functions as set out in the Act. It should be noted that the above limitations apply only to the Ombudsman's investigatory powers and not to the policy sphere, research, advocacy or other functions. Those limitations and exclusions of greatest concern to the Ombudsman's Office are: children in places of detention; the administration of the law relating to asylum, immigration, naturalisation or citizenship; the Garda Síochána; the Defence Forces; and the provision relating to a Ministerial veto on investigations. With regard to children in detention, the report considers that these particularly vulnerable children should have recourse to the Ombudsman on the same basis as all other children in the State and the Ombudsman promises to pursue this matter further in a future report to the Oireachtas.

Schedule 1, Part 2 of the 2002 Act excludes certain public bodies from the Ombudsman's powers and concerns are expressed in the Report regarding the exclusion of the Garda Síochána and the Defence Forces from her remit. While the Children Act 2001 lays down a significant role and function for the Gardai in relation to children who engage in offending behaviour, they have considerable powers in relation to the most vulnerable children in the State, including the power to detain. Given the pivotal role of the Gardai in these spheres, the Ombudsman's Office is concerned that it has been precluded by the 2002 Act from investigating any action taken by the Gardai which would normally fall within the Ombudsman's remit.[50] The Office states that in the event of an Garda Síochána being brought within the scope of the Act, any overlapping of mandates between the Ombudsman's Office and the proposed new Garda complaint mechanism could be addressed through the medium of a memorandum of understanding between both bodies.[51]

Part 2 of Schedule 1, together with section 11(1)(b) of the Act, precludes any investigation by the Ombudsman in relation to the Defence Forces. As children aged 17 may be recruited into the Defence Forces, the Office has concerns that actions taken in egard to such children lie outside its powers and, while it welcomes the establishment of an Ombudsman for the Defence Forces, it considers that such a body may not always be "the most appropriate complaints mechanism for all complaints by all children in the Defence Forces."[52]

---

[50] *Annual Report of Ombudsman for Children 2005*, para.5.3, p.25.
[51] *Ibid.*
[52] *Ibid.*, para.5.6, p.27.

FREEDOM OF INFORMATION ACT AND SCHOOLS: BALANCING EDUCATION AND SECRECY

ESTELLE FELDMAN[*]

INTRODUCTION

At first glance the Freedom of Information Act 1997 does not apply to schools. After all, no schools are listed among the public bodies prescribed for the purposes of the Act. Nevertheless, the Department of Education and Science is included in the access to information regime which means that, at the very least, schools are concerned with the Act at arm's length. More specifically for a sector of schools there is, in fact, a direct relationship. These are schools within the control of a prescribed public body such as a hospital school, and schools managed by organisations caring for those with special needs. Furthermore, as a school is, in effect, an amalgam of the partners in education, there may be times when a Board of Management, teachers or parents, acting collectively or individually may wish to take advantage of the rights conferred by the Freedom of Information Act.

The perspective taken in this chapter is a management rather than a legal one and the backdrop for this perspective are two Supreme Court appeals, various High Court judgments, various reports and deliberations of the

---

[*] Research Associate, School of Law, Trinity College and Lecturer in Constitutional Law in Portobello College, Dublin. This chapter is an amalgam of papers prepared for the TCD School of Law Conferences for the Primary and Post-primary sectors from 2003 to date. It quotes extensively from Feldman, "Freedom of Information: The Challenge for a New Management Culture", presented at the first Annual Freedom of Information Conference 2002 organised by the TCD School of Law, and from Feldman, "Record-Keeping, Agreed Procedures, Consistent Application ... It's only common sense", a paper presented to the Irish Higher Education Authority seminar, One Year On – Where Do We Go From Here?, Dublin 2002.

Information Commissioner,[1] the Education Act 1998 and varied material accessible on Freedom of Information websites on the Internet.[2]

It must be borne in mind that the fact base of a particular court judgment or Information Commissioner's review may not immediately appear to have direct relevance to a particular school or individual. Nevertheless, general principles of importance may be drawn from a variety of decisions. For instance, a High Court judgment on an appeal against a decision of the Information Commissioner regarding the rights of parents to access medical records has wider application[3]; the Supreme Court appeal on this judgment was heard in early November 2005 and the decision, which is likely to have serious implications for the constitutional relationship between the rights of children and the rights of parents, is awaited.

The Information Commissioner has issued a number of decisions affecting persons within the schools sector. These decisions, easily accessible on the official website,[4] are comprehensive and cover a wide range of issues that might be of interest to schools such as release of marking systems or of job interview records.[5] It should be remembered that each case does vary and, during review, it is clear that the Information Commissioner[6] is at pains to allow for these variations. Certainly, in the course of reviews of decisions affecting schools and persons within the schools sector she has sought and considered submissions from the affected partners in education.

As noted, general principles of importance may be drawn from the materials considered which may be applied in a variety of situations. It is these that this chapter seeks to highlight. They tend to illustrate why the Freedom of Information Act is something to be viewed as a positive opportunity rather than as a troublesome if not a dangerous burden.

---

[1] For analysis of civil judgments, and annual commentary on the Office of the Information Commissioner, see Feldman, "Information Law and the Ombudsman" in Byrne and Binchy (eds.), *Annual Review of Irish Law 1999* to date (Roundhall Sweet & Maxwell, Dublin).
[2] Example, Central Policy Unit of the Department of Finance website at www.foi.gov.ie.
[3] *NMcK v. Information Commissioner* [2004] I.E.H.C. 4 see below at p.256.
[4] www.oic.gov.ie . Linked High Court judgments are also included.
[5] See for example Case 98187, *Ms ABH and the Office of the Local Appointments Commissioners*, March 30, 1999; Case 98082, *Mr ABD and the Office of the Local Appointments Commissioners*, February 11, 1999. See also Case 98020, *Mr AAF and the Office of the Civil Service and Local Appointments Commissioners*, October 12, 1998.
[6] The Government appoined the Ombudsman, Mr Kevin Murphy, as first Information Commissioner. On his retirement in 2003, he was succeeded in both functions by Ms Emily O'Reilly.

The Freedom of Information Acts 1997 and 2003

The Long Title of the Freedom of Information Act describes it as: "An Act to enable members of the public to obtain access, to the greatest extent possible consistent with the public interest and the right to privacy, to information in the possession of public bodies". This appears to be the only Act on the Statute Book that is directed at "members of the public" and that has as its express object "to enable members of the public". Consequently, anyone who is unfamiliar with the Act might reasonably expect it to be in fairly clear and simple terms, even, perhaps, in a form that is accessible and transparent to those of us who are not experienced administrative and constitutional lawyers. Indeed, in a public statement at the time of the introduction of the Bill the sponsoring Minister stated: "I appreciate that navigating a legal text of some complexity is not always easy for those of us who are not lawyers."[7]

In defence of the Act, it was drafted at a time when openness, transparency and accountability were only beginning to be spoken of as the desired culture of the public service. Nevertheless, for all its positive points, one cannot escape the fact that in some respects the text is extraordinarily convoluted, *e.g.* section 25 dealing with the procedures for Ministers to issue certificates exempting records and section 34 dealing with the Information Commissioner's review of decisions on appeal. In these two sections, approximately seven pages of a 63-page Act, there are 85 cross-references to other sections, subsections or paragraphs of the Act. It might be argued that all these cross-references are necessary. However, for an Act that was heralded as a culture change in the openness of the public service, clarity of exposition in its drafting does not appear to have been a priority.

The Amendment Act

Adding the Freedom of Information (Amendment) Act 2003 into this mix does not facilitate understanding. For instance, section 10(b) amends section 15(6)(d)(ii) of the Principal Act in the following terms:

"(*b*) in subsection (6), in paragraph (*d*), by substituting the following subparagraph for subparagraph (ii):

'(ii) the period of 12 months or of such other length as may be determined beginning on the expiration of the period aforesaid

---

[7] Ms Eithne Fitzgerald, *The Irish Times* letters column, January 4, 1997.

and each subsequent period of 12 months or of such other length as may be determined beginning on the expiration of the period of 12 months or of such other length as may be determined immediately preceding'."

These are the terms of an amending Act that was drafted in 2003 subsequent to several initiatives within the legal sphere calling for plain language. The Act is not simple. It is not straightforward and it is not easy to understand either as a matter of plain English or as a matter of legal application. An example of the problem in action is the following extract from a High Court judgment in an appeal against the Information Commissioner: "A decision specified in subsection (1) includes a decision under section 14 which includes, at section 14(1)(f) a decision under section 18 in relation to the contents of a statement furnished under subsection (1) of that section or to refuse an application under that subsection."[8]

Hence, because the Act is so complex and abstruse it is all the more important that it is administered in a spirit of openness, transparency and accountability and by an organisational culture that reflects those values.

Administering the Act

One of the pitfalls facing FOI[9] decision-makers is that they may feel constrained to exercise the black and white letter of the Freedom of Information Act rather than follow common sense. As just noted, a great deal of the Act is not only obscure but, overall, it requires an extraordinary skill in mental gymnastics to keep all the sections and subsections and amendments in mind. Thus, there is a considerable danger that, in practice, guidelines and guidance notes written in plainer English will replace the Act as the easier option for understanding.

These helpful hints, perhaps at times even policy statements, issued by various government departments and other public bodies, including the Central Policy Unit of the Department of Finance, are not the law. An example was the information note from the Department of the Taoiseach on the application of the new fees. It stated in the final line: "Fees are not refundable if a decision is varied or annulled at internal or external review stage." Such a statement is not included in the Amendment Act nor in the Regulations on

---

[8] *Killilea v. Information Commissioner* [2003] I.E.H.C. 63.
[9] The acronym, FOI, is the universally accepted abbreviated term to describe freedom of information.

Fees. The validity of the statement as a policy guidance was, therefore, questionable.[10]

Fees: A requester's nightmare

Under the amending Act a compulsory scale of up-front fees has been introduced.[11] The Information Commissioner has noted on a number of occasions that, apparently as a consequence, the number of requests under the Act has dropped. According to the fees Regulations, a request must be accompanied by the appropriate fee but no fee is to be charged for requests for personal information, nor for applications for reasons for decisions,[12] nor for requests to amend records;[13] additionally, the fee varies depending on whether the requester does or does not hold a medical card. A fee must also be paid at each stage of review.

What is personal information?

Complying with these regulations undoubtedly creates an additional administrative burden for all organisations coming within the FOI regime. An FOI Officer on receipt of a request must now decide the precise nature of the records requested BEFORE the request can be formally treated as an FOI request. Not only is more than one page of the Principal Act devoted to the interpretation of "personal information" but it includes 14 positive sub-clauses and three negative sub-clauses. It is doubtful that an FOI Officer, let alone a requester, is conversant with these subtle complexities; moreover, the Information Commissioner has ruled that personal information is something that may be implied in a record.[14]

To which Schools does the Freedom of Information Act apply?

To qualify as a public body that is subject to the direct application of the Freedom of Information Act a school must be:

---

[10] Information Note Freedom of Information (Fees) Regulations 2003, Department of the Taoiseach, July 2003. This note disappeared from the Internet subsequent to the TCD School of Law FOI Annual Conference 2003 at which it was highlighted by the author.
[11] S.I. No.264 of 2003. Freedom of Information Act 1997 (Fees) Regulations 2003.
[12] Freedom of Information Act, s.18.
[13] *Ibid.*, s.17.
[14] Case 000365 – *Ms ACH and Others and the Department of Education and Science*, October 16, 2001. Below at p.264.

- listed among the hundreds of public bodies in the First Schedule of the Act as originally published and as subsequently amended by a series of statutory instruments[15];
- if not listed by name, must be directly managed by one of the listed bodies, or
- the management must be under a contract for services to a listed body.[16]

In late 1999 a number of health care organisations were added by statutory instrument[17] to the list of prescribed bodies in Schedule 1 of the Act. The First Schedule of the statutory instrument includes a number of hospitals that have recognised schools. All activities of these bodies including their schools, unless otherwise exempted, came directly within the freedom of information regime with their parent body. The Second Schedule of the statutory instrument lists a number of organisations that care for those with special needs. The functions of these bodies came within the ambit of the Act in so far as they relate to the provision of mental health services or services for persons of intellectual disability. As a consequence, any school within these organisations providing these functions is directly subject to the provisions of the Act.

Accurate record-keeping and sensible procedures

The Act does not impose specific requirements on public bodies in relation to records management. It is, nonetheless, clear that proper records management is vital to the success of the Act. Indeed, whether subject to the Act or not, to be effective, organisations of all kinds require accurate record-keeping and sensible procedures which are applied in a consistent manner across the board. These are the principles that are stressed time and time again by judges and by information commissioners in all jurisdictions.

What is also required, especially in highly stressful environments such as schools where personal worth is often put on the line, is a management approach that is sensitive to teachers and students and alike. In well-managed organisations, and schools are not exceptions to this rule, decision-makers are conscious that their actions have qualitative consequences; thus, as a matter of course they keep their staff, students and parents informed and ensure that anyone affected by an institutional decision is made aware of the

---

[15] Freedom of Information Act, s.3.
[16] Ibid., s.6(9).
[17] S.I. No. 329 of 1999, Freedom of Information Act 1997 (Prescribed Bodies) Regulations 1999.

rationale underlying such decisions. Thus, staff and students are already aware of any information retained about them and these and other records are well maintained to facilitate tracking decisions.

Sound management practice

It cannot be overstressed that if the school is already well managed application of freedom of information will merely reinforce sound practices.

This would be the case with any primary school where the Board of Management seriously embraces the Constitution of Boards and Rules of Procedure which was agreed by the partners in education. It suffices to quote section 8 and 9 of the document:

> "8. *Confidentiality*
>   (a) Individual members of the Board are required to keep confidential the matters discussed at meetings unless otherwise agreed by the Board.
>   (b) Where the Patron is satisfied, after due investigation, that any member of the Board infringed this injunction of confidentiality, he/she may, subject to the consent of the Minister remove that person from membership and shall not subsequently nominate that person as a member of any Board of Management.
>
> 9. *Board communications/transparency*
>   (a) Good management practice will require frequent communications to parents, staff and the school community.
>   (b) The Board shall put in place procedures to support good communication within the school community.
>   (c) The Board, at the closure of each Board meeting shall determine the information to be conveyed to parents, teachers and the school community, and the manner and terms in which it should be conveyed.
> **Note:** In authorising the dissemination of information under (b) above, the Board shall pursue a policy of openness and have a positive approach to sharing information with the school community. The provisions of section 8(a) regarding confidentiality need not necessarily conflict with the operation of such a policy; 8 above is intended to protect against inappropriate disclosure rather than to obstruct good communi-cations and transparency."[18]

---

[18] Boards of Management of National Schools Constitution of Boards and Rules of

With regard to post-primary schools, a well-managed school is compliant with the provisions of the education legislation. For example, the Education Act 1998 not only gives statutory recognition to the National Parents Councils, but also establishes procedural rights for the constructive involvement of parents in individual schools. These include the following:

- Parents have a statutory right to establish parents' associations in schools.
- Parent representatives have a statutory right to participation in boards of management, including deciding on their membership.
- Parents are entitled to receive copies of any reports on the operation and performance of the school produced by the board of management and to have access to the school accounts on the same basis as the Minister. They are involved in the preparation of the school plan, copies of which are also circulated to them.
- Parents have a right of access to their children's school records.
- Parents must be consulted in relation to the assessment of the psychological needs of their children and must be advised by the psychologists concerned in relation to the education and psychological development of the children.
- Parents have the right to appeal to the board of management against a decision of a teacher or member of staff of the school and to the Secretary General of the Department of Education and Science against certain actions taken by the board of management.

Principal Rights under the Act

The Freedom of Information Act confers three significant rights on members of the public:

- to access official records held by Government Departments and other listed public bodies,[19]
- to have personal information corrected or updated where such information is incomplete, incorrect or misleading,[20]
- to be given reasons for decisions that affect them taken by public bodies.[21]

Procedure. November 2003. Department of Education and Science website: www.education.ie.
[19] Freedom of Information Act, s.6.
[20] Ibid., s.17.
[21] Ibid., s.18.

Process of releasing information

Any request for information must be in writing and state that the request is being made under the Freedom of Information Act.[22] If the initial request is refused in whole or in part there is recourse to an internal review.[23] If this also results in refusal an appeal for review may be taken to the Information Commissioner.[24] The Information Commissioner's decision, which is binding, may be appealed on a point of law to the High Court.[25] Initially, there was no right of appeal to the Supreme Court but this was remedied by the amending Act.[26]

Rights of third parties

Any third party such as a school, or such as a student, teacher or parent, who is mentioned in the records, or who would be directly affected by the release of the records, must be approached for their agreement to release.[27] If the third party is opposed to release the same system of appeal is available as applies to the requester. Thus, the Act contains a series of checks and balances that, when properly administered, ensure that personal information, privacy of individuals and confidential information is exempt from release in most circumstances. Even when there might appear to be an overriding public interest in the release of records, personal information and information specific to individual schools is not released or is redacted, *i.e.* blacked out, to the extent that clues as to identity which could result in harm are also withheld.[28] All can be reassured that the Information Commissioner is most diligent in protecting requesters and third parties.

DEPARTMENT OF EDUCATION AND SCIENCE AND THE
FREEDOM OF INFORMATION ACT

The Department of Education and Science as a government department is, obviously, a listed public body for the purposes of the Act. This means that all records held by the Department come within the regulatory regime. This

---

[22] *Ibid.*, s.7.
[23] *Ibid.*, s.14.
[24] *Ibid.*, s.34.
[25] *Ibid.*, s.42.
[26] *Ibid.*, s.42 as amended in 2003.
[27] *Ibid.*, s.29.
[28] See Freedom of Information Act Pt III: Exempt records particularly ss.26, 27, 28.

does not mean that all such records are freely available to whomsoever may request them.

Openness and transparency

A visit to the Department of Education and Science website[29] is recommended for anyone wanting to access information about educational services in Ireland. Indeed, it seems as if the provisions of the Freedom of Information Act might well have become superfluous in many dealings with the Department. The Department's section 15 and section 16 manuals, the publications required under the Act that essentially detail what records are accessible under the Act and the rules and procedures used for decisions of the Department, are easily downloadable from the website.

Education Act 1998

The Education Act 1998 conferred considerable rights on parents and students to access school records. Section 9(g) requires schools to "ensure that parents of a student, or in the case of a student who has reached the age of 18 years, the student, have access in the prescribed manner to records kept by that school relating to the progress of that student in his or her education."

Unfortunately, expansive availability of information has not always been the way in the Department.

SCHOOL LEAGUE TABLES OR THE CLASH OF THE ACTS

Minister for Education and Science v. the Information Commissioner,[30] was a High Court appeal taken by the Minister of the day[31] against the Information Commissioner's decision directing the Minister to give *The Sunday Times*, *The Sunday Tribune* and *The Kerryman*, access to certain records held by the Minister concerning the results of the Leaving Certificate Examinations held in 1998. The substantive matter was already moot by the time of the High Court hearing in July 2000. In other words, whatever way the High

---

[29] www.education.ie
[30] [2001] I.E.H.C. 116.
[31] Ministers of Education and Science from 1998 to date: 1998–200: Mr Micheál Martin; 2000–2002; Dr Michael Woods; 2002–2004: Mr Noel Dempsey, and 2004 to date: Ms Mary Hanafin.

Freedom of Information Act and Schools

Court decided, the timeliness for the media of publication of the Leaving Certificate results was long past its sell-by date. Known popularly as the *School League Tables* case, the circumstances of the Information Commissioner's review and the High Court action caused public furore.

Denying parents information

The Minister and his advisers could have chosen one of two approaches to the requests by the media: be secretive or be open. Sadly, they took the first route apparently deciding that parents, although products of our educational system, are unable to handle critically the implications of school league tables published in the media that are of a uni-dimensional character, *i.e.* based solely on Leaving Certificate results. The Department and Teachers' Unions could have taken a more generous approach whereby a comprehensive body of information could be released regularly indicating factors such as class sizes, remedial classes, sports curricula, involvement in debating societies, theatrical productions, chess clubs, social and charitable activities, etc., etc. The reasons for a choice of school encompass a variety of factors, not least location and family connections, and if there are parents who select a school solely based on the criterion of academic results in the Leaving Certificate surely that is their right so to do.

The decision of the Minister to appeal the Commissioner's determination was deplored in an editorial of *The Irish Times* in the following terms: "There is a sense in which the Minister, with the support of the educational establishment, is turning his face against the principles of openness, transparency and accountability which are now a routine part of some other aspects of public administration."[32] Bearing in mind that this decision was, indeed, taken by the then Minister for Education and Science in the supposed new era of freedom of information, it is instructive to note that the Department took even more draconian action in favour of secrecy.

Legislative opportunism

Section 53 of the Education Act 1998 confers discretion on the Minister in relation to examinations, to refuse access to any information which would enable the compilation of information (that is not otherwise available to the general public) in relation to the comparative performance of schools in respect of the academic achievement of students, notwithstanding any other

---

[32] *The Irish Times*, November 3,1999.

enactment. Section 53 is in direct contradiction to section 8(4)(b) of the Freedom of Information Act that requires that any belief or opinion of the head of the public body as to what are the reasons of the requester for the request shall be disregarded. The timing of the amendment introducing section 53 coincided with the process of the requesters' appeal against a refusal by the Department of Education and Science to provide information relating to examination results.

League tables emerge

A year or so after the High Court judgment was delivered this debate re-emerged in full cry with the publication in *The Irish Times* of details of numbers of university entrants from specified schools in.[33] The information was obtained through the exercise of the Freedom of Information Act. Subsequently, School League Tables for each county were published by the *Farmers Journal* using this information in combination with additional information on numbers in each school sitting the Leaving Certificate obtained from the Department, also by means of a freedom of information request.[34] Such was the interest in this publication that some Dublin city centre newsagents were sold out of copies of the *Farmers Journal* by lunchtime on the first day of sales, and this stock-out resulted in some newsagents in the outlying urban areas failing to receive any copies.[35]

Primary School league tables

The case of *Sheedy v. Information Commissioner*[36] is also about the clash between section 53 of the Education Act 1998 and the terms of the Freedom of Information Act, this time in respect of the possibility of primary school league tables. The High Court affirmed the Information Commissioner's decision to release a primary school inspection report but this judgment has been reversed on appeal to the Supreme Court. This was the first opportunity since the Freedom of Information Act was passed for the Supreme Court to adjudicate the Act's terms; the appeal judgment centred on whether or not section 53 of the Education Act trumped the Freedom of Information Act.

The case began life when *The Irish Times* requested copies of five primary

---

[33] *Ibid.*, September 17, 2002.
[34] *Farmers Journal*, January 25, 2003.
[35] The author had to go directly to the publisher to obtain a copy following a fruitless search within the dense farmlands of Dublin 2 and 24.
[36] Unreported, High Court, Gilligan J., May 20 2004.

school Tuairiscí Scoile from the Department of Education and Science. The request was refused and appealed by the newspaper to the Information Commissioner. He set aside the Department's decision and directed that access be given to redacted versions of the Tuairiscí Scoile for all five schools, including Scoil Choilm. All personal information, within the meaning of section 28 of the Freedom of Information Act,[37] was excluded from the redacted reports. The applicant is Principal of Scoil Choilm and it is against this decision of the Information Commissioner that Mr. Sheedy brought an appeal to the courts.

Contents of Tuairiscí Scoile

The reports gave an overall impression of the schools but they did not contain any specific references to the academic achievements of students in each school. The reports were prepared in accordance with circular 12/83 which provides that: "A school report containing an assessment of the organisation and work of the school as a whole is to be furnished to the Department at regular intervals of approximately four years." The reports included an introduction dealing with factual background material about the history and location of the school, accommodation, the principal and staff, organisation preparation and planning, languages (English and Irish), mathematics, social and environmental studies, aesthetic and creative activities, special needs pupils, physical education, a post-inspection meeting and a conclusion.

In his decision the Commissioner had noted:

> "[W]hile the reports gave an overall impression of the schools they did not contain any specific references to the academic achievements of students in each school. The Commissioner went on to find that the comments in the reports were of such a general nature that no meaningful comparison could be drawn between the schools. He did not accept that the information in the reports could be described as information given in confidence to the Inspectors as the reports were the Inspectors' own opinions and observations formed during the course of visits to the schools."[38]

---

[37] S.28(1) provides:" Subject to the provisions of this section, a head shall refuse to grant a request under s.7 if, in the opinion of the head access to the record concerned would involve the disclosure of personal information (including personal information relating to a deceased individual)".
[38] Case 000238, *The Irish Times and the Department of Education and Science*, March 5, 2003.

High Court appeal

Section 53 of the Education Act 1998, as described above, confers discretion on the Minister for Education and Science in relation to examinations, to refuse access to any information which would enable the compilation of information (that is not otherwise available to the general public) in relation to the comparative performance of schools in respect of the academic achievement of students, notwithstanding any other enactment.

In *Sheedy*, Gilligan J. noted that to come within the ambit of section 53 the relevant information would have to enable the compilation of information in relation to the comparative performance of schools in respect of the academic achievement of the students enrolled therein. He observed that the Commissioner carefully evaluated the information in issue in the light of the terms of section 53 and the statutory requirement[39] to give effect to its restrictions by refusing to grant access to the reports if "any empirical league table of schools, even one based on overall impressions, could be compiled." Gilligan J. distinguished between the Information Commissioner's decision, which dealt with all five school reports, and the case before him, which dealt with only one. Nevertheless, he agreed with the Commissioner stating:

> "I also have had the benefit of reading the redacted version of the Inspector's report relating to Scoil Choilm and I take the view that the appellant has failed to demonstrate that granting access to the school report from Scoil Choilm would enable the compilation of information in relation to the comparative performance of schools in respect of academic achievements of students."

Section 21(1) FOI exemption if access might prejudice future reports[40]

Section 21(1)(a) of the Freedom of Information Act provides that access to a record may be refused if, in the opinion of the head of the public body, access could reasonably be expected to "prejudice the effectiveness of tests, examinations, investigations, inquiries or audits conducted by or on behalf of the public body concerned or the procedures or methods employed for the conduct thereof."

---

[39] S.32(1)(a) of the Freedom of Information Act requires the Information Commissioner to take account of any other enactments.
[40] See below, p.254.

Section 21(2) provides:

> "Subsection (1) shall not apply in relation to a case in which in the opinion of the head concerned, the public interest would, on balance, be better served by granting than by refusing to grant the request".[41]

In considering these clauses, Gilligan J. stated that it is well established that this exemption is to be exercised sparingly. The onus was on the appellant to show that a significant adverse effect could result in the granting of access to the records. He held that no satisfactory evidence had been presented in this regard. In arriving at this conclusion he commented that the Commissioner had dealt extensively with this aspect and:

> "in particular that pursuant to s. 13 of the Education Act 1998 inspectors have sufficient powers to require the co-operation of schools and that accordingly from the appellant's perspective it is not a matter of choice as regards information that is given to the Department inspectorate but in fact is a matter of statutory obligation."

The judge noted further that in his decision the Commissioner specifically refers to the fact that if he were to find that section 21 exemptions applied, in the absence of any countervailing public interest, and if he had to decide a case on whether the public interest would be better served by release he would find in favour of release.

> "I do not consider, having regard to the detailed consideration that was given to this matter by the Information Commissioner, that he can be faulted in any regard in the decision as arrived at."

Section 26(1) FOI exemption if information given in confidence

When the Department of Education had refused access to the various school reports it had argued that the information in the reports was given in confidence to the inspectors and that the information would not have been given if the parties concerned believed the reports would be published: the reports would be of little value in the absence of the information supplied by the school. Gilligan J., in dismissing the "given in confidence" argument, agreed with the Commissioner that it is reasonable to conclude that the

---

[41] S.21(1)(b), refers to significant adverse effects on management functions and s.21(1)(c) refers to disclosure of negotiating positions.

information was not imparted in circumstances in which the appellant could reasonably have expected that an obligation of confidence arose. The appellant ought to have been aware that:

> "the information was being supplied to comply with the inspector's functions pursuant to s. 13 of the Education Act, 1998, and this would involve the inspector reporting to the Minister, the board, patrons, parents of students and teachers as appropriate and conceivably in disseminating information on a wider basis."

The High Court held therefore that the Commissioner had not erred in law in any respect.

Supreme Court appeal

While the Supreme Court reversed the judgment of the High Court on the substantive issue ruling that the report on Scoil Choilm should not be released based on section 53 of the Education Act 1998, the court affirmed both the Information Commissioner and the High Court's view on the sections of the Freedom of Information Act that had been raised.

Kearns J. delivered the judgment on behalf of the court with Fennelly J. dissenting. The latter considered that the Freedom of Information Act holds special significance.

> "The passing of the Freedom of Information Act constituted a legislative development of major importance. By it, the Oireachtas took a considered and deliberate step, which dramatically alters the administrative assumptions and culture of centuries. It replaces the presumption of secrecy with one of openness. It is designed to open up the workings of government and administration to scrutiny. It is not designed simply to satisfy the appetite of the media for stories. It is for the benefit of every citizen. It lets light in to the offices and filing cabinets of our rulers."

Consequently, he did not agree that section 53 ought to be applied in order to deny disclosure of the information requested. He did agree that the grounds of appeal based on sections 21 and 26 of the Freedom of Information Act should be dismissed.

With regard to the section 21 of the Freedom of Information Act, exemption if access to a record might prejudice future reports, Kearns J. held that the High Court was "absolutely correct" in finding as it did. In so doing he stated that:

> "the onus to produce evidence of prejudice fell on the Department and in the absence of same the Commissioner was entitled, under s. 34 of the Act of 1997, to hold against the Department. A mere assertion of an expectation of non co-operation from teaching staff could never constitute sufficient evidence in this regard, particularly in the circumstances shown to apply, namely, that as a consequence of both Circular 12/83 and s.13 of the Act of 1998, there was no choice left to schools or their staff as to whether or not to co-operate with the Department's inspectors in terms of furnishing the information sought."

Kearns J. was also in complete agreement with the High Court in respect of its finding on section 26, exemption if information given in confidence. He noted that this section:

> "is triggered where information is given or imparted in confidence, so that the Commissioner's first task was to inquire and assess whether or not the material or information going into the tuairisci scoile had that quality [of confidence] or not. ... He took the position that while some of the views *might* have been imparted to the inspectors in confidence, he thought it unlikely given the purpose of the reports and the circumstances of their creation. However, he went further and based his decision on his own reading of the reports. Having examined the contents of the reports, he was thus in a position to state that he was satisfied that they did not contain any information that could be said to have been imparted in circumstances imposing an obligation of confidence or have the necessary quality of confidence about it. ... In reaching his decision the Commissioner had careful regard to the fact that the reports were prepared by inspectors in the course of their statutory functions and that they represented the fruits of the inspectors' own opinions and observations formed during the course of their visits to the schools. He concluded, as in my view he was entitled to do, that these opinions and observations were not imparted to them by anyone. He further noted that much of the information would in any event already have been in the possession of the Department and that it did not consist of private or secret matters."

In summary, both the High Court and the Supreme Court accepted the Information Commissioner's reasoning with regard to the provisions of the Freedom of Information Act. However, the majority in the Supreme Court held that because of section 53 of the Education Act 1998 the inspection report on Scoil Choilm should be withheld from disclosure.

Discretionary nature of section 53

Following publication of the Supreme Court judgment the current Minister of Education and Science, Ms. Mary Hanafin TD, noted that the judgment clarified that section 53 gave discretion to the Minister whether or not to release information on schools. She continued:

> "I am totally opposed to the publication of crude league tables based on examination results. Such league tables are damaging to schools, and we need to make available more balanced information that can take account of the wide range of work undertaken by schools. Unlike league tables, which tell us little about the wide range of work that schools undertake, school inspection reports provide balanced evaluations on the work of schools. In this context, I am convinced that wider availability of school inspection reports, rather than crude league tables, could be very beneficial for students, teachers, parents and schools. As the Supreme Court makes clear, the discretionary power of the Minister to use Section 53 in a balanced way makes this possible."

The Minister concluded:

> "This is, of course, a complex matter and I intend to proceed in a planned and well-thought out way. I intend to consult with the education partners on how best we can make school inspection reports more generally available. I have asked the Inspectorate of my Department to enter into consultations with the education partners as soon as possible on how best we can achieve this".[42]

SEPARATED PARENTS' RIGHTS OF ACCESS TO RECORDS

N. McK. v. Information Commissioner[43] allowed an appeal of a separated parent against a decision of the Information Commissioner that affirmed the refusal of the Adelaide & Meath Hospital, Dublin incorporating the National Children's Hospital to grant access to medical records relating to his daughter.

---

[42] Department of Education and Science *Press Release*, May 30, 2005.
[43] [2004] 1 I.R. 12.

This judgment, which was the subject of an appeal to the Supreme Court, has significance for any body holding children's records, especially schools given the terms of section 9(g) of the Education Act.[44]

Access to minor's records shall be granted

This case involved consideration of the Freedom of Information Act 1997 (section 28(6)) Regulations, 1999,[45] in particular, article 3(1) which states that a request for access to a record which involves the disclosure of personal information shall be granted, *inter alia*, where:

> "(a) the requester is a parent or guardian of the individual to whom the record concerned relates and that individual belongs to one of the following classes of individuals:
> (i) Individuals who, on the date of the request, have not attained full age (within the meaning of the Age of Majority Act, 1985 ...) access to whose records would, in the opinion of the head having regard to all the circumstances and to any guidelines drawn up and published by the Minister, be in their best interests".

Quirke J. held that these terms are *prima facie* "imperative and positive requiring that access to appropriate records *shall* be granted where the requester is a parent or guardian and where the record relates to a minor (as in this case)." The only relevant qualification upon this requirement is that such access:

> "'... would, in the opinion of the head, having regard to all the circumstances and to any guidelines drawn up and published by the Minister, be in [the minor's] best interests...'
> It has been acknowledged that no guidelines of the kind contemplated in the Regulations have been drawn up or published so it follows that the regulation imposes an obligation upon the [Information Commissioner] to form an opinion as to whether access to the records would, having regard to all the circumstances, be in the minor's best interests."

Quirke J. held that the Information Commissioner had misconstrued these

---

[44] See Education Act 1998, above, p.248.
[45] S.I. No.47 of 1999.

provisions by placing an onus on the applicant to prove that granting of access would be a tangible benefit to the child:

> "The respondent is not of the opinion that access by the appellant to the records will accrue to *the detriment* of the minor. The respondent construes the section as requiring that access must invariably be *denied* unless and until *'tangible'* evidence has been furnished demonstrating that the access will result in a benefit to the minor.
> I do not believe that this construction is the correct one. It imposes upon an applicant such as the appellant in this case, the obligation to discharge an onus, which is not apparent from the terms of the legislation. The Act and the Regulations, when read together, provide that access *'shall'* be granted where, in the opinion of the deciding officers it is in the best interests of the minor *'having regard to all the circumstances'*."

Strained family relationship irrelevant

The background to the case is that during separation proceedings between the applicant and his wife, an allegation was made that the applicant had sexually abused his daughter. He vigorously denied and still denies this allegation and the Gardaí, having investigated the allegations concluded that there was "no evidence to warrant a prosecution".

The applicant was granted supervised access to his children. Subsequently, the wife died and by agreement the two children of the marriage went to live with the late Mrs McK's brother and his wife, with whom Mr McK had a strained relationship, and it was agreed, *inter alia* that they and the applicant would be appointed as joint guardian of the two children. In January 2000, the daughter, then aged 12, was admitted to hospital. The applicant had failed in his appeal to the Information Commissioner following the hospital's refusal to grant him access to his daughter's records and he had then appealed on a point of law to the High Court.

With regard to the applicant's history, Quirke J. stated:

> "Although a complaint has in the past been made about the appellant, it remains unsubstantiated and the appellant comes before this Court enjoying the presumption of innocence which is enjoyed by every citizen of the State. The evidence indicates that he is concerned with the welfare of both of his children and avails of his rights of access to them in a conscientious fashion."

Quirke J. rooted his judgment in the Supreme Court judgment of Hardiman J. in *North Western Health Board v. H.W.*[46] which declared that any legislation vindicating and defending the rights of children must be interpreted in the light of the Constitution particularly Article 41 (The Family) and Article 42 (Education).

Parental primacy

Quirke J. quoted extensively from this judgment and the following points with regard to the role of the family are of particular significance:

> "... a presumption exists that the welfare of the child is to be found in the family exercising its authority as such. ... The presumption ... is not, of course, a presumption that the parents are always correct in their decisions according to some objective criterion. It is a presumption that where the constitutional family exists and is discharging its functions as such and the parents have not for physical or moral reasons failed in their duty towards their children, their decisions should not be overridden by the State or in particular by the Courts in the absence of a jurisdiction conferred by statute."

Having noted that there had been no suggestion of such a failure of duty on the part of the appellant Quirke J. continued:

> "Accordingly the appellant, as a parent, joint guardian and joint custodian of the child concerned enjoys the parental primacy identified by Hardiman J. in *North Western Health Board v. H.W.* ... and the presumption that he has the welfare of his child at heart in the absence of evidence to the contrary.
> The presumption is of course rebuttable, but there is no suggestion of rebuttal in this case.
> Reluctance by another family member to agree to access does not, in the absence of any supporting evidence, amount to rebuttal sufficient to displace the presumption referred to."

Supreme Court appeal

The reserved judgment of the Supreme Court appeal which was heard in early November 2005 is awaited. Irrespective of whether the judgment affirms or reverses the High Court decision it is anticipated that the judgment will

---

[46] [2001] 3 I.R. 622.

include significant comment on Articles 41 and 42 of the Constitution which deal with the rights of the family and the right to education. In particular it is expected that the court will comment on the rights of children to preserve confidentiality of information as against the rights of parents as enshrined and inferred in the Constitution and as based in earlier court judgments.

Partners in Education

A school the management of which is under a contract for services to a body listed under the Freedom of Information Act is also subject to the Act. Since all recognised schools are subject to the regulation of the Department of Education and Science and most are not managed directly by the Department, a critical question is whether the relationship is a contract for services.

Relationship of Department of Education and Science with Boards of Management and with teachers

This issue has been considered by the Information Commissioner who declared himself satisfied that a contract for services does not exist between a Board and the Department. It informed the Commissioner that:

> "[A] board carries out various functions many of which are carried out on behalf of the Minister for Education and Science with a view to ensuring that good quality educational services are provided to pupils. [The Department] accepted that the Chairpersons of boards have a responsibility to ensure that schools are operating properly and are also involved in certifying various returns for the Department. It stated, however, ... that as Chairpersons or other members of boards are not remunerated by the Department for their roles they are not acting as contractors for the Department. I accept this to be the case. I am also satisfied that teachers are engaged under contracts of service with the boards rather than under contracts for services with the Department."[47]

---

[47] Case 98169, *Ms ABY and the Department of Education and Science*, July 6, 2000; see below pp.261, 266 *et seq*. See also letter decision, Case 99173, *Mr X and the Department of Education and Science*, July 17, 2001.

All records held by the Department of Education and Science are subject to the Act

Boards of Management should be aware that all of their communications with the Department may come under scrutiny for the purposes of the Act. This includes notes taken of telephone conversations. In the course of dealing with a request regarding a complaint against a teacher, the Department agreed to release a hand-written note of a telephone conversation between an official of the Department and the Chairman of the Board of Management concerning, *inter alia*, a meeting of the Board with the exception of the last three lines which it claimed contain information which did not relate to the requester. The Information Commissioner upheld the decision of the Department.

Lest members of Boards of Management feel a cold chill at the thought that all their communications could become public knowledge, the Commissioner also made some general comments of relevance:

> "I do not accept that every communication between a board of management and the Department is made in confidence. Where, as in this case, there is no express understanding of confidentiality between the parties but it is alleged that confidentiality is implicit, then it is legitimate to look at the nature of the relationship between the parties, the content of the information and the practice of the public body in relation to such communications.
>
> It seems to me that there is nothing in the nature of the relationship between the Department and a board of management which would suggest that all communications between them are or are intended to be confidential. Nor do I accept that it is the invariable practice of the Department to treat <u>all</u> such communications as confidential. However, I do accept that the Department's practice has been, and is, to treat a teacher's response to a complaint as confidential. Having regard to this practice, and having regard to the nature of the information conveyed, I find that the Board furnished the teacher's response to the Department in confidence and on the understanding that it was to be treated as confidential."[48]

Parents

Of course, within the context of the Freedom of Information Act, parents are in a different category to Boards of Management and to teachers. Whether

---

[48] Case 98169, *Ms ABY and the Department of Education and Science*, July 6 2000.

or not the records relating to parents' groups or individual parents are subject to access by requests under the Act is regulated in the standard manner, *e.g.* do the records contain personal information or were they submitted in confidence?

Hence, any parent concerned in this regard should be treated in precisely the same fashion with respect to the Act as any other member of the public. Naturally, a parent or guardian has particular rights in respect of the records of a minor child or of a child over 18 who by reason of some disability is dependent on the parent.[49] Such situations are covered by both the Education Act, as already noted, and by section 28 of the Freedom of Information Act.

Any parent who is unsure of their rights need only ask the designated freedom of information officer in the body from which they request records: within the freedom of information regulations is a requirement that requesters must be assisted when necessary.[50] It should always be borne in mind that it is prohibited by the Act for a public body to consider the use to which information will be put by the requester.[51] Thus, anyone who is anxious about making inquiries should be reassured in this knowledge. Nevertheless, quite often members of the public are facilitated by freedom of information officers asking them to withdraw formal freedom of information requests and by talking to them about what they want and for what purpose, something that the Act itself prohibits. It can be noted for the computer literate that most freedom of information websites will specify the rights of requesters in simple terms.

SELECTION OF INFORMATION COMMISSIONER'S DECISIONS INVOLVING SCHOOLS

Request by a newspaper for release of records relating to Whole School Evaluation (WSE)

It is worthwhile to quote extensively from the Information Commissioner's findings as they illustrate the balancing act required between differing rights under the Act and the public interest:

> "I accept the Department's evidence that the schools, the reports on which are the subject of this review, volunteered to participate in the project on the understanding that the reports would not be published.

---

[49] See above *NMcK v. Information Commissioner* [2004] I.E.H.C. 4, *supra*, p.256
[50] Freedom of Information Act, s.7(7).
[51] This is an intriguing aspect of the *School League Tables* case considered *supra*, p.248 *et seq.*

I accept that the Department did not warn them that the reports might run the risk (as the schools might see it) of being released under the FOI Act. It is clear that the WSE project is a controversial one. In the normal course, it represents the kind of development which one would expect to be the subject of a pilot project of some kind. I am satisfied that any such pilot project would have to be conducted on a voluntary basis. It seems to me that to release information about parties, who had participated on a voluntary basis in a pilot project designed to test a new and a controversial concept, runs a very real risk of prejudicing the Department's future capacity to secure such co-operation. ...

On a general level, I accept [the] arguments that there is a public interest in information about schools being available, and in the public having access to records under the FOI Act. However, these aspects of the public interest cannot prevail in all circumstances and regardless of the content of the information or the circumstances in which it was created or procured by a public body. As regards the question of an informed public debate, particularly on the question of parental involvement, I am of the view that the Department's report on the pilot project published in September 1999, which contains an analysis and critique of the individual reports, provides a solid basis for an informed public debate. In saying this I do not wish to suggest that the public's right, under the FOI Act, to information about a pilot project conducted by a public body can always be satisfied by the publication of a final report on the project. However, I am satisfied that access to the individual reports at this stage is not necessary to assist an informed public debate.

Having regard to the above and, in particular, to the possibility of damage to the Department's capacity to secure co-operation in relation to future pilot projects, I am satisfied that the release of these reports would be contrary to the public interest."[52]

Poor working atmosphere in school

The details of this case illustrate some of the protections for third parties provided under the Freedom of Information Act:

"A number of teachers in a school in the West of Ireland wrote a letter to the Minister for Education and Science under the terms of the Safety,

---

[52] Case 98099, *Mr John Burns and the Department of Education and Science*, September 13, 2000.

Health and Welfare at Work Act, 1989 regarding working conditions in their school. The Department sent an acknowledgement to all the teachers in the school, following which a number of the teachers who had not signed the letter requested a copy of the letter under the FOI Act from the Department. The Department decided that the letter had been sent to it in confidence but that the public interest was better served by the release of the letter than by withholding it. The Department decided to release the letter.

The Commissioner found that the information in the letter did not amount to personal information about the signatories as the letter expressed their views as a group and did not attribute personal experience or viewpoints to any specific individual signatory. He found that the letter contained no specific allegations about any of the other teachers but that the school principal was identifiable by inference. He considered that, as the views of a person about an individual amounts to personal information about that individual, the fact that the Principal was referred to implicitly meant that the information contained in the letter amounted to personal information about her. The Commissioner found that no other teacher was identifiable either from a specific allegation or by inference and, accordingly, that the letter did not contain personal information about any teacher other than the Principal.

The Commissioner found that the letter had been given in confidence but that the public interest was better served by release of the content of the letter to the Principal. He found that while the content of the letter should be released to the Principal, the identities of the signatories should not be released. The Commissioner found that the release of the content of the letter to the requesters, other than the Principal, would breach the privacy rights of the Principal and that the public interest was best served by withholding the contents of the letter from the other requesters."[53]

Teacher's request for personal files

A teacher in a comprehensive school sought his personal file from the Department of Education and Science, which was released to him. He also sought, from the Department, the personal file held on him by the Board of Management and the personal file held on him by the school Principal. The

---

[53] Case 000365, *Ms ACH and Others and the Department of Education and Science*, October 16, 2001.

Department refused his request for the records held by the Board of Management and the Principal on the grounds that neither were held or controlled by the Department, but were the property of the Board of Management, which is not subject to the FOI Act.

In summary, the Information Commissioner's authorised officer found that:

> "the method of appointment of teachers to the school (whereby the Board of Management interviews prospective candidates, and recommends the most suitable for appointment to the Minister for Education and Science) was not evidence that the Board of Management was under the control of the Department. He also found that the Deed of Trust, which governs the relationship between the Department and the school, was not equivalent to a contract for services, given that the teachers' salaries are met from grants paid to the school, and given that the Board of Management members are not remunerated by the Department for their work."

Having examined the Deed and its Schedule the Commissioner noted as follows:

> "The Schedule states that the Minister shall appoint a BoM which 'is charged with the direct government of the school, the appointment and removal of teachers, subject to the approval of the Minister ..'. It also stipulates that the BoM 'shall enter into an agreement ...with each member of the teaching staff of the school and the services of any member of the staff cannot be dispensed with by the Board except in accordance with the terms of this agreement.'"

With regard to the employment of teachers the Commissioner found that:

> "The Deed of Trust requires that the BoM will interview prospective teachers and will 'recommend for the approval of the Minister the appointment of the candidate' who appears most suitable. According to the Deed, this arrangement must be complied with in order for the school to receive funding. Additionally, as the Deed stipulates that any teacher who is appointed must sign an 'agreement' with the BoM in relation to his or her appointment, I accept the Department's argument that it is not the employer of such a teacher but that the actual employer is the Board of Management. It appears to me, therefore, that the system of appointment of a teacher does not demonstrate that the BoM is

under the control of the Department. I have found no other evidence to suggest that either the BoM or its records are under the direct control of the Department".

Finally, with regard to control of records, the Department informed the Commissioner that the submission of a number of minutes of BoM meetings in comprehensive schools has evolved over the years as a voluntary practice. The Commissioner examined the Deed of Trust and found that:

> "there is no express stipulation therein that the BoM must submit minutes of meetings to the Department. In these circumstances, I would not expect all minutes of the BoM meetings to be sent to the Department."[54]

Complaint against a teacher

A parent applied for access to the Department of Education and Science's file concerning a complaint she had made about a national schoolteacher. The Department refused access to certain records given to it by the Board of Management of the school concerned including the teacher's response to the complaint. It argued that release would have an adverse impact on the receipt of similar information from teachers and Boards of Management in similar cases. It contended that it is necessary for a Board to be able to carry out an enquiry in relation to one of its employees in a confidential manner. It also argued that where the Department becomes involved in carrying out inquiries in relation to a case already considered by a Board it must respect that confidentiality.

The Commissioner accepted that the information given to the Department by the Board was given in confidence and that it was reasonable for the Board to expect that it would treat that information with the same degree of confidence expected of the Board. He found that release of the teacher's response to the Board could reasonably be expected to prejudice the procedures adopted by the Department for the investigation by it of complaints against teachers. He was not satisfied that the release of the teacher's response would have a significant, adverse effect on the functions relating to management of the Department. Nevertheless, he found that the Department was justified in refusing access to this record on other grounds.

Again, it is instructive to quote a substantial part of the findings as it

---

[54] Letter decision, Case 99173, *Mr X and the Department of Education and Science*, July 17, 2001.

focuses attention on issues of accountability and transparency:

> "I am of the view that there is a clear public interest in a public body, in this case the Department, being able effectively to investigate complaints made to it.
> In this case all parties appear to be in agreement that a complainant should be informed as to the outcome of his/her complaint, yet the NPC [National Parents Council] has put it to me that parents are generally not advised in any manner in relation to the outcome of a complaint and that it is only where a parent persists that that they will get an answer from the Department. If so, this is clearly an unsatisfactory situation.
> While the choice of investigation procedure rests with the public body, in this case the Department, it seems to me essential that there be clarity and certainty for all the relevant parties in relation to the procedures to be adopted and the time scales within which matters are likely to be brought to a conclusion. I am not necessarily saying here that a complainant should always be made privy to all of the papers considered during the course of the investigation procedure or that strict time scales should always be adhered to. Those are matters for consideration in the context of procedural design. However, I am of the view that, having regard to the range of complaints that could be made against a teacher in the performance of his/her duties, the potential for an adverse effect on the well being of the child concerned, the reputation of the teacher and of the school generally, it is in the interests of all the relevant parties that such design should incorporate procedures which would allow for the expeditious conclusion of investigations into complaints. There is a clear public interest in members of the public exercising their rights of access under the FOI Act and I am in agreement with the Department that there is a public interest in the accountability of officials (which I take to include all those paid out of public moneys) and the scrutiny of the decision making process. However, in the case of an investigation into a complaint against a teacher, I am satisfied this particular public interest can be best achieved through the use of transparent procedures and a clear notification of the outcome to all the relevant parties within a reasonable time frame.
> Both the Department and the INTO have commented on the potential for the notification of an outcome to affect seriously the standing of the teacher in the local community and the employer/employee relationship between a teacher and a board of management. I accept the argument of the NPC that the notification of decisions to

the relevant parties could be as useful to teachers as to parents and that clear decisions would serve to vindicate teachers. The INTO put it to my staff that it would be counterproductive to the deliberation process if all or some of the matters considered by the Board or the Department and which would generally be contained in the rationale for the decision were to be released under FOI. While I accept that it would not be in the public interest for the deliberations relating to an investigation to be made available while such deliberations are in progress, I cannot agree that it would be counterproductive for the rationale behind a decision to be released. It seems to me to be essential that the rationale underlying such a decision be set out for the purposes of both clarity and certainty."[55]

Section 21 Decisions

Section 21(1)(a) of the Freedom of Information Act provides that access to a record may be refused if, in the opinion of the head of the public body, access could reasonably be expected to: "prejudice the effectiveness of tests, examinations, investigations, inquiries or audits conducted by or on behalf of the public body concerned or the procedures or methods employed for the conduct thereof."

Section 21(2) provides that: "Subsection (1) shall not apply in relation to a case in which in the opinion of the head concerned, the public interest would, on balance, be better served by granting than by refusing to grant the request".[56]

Requirement to identify potential harm that might arise

Is decision-maker's expectation reasonable?

Section 21 exemption was relied on by the Department of Education in refusing a request from the Principal of St. Catherine's College of Education for Home Economics for records relating to a consultant's report and the Ministerial decision to close the College.[57] The Information Commissioner, in finding for the applicant, *inter alia*, noted the following:

---

[55] Case 98169, *Ms ABY and the Department of Education and Science*, July 6, 2000.
[56] S.21(1)(b) refers to significant adverse effects on management functions and s.21(1)(c) refers to disclosure of negotiating positions. Also *supra*, p.253
[57] Case 031109, *Ms Madeleine Mulrennan and the Department of Education & Science*, August 10, 2004.

> "In arriving at a decision to claim a section 21 exemption, a decision maker must, firstly, identify the potential harm to the functions covered by the exemption that might arise from disclosure and, having identified that harm, consider the reasonableness of any expectation that the harm will occur. The test of whether the expectation is reasonable is not concerned with the question of probabilities or possibilities. It is concerned simply with whether or not the decision maker's expectation is reasonable."

Public interest test

The Commissioner also considered the public interest test with particular reference to the circumstances of the decision to close the College.

> "There is a significant public interest in members of the public knowing how a public body ensures that its decisions are predicated on ensuring value for money; in members of the public knowing how a public body performs its functions particularly in a context where a decision has consequences for existing employees and their families and, in ensuring openness, transparency and accountability in relation to the expenditure of public money. The Commissioner found that the records sought concern a decision to close a third level college and it is a decision which has very significant implications for existing staff and for potential future students; and is a decision, also, which seems likely to have significant financial implications into the future for the Exchequer. In these circumstances, the Commissioner believed the public interest arguments in favour of openness and accountability were particularly strong and, had it been necessary to apply the public interest test, the public interest in granting the request would have prevailed."

Access refused to internal audits of Department of Education and Science

Section 21 exemption was also relied upon when Deputy Enda Kenny was refused access to reports of internal audits undertaken by the Department of Education and Science between January 2000 and March 2003.[58]

---

[58] Case 030693, *Deputy Enda Kenny and the Department of Education and Science*, May 24, 2004.

"Access to the reports was refused on the grounds that, among other things, disclosure could result in harm to the capacity of the Internal Audit Unit to discharge its functions, disclosure could damage the existing expert/client relationship between the Internal Audit Unit and its clients and disclosure could result in destabilisation and circumvention of existing accountability arrangements."

In arriving at her decision, which annulled the Department's decision and released records to Deputy Kenny, the Information Commissioner noted as follows:

"[I]nternal audit reports have been released by other Government Departments in the past and I am not aware of any suggestion that their release has resulted in any of the harms envisaged by the Department in this case. Further, it is clear that some other Government Departments did not anticipate that release of audit reports would have the prejudicial effect on the audit process anticipated by the Department in this case.

The fact that accountability arrangements may already exist in respect of audit reports is not grounds for refusing access under the FOI Act. Further, I do not accept that the work of the Office of the Comptroller and Auditor General, and/or others involved in scrutinising audit reports, would be prejudiced or compromised by the release of such reports under the FOI Act. Although the Department has argued that release of the records would prejudice the procedures and methods which it uses in carrying out such audits, it has not detailed specifically which procedures would be prejudiced or how they would be prejudiced. The Department has also argued that release of the records would impair the existing expert/client relation between the Internal Audit Unit and its clients. I do not accept that release of these records would lead to the Department's Internal Audit Unit staff being perceived as anything other than honest, objective and professional. As the Department has pointed out, some audit reports are already made available to the Public Accounts Committee without any apparent prejudice to the relationship between the Internal Audit Unit and its clients. Furthermore, it is reasonable to assume that all staff of public bodies will co-operate with audit inquiries where such inquiries relate to their work areas or functions. I consider that it is not sustainable that anything other than full co-operation would be given by public employees to the Department's Internal Audit Unit."

Understanding Realities

Data versus information

The speed with which technology is impacting on communication is, in effect, a two-edged sword. There is an increasing amount of data being conveyed on the information highway but the extent to which this amounts to "information" is questionable. Public bodies need to be conscious that a real problem confronting most members of the public is that they may not be able to formulate their requests so as to elicit the information they seek. This is the case whether or not the Freedom of Information Act is brought into play.

Consider for example:

- when parents query their child's marks in an exam, perhaps what they want is not so much to query the marks but to have someone they trust discuss aspects of the child's behaviour;

- when a member of staff queries why they were not promoted, perhaps what they actually want is not to question the dubious antecedents of the interview board and the general incompetence of the Principal and every member of the Board of Management in sight. It is possible that what they want is an intelligent conversation with somebody trustworthy and a genuine appraisal of their career prospects and whether or not they should continue as a teacher.

In such scenarios the requester of information does not set out to be a troublemaker. Unfortunately, all too often that is how they are treated and with certain predictability that is what they become.

Secret versus confidential

One of the great fallacies permeating both the public and private sector is that there are "secrets". This false presumption leads to the situation where information is withheld on a blanket basis. There is a necessity in all walks of life to maintain confidentiality but that is quite different from the presumption of secrecy. A serious flaw in the Freedom of Information Act is that it gives little discretion for public bodies to retain the confidentiality of the early stages of policy innovation or other pre-decision deliberations. There is no denying the chilling effect in a situation where anything that is said or done may find its way into a newspaper headline. There are very real negative effects to openness if every one on a committee feels constrained to talk in code and minutes are truncated so much that they are no longer a true and accurate record of proceedings.

CONCLUSIONS

Whether or not a school and the school community view freedom of information as a positive or a negative depends on whether or not that school and its community has an open culture. That in turn depends on how it treats its own people, its human resources. The watchword for everyone must be to deal with others, student, teacher or parent, as each person would want to be treated themselves in similar circumstances. It is simple cause and effect. My attitude is a direct cause of creating an environment suitable for an open culture. That does not mean that you will always get what you ask for. It means that I will make the effort to give you what you have requested and will refuse only if I am strictly precluded from so doing; in case of refusal I will make every effort to enable you understand the cause of the refusal.

The issues raised in this paper have general application that applies irrespective of whether the school is directly or indirectly concerned with the Freedom of Information Act. What is necessary in all cases is that the school and all the partners in education become wedded to a concept of accountability to each other. But, without openness there can be no accountability.

SUBJECT INDEX

ASTI,
   surveys, 4
Absenteeism, 106
Assault, 147 *et seq., see also*
   Criminal liability
   causing harm, 147
   causing serious harm, 148
Autonomy,
   pupils and, 57 *et seq.*

Bullying, 21–24, 145 *et seq.*, 210, 211, 214, 215

Civil liability, 151, *et seq., see also*
   Criminal liability
   basis of, 152
   generally, 151
   negligence and, 152 *et seq., see also* **Negligence**
Corporal punishment, 146, 199, 120, 225
Criminal liability, 146 *et seq., see also* **Civil liability**
   Assault, *see* **Assault**
   offences, 148
   defences, 148 *et seq.*
   use of force, 148 *et seq.*

Department of Education and Science, 136, 137, 146, 166, 172, 175–177, 188, 227, 233, 234, 239, 243, 246, 247, 248, 250, 251, 256, 260, 261, 263, 264, 266, 268, 269
   access refused to internal audits of, 269
   records held by, 262
   relationship with boards of management and teachers, 260

Detention, 94, 103, 114, 149, 190, 199, 210, 234, 235, 238
   In-school, 191
Disability, *see also* **Discrimination** and **Equality**
   pupils with, 54 *et seq.*, 102, 119–123, 125, 30, 131, 142, 143, 183, 184, 195, 202, 205, 225, 230, 244, 262
Discipline, 145 *et seq.*, 180 *et seq., see also* **Exclusion** and **Expulsion**
   bullying and, 145 *et seq., see* **Bullying**
   codes of behaviour, 172
   detention, *see* **Detention**
   exclusion, *see also* **Exclusion**
   expulsion, *see* **Expulsion**
   individual students rights and the common good, 180 *et seq.*
   necessary, 159–166
   procedures, 166
      fairness of procedures, 167–169, 186–188
      general, 166
      immediate action, 167
      injunctive relief, 173
      scope of judicial review and, 169
      wrongdoing off school premises, 170–173
   reasonable force, 198 *et seq.*
Discrimination, *see also* **Equality** and **Harassment**
   employment and, 130 *et seq.*
   educational establishment and, 124 *et seq.*
   definition of, 124
   meaning of, 121, 132 *et seq.*
   provision of on grounds of, 118, 120 *et seq.*, 130

Discrimination—*contd.*
provision of on grounds of—*contd.*
    age, 120
    disability, 120, *see also*
        Disability
    family status, 120
    gender, 120
    martial status, 120
    race, 120
    religion, 120
    sexual orientation, 120
    travelling community, 120, *see*
        Travellers
    victimisation, 120
Drugs, *see* **Sports**
    dietary supplements, 74 *et seq.*
    use of, 74 *et seq.*
Duty of care, 1 *et seq.*, *see also*
    Negligence and Supervision
    careful parent test, 3
    disability and, *see* **Disability**
    occupiers liability, 35 *et seq.*, *see*
        Occupiers liability
    reasonable care, 18
    safety, health and welfare at work,
        47 *et seq.*, *see* **Safety, health
        and welfare at work**
    supervision and, 3 *et seq.*, *see*
        Supervision

**Educational Welfare Officers
    (EWOs)**, 106 *et seq.*, *see*
    Minimum education and
    **National Education Welfare
    Board (NEWB)**
    numbers of, 106 *et seq.*
Equality, 118 *et seq.*, *see also*
    Discrimination and
    Harassment
    Director of Equality Tribunal,
        enforcement procedures and,
        126 *et seq.*, 139 *et seq.*
    remedies by, 126 *et seq.*,
        139 *et seq.*
    employment and, 130 *et seq.*

Equality—*contd.*
    Equality Authority, 26 *et seq.*
Exclusion, 35, 40,41, 51, 145 *et seq.*,
    158, 180, 184,188, 189, 203,
    206, 213, 234, 235, 238, *see
    also* **Bullying, Civil liability,
    Criminal liability** and
    Suspension
    legality of, 195–198
    necessary, 158, 159
    Ombudsman for Children and, 232,
        see **Ombudsman for
        Children in Ireland**
    statutory mechanism and, 175
Expulsion, *see also* **discipline**, 14,
    124, 141, 169, 171 *et seq.*, 178,
    180, 182, 183, 187, 189, *see
    also* **Discipline, Expulsion** and
    Suspension
    appeals against, 178, 188
    recognised school from,
        182–186
    statutory mechanism and,
        175

Freedom of information, 239 *et seq.*
    administration of Acts for, 242
    Department of Education and
        Science and, 239, 243, 246,
        247, 248, 250, 251, 256,
        260, 261, 263, 264, 266, 268,
        269
    openness and transparency of,
        248
    claims against teachers, 266
    data versus information, 271
    exemptions to, 252 *et seq.*
    fees and, 243
    information commissioner's
        decision, 262, 262
    partners in education and, 260 *et
        seq.*
    personal information, 243
    principal rights and, 246
    public interests and, 269

Subject Index

Freedom of information—*contd.*
  record-keeping, 244
  releasing information, 247
  right top access school records, 248
  school league tables and 248, *see* **School league tables**
  schools and application of, 243
  secrecy v confidentiality, 271
  separated parents and, 256, *see* **Separated parents**
  teacher's request fro personal files, 264
  third party rights, 247

Harassment,
  meaning of, 123, 124, 138
  sexual, 123, 138
  unwanted conduct, 123
Health and Safety Authority, 488, *see also* **Safety, health and welfare at work**
Human rights, 57, 60, 92, 99, 128, 196, 197, 198, 204, 207, 224, 236

INTO, 194, 267, 268
Insurance,
  sports and, 89, *see also* **Sports**

Minimum education, 92 *et seq.*, *see also* **Educational Welfare Officers** and **National Education Welfare Board (NEWB),**
  constitutional right to, 95 *et seq.*
  duties on schools and principals, 109–110
  early school leaving and, 93
  legislative provision for, 102 *et seq.*
  limits to state's obligations, 101, 102
  prosecution for failure to attend school, 107–109

Minimum education—*contd.*
  separation of powers doctrine and, *see* **Separation of powers**
  young persons in employment and, 110

National Education Welfare Board (NEWB), 95, 104 *et seq.*, 116, 117, 177 *et seq.*, 182, 188, *see* **Minimum education**
  central role of, 105
  duty of, 104
  educational welfare officers, 106 *et seq.*, *see* **Educational Welfare Officers**
  functions of, 104 *et seq.*
  powers of, 104
Negligence, 1, 52 *et seq.*, *see also* **Duty of Care** and **Supervision**
  liability and, 152 *et seq.*, *see also* **Civil liability**
  balancing supervision and humaneness, 156
  small children and supervision, 155
  standard of care, 155

Occupiers liability, 35 *et seq.*, *see also* **Duty of Care**
  criminal entrants, 43
  principles of, 38 *et seq.*
  recreational users, 35, 44 *et seq.*
  definition of, 44
  recreational activity, 44
  trespassers, 35
  duty of school management to, 42
  visitors, 35
Ombudsman for Children in Ireland, 222 *et seq.*
  exclusions and, 232, *see also* **Exclusion**
  first annual report of, 237
  functions of, 226
  promotional, 227, 228

Ombudsman for Children in Ireland—contd.
functions of—contd.
investigatory, 228
human rights and, 224, see also **Human rights**
independence of, 235
limitations on powers of, 233
ministerial veto and, 235
origins of, 224
recent reforms in Ireland of children's rights, 225
role of, 226

Privacy,
pupils of, 57 et seq.

Safety, health and welfare at work, 47 et seq., 190, 191, see also **Duty of Care and health And Safety Authority** and **Sports**
obligations of employees, 48 et seq.
obligations of employers and, 47 et seq., 50 et seq.
safety statements and, 48
second level schools and, 48
strict liability, 50
School,
function of, 230–232
School attendance, 92–95, 97, 98, 103–109, 113–115, 141, 168
compulsory, 41
England, in, 202 et seq.
prosecutions and, 213 et seq.
right to education and, 204–213
problem students and, 194, 195
School League Tables, 248 et seq.
denying parents information and, 249
emergence of, 250
legislative opportunism, 249
primary school, 250
Tuairiscí Scoile and, 251
School transport, 32, see also **Supervision**

Separated parents,
right of access to records, 256 et seq.
access to minor's records, 257
parental primacy, 259
strained family relationship irrelevant, 258
Separation of powers, see also **Minimum education**
doctrine of, 111 et seq.
Sports (Secondary Schools), 63 et seq.
code of ethics for good practice and, 90
Irish Sports Council, 90
insurance, 89
premises, use of,
liability and, 84
safety levels of facilities, 85, 88
safety of areas peripheral to sorts arena, 86, see also **Safety, health and welfare at work**
swimming pools, 86
sports teachers,
general standards for, 64 et seq.
teaching sports and duties, 66
appropriate matching of players, 698
coach as a referee, 71
coaching qualifications, 72 et seq.
dietary supplements, 74
drugs, see **Drugs**
duties in respect of equipment, 75
fitness of pupils, 68
injury avoidance principles, 66
weather permitting, 70
supervision, 76 et seq., see also **Supervision**
absence of, 77
adequate, 79
appropriate levels of, 79 et seq.
mandatory, 78

Subject Index

Sports (Secondary Schools)—*contd.*
Supervision—*contd.*
provision of appropriate medical care, 84
unauthorised sport, 83
Strike action, 192–194
Supervision, 3 *et seq.*, *see also* **Duty of Care**
injuries sustained off the premises, 25 *et seq.*
modification of scope of, 40 *et seq.*
negligence and, 38 *et seq.*, 155 *et seq.*, *see also* **Negligence**
on school premises, 4 *et seq.*
outside hours, 26 *et seq.*
school tours and, 33 *et seq.*

Supervision—*contd.*
school transport, 32
sports and, 76 *et seq.*, *see also* **Sports**
Suspension, *see* **discipline, exclusion and expulsion**
appeals against, 178, 188
statutory mechanisms and, 175 *et seq.*

Travellers, 93, 94, 119, 120, 127, 128, 131, *see also* **Discrimination**

Violent pupils, 21, 24, 146 *et seq.*, *see also* **Assault** and **Criminal Liability**